IMAGES
of America

AROUND RANDOLPH TOWNSHIP AND GUYS MILLS

On the cover: Guys Mills Congregational Church members in the late 1930s pose for the camera's shutter. Pictured are, from left to right, (first row) Betty Jane Jones, Thelma Parker, Joyce Burchard, Jean Boyd, Carolyn Boyd, Jack Boyd, and Don Boyd; (second row) John Boyd, Myrtle Boyd, Mary Lingo, Hank Lingo, Rev. Frank Ritter, Mrs. Ritter, Elsie Reagle, and Willard Burchard holding daughter Janice; (third row) unidentified, Ed Cooper, Mary Cooper, Florence Boyd, Leatha Burchard, and Gladys Woodcock; (fourth row) unidentified, Judd Lingo, Mabel Lingo, Doris Hall, Mildred Hotchkiss, Virginia McFadden, Margaret Birtsel, and Lenore Schweitzer; (fifth row) Mae Woodcock, Audine Hall, Ruth Graham, Romaine Hotchkiss, Laura Roueche, Bertha Graham, and David (Gerald) Bird Sr. (Courtesy of Carolyn Miller and Leatha Humes.)

IMAGES
of America

AROUND RANDOLPH TOWNSHIP AND GUYS MILLS

Cheryl Seber Weiderspahn

ARCADIA
PUBLISHING

ISBN 978-0-7385-6217-9

Published by Arcadia Publishing
Charleston SC, Chicago IL, Portsmouth NH, San Francisco CA

Printed in the United States of America

Library of Congress Control Number: 2008935289

For all general information contact Arcadia Publishing at:
Telephone 843-853-2070
Fax 843-853-0044
E-mail sales@arcadiapublishing.com
For customer service and orders:
Toll-Free 1-888-313-2665

Visit us on the Internet at www.arcadiapublishing.com

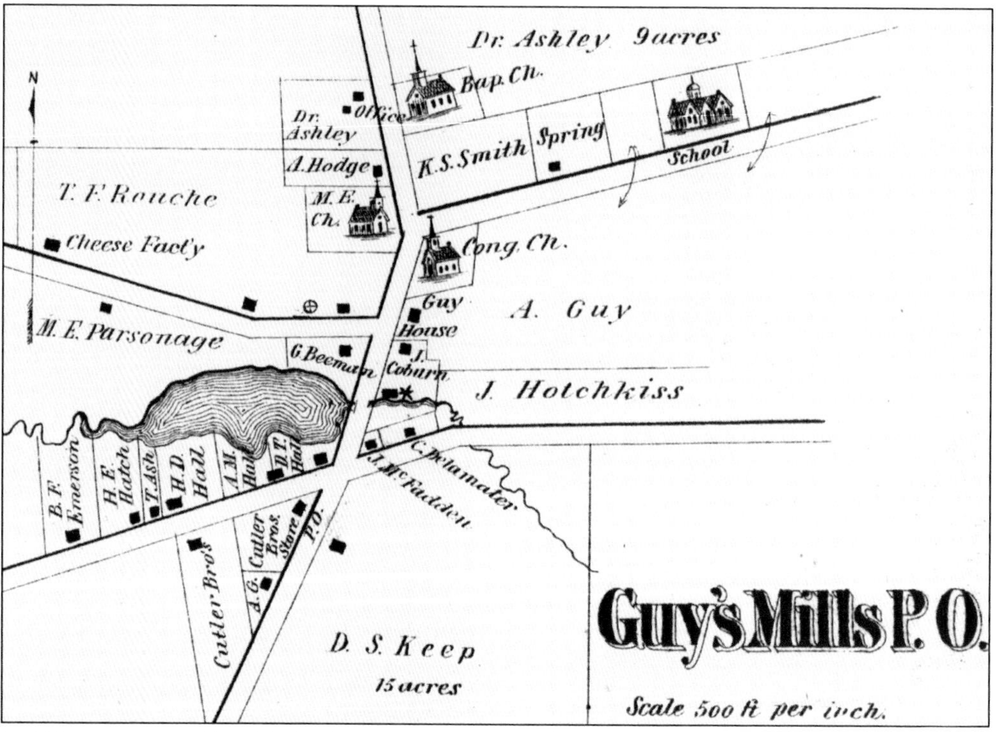

In 1876 downtown Guys Mills, the creek was dammed to create the millpond. In fact, this valley between two steep hills is precisely what lured Jacob Guy to move here in 1815 and build the sawmill. The mill wheel caught the overflow and powered the mill, a huge three-story frame building standing on the site of the current Olde Grist Mill gift shop named in honor of mill. The Baptists on Ashley Hill baptized by emersion in the millpond. Cutler's Department Store, Hall's Store, Guy House Hotel, physicians, blacksmiths, wagon makers, carpenters, a cheese factory, and a school made this a progressive town. (Courtesy of Crawford County Historical Society.)

Contents

Acknowledgments 6

Introduction 7

1. They Settled the Wilderness: Early Bird's-eye Views 9

2. They Nurtured: Families and Homes 17

3. They Worshipped: Church History 33

4. They Learned: School History 45

5. They Hosted: The Guy House Hotel 59

6. They Communicated: Post Office History 67

7. They Developed the Area: Businesses and Trades 73

8. They Protected: Randolph Volunteer Fire Department 93

9. They Played: Music, Sports, and Civic Organizations 99

10. They Celebrated: Independence Day 113

ACKNOWLEDGMENTS

My personal collection of photographs became the core for this book. These images are labeled "author's collection."

The Crawford County Historical Society graciously opened their archives, and I gratefully acknowledge Anne Stewart's and Larry Wonder's cooperation. These images were professionally scanned by Tim Kirk and are labeled "Courtesy of CCHS."

Warm heartfelt thanks go to Norman and Arlean Childs. Early in my quest for photographs, they came from Illinois to combine our historical collections. We had never met, but our common passion for Randolph history bound us immediately. Authors in their own right, visit them at www.childsfamilygenealogy.com for their books. These images are labeled "Courtesy of the Childs family."

The *Meadville Tribune* willingly granted permission to use pictures that were taken by photographers for the newspaper over the years. The photographer or studio is acknowledged, if known, along with the newspaper for allowing the inclusion of these photographs.

Many thanks go to Erin Vosgien, junior publisher for Arcadia Publishing and my editor for this book, for many prompt and professional answers over the phone and by e-mail.

In addition, photographs and memories were graciously shared by the following individuals whose homes or hearts are in Randolph Township: Barbara Anderson, Dorothy Anthony, Iris Armburger, Tammy Bakus, Erna Bancroft, Wenna Bean, Judy Beuchat, Ray and Jayne Beuchat, Marybelle Bird, Norman and Myrtle Bogardus, Dorcy Bowersox, John Bowser, David and Marilyn Boyd, Russell and Virginia Boyd, Kathleen Britton, Clint Brown, Dave Brumagin, Marjorie and Clair Burchard, Frank Byham, Oletha Davis, Faith Builders Educational Programs, John Foulk, Doug Gilbert, Shirley Gregory, Sharon Hayes, Sally Hotchkiss, Leatha Humes, Donna Hunter, Darlene Jablon, Helen Kelley, Brian and Judy Kirberger, Donna Mailliard, Ed Mangus Sr., Janet Marvin, Andrew and Katie Mattis, Tom Mattis, Peggy McKinley, Eli Mihailov, Wilford and Carolyn Miller, Bonnie Murphy, Betty Nelson, Steve Potts, Bonnie Proper, Coralee Rittenhouse, Mark Roche, Ron and Virginia Sanner, Harold Seber, John N. Seber, John L. and Opal Seber, Dorothy Sliter, Gary and Joyce Sliter, Harold and Shirley Smith, Lucile Stallard, Marilyn Steadman, Mae Sutley, Kim Templin, Robert W. Waid, Pauline Webster, John Wentworth, Sally Wentworth, Barbara White, Dorothy White, and Dorothy Wilson.

INTRODUCTION

From 1795 through the early 1820s, small groups of settlers immigrated from New York and other New England states. A dozen settlers attempted an existence in this primeval forest. These pioneers experienced starvation and poverty, merciless winters and isolation, pestilence and illness, hostile Native American raids, and attacks by wild animals. Some succumbed to the hardships. With fortitude and perseverance, others tamed and civilized the land and populated it with descendants who still live here today.

One influential early pioneer was Jacob Guy Esq. (1779–1850), a well-educated New Englander. Early accounts claim that Guy owned as much as 10,000 acres (nearly half) of Randolph Township. Dubbed a "Land Baron," he constantly bought land and resold to incoming settlers. Jacob Guy's early foresight enabled his crossroads, once known as Guytown, to mature and become the hub of all Randolph Township. He was remembered as a keen bookkeeper, shrewd businessman, surveyor, justice of the peace, political activist, mill proprietor, and store merchant. Jacob and Susanna Guy's union brought forth nine children, and records show that the Guy offspring continued to contribute to the area by becoming a schoolmistress, a hotel proprietor, a tavern owner, a sawmill operator, farmers, and an Episcopal minister.

Life in the unbroken wilderness began to change. The 1820s and 1830s saw a rapid influx of settlers. Slowly Randolph was dotted with small clearings, then self-sufficient farms. Ambitious tradesmen sold services and scores of businesses sprouted up. With a high priority in education and spiritual fervor, schools and churches soon followed. The close-knit crossroad communities of Guys Mills, Black Ash, Mount Hope, Brawley Stand, and Hickory Corners flourished. These rural villages were self-sufficient prior to the advent of the automobile. This area pioneered in independently owned local phone, newspaper, electric, and water systems.

Randolph Township was touched by the great oil boom to the east. Edwin Drake's historic Titusville oil discovery in 1859 changed the landscape and economics of the area. The Guy House Hotel was a main overnight stopping place for fortune seekers between the county seat in Meadville and the Titusville Oil Fields. John D. Rockefeller inspected an oil well in Guys Mills to investigate the possibility of obtaining a lease. Barrel makers could not keep up with the demand. Eastbound wagons of empty barrels and westbound wagons of barrels full of crude crisscrossed Randolph Township.

So, *Around Randolph Township and Guys Mills* celebrates the ambitious vision, the moral courage, and the physical stamina of those early forefathers.

Therefore this story is painted in broad strokes. It was no easy chore to condense over 200 years of milestones into 128 pages! I labored to provide the reader with an appreciation and understanding of the past and a connection to these communities. I have attempted to instill a pride in our beautiful area and its colorful past. You will notice that the history of this area is well seasoned with a healthy sense of humor. Perhaps it was this humor that carried them through the hardships and struggles.

Following the standardized format of Arcadia's Images of America series, this photograph essay is a visual history of yesteryear. Because a picture truly is "worth a thousand words," this book gives unlimited insight into our past. Care was given to compose the captions to be entertaining readable accounts as well as a historically accurate reference.

Because photography was rare in this area prior to 1900, there were times that I would like to have included an event, person, building, or business, but no photograph was available. I contacted over 20 people before finding a photograph of the Black Ash Methodist Church! And in requests for photographs of other subjects, the trust and generosity of my fellow Randolphians overwhelmed me. The number of allotted pages did not allow me to use all of the hundreds of old photographs that were loaned to me. You will notice that there are no current photographs in this book. I could have run around the township snapping pictures, but my goal was to provide only vintage images. The vast majority of these vintage images have never been published or presented to the public. With only a couple exceptions, all the 210 photographs contained in this book are prior to 1970.

On a personal level, writing about John Brown not being the choirmaster at Guys Mills Congregational church (see page 41) was perhaps the most difficult part of writing this book. An image of this congregation appears on the cover of this book. That is my hometown church and even I had helped spread the myth. I selfishly considered remaining silent and to letting the legend remain intact. But truth is truth, facts are facts, and a responsible historian reports facts.

I fondly remember spending many childhood hours crosswise on my bed with my elbows propped on my bedroom windowsill. From my vantage point, I could watch the people of Guys Mills scurry around below like ants on an anthill. I suppose this is when my love affair with the area began. I lived here, went to school here, married here, and dedicated my children here. I could go on and on about my passion for Randolph Township.

Today Randolph is a tranquil scenic township where family ties are strong, and good friends are precious. Our beloved Randolph Township has a rich past. May her future be one full of prosperity and memories to preserve.

Rev. T. H. Delamater, pastor of the Guys Mills Congregational Church, wrote this about Randolph Township in 1876: "A howling wilderness around, / Where smiling plenty now is found; / Primeval forests held their sway, / And obstacles beset their way, / And yet that noble little band, / Who settled first in this fair land, / Felt it was their duty clear / To plant a Christian mission here."

One

THEY SETTLED THE WILDERNESS
EARLY BIRD'S-EYE VIEWS

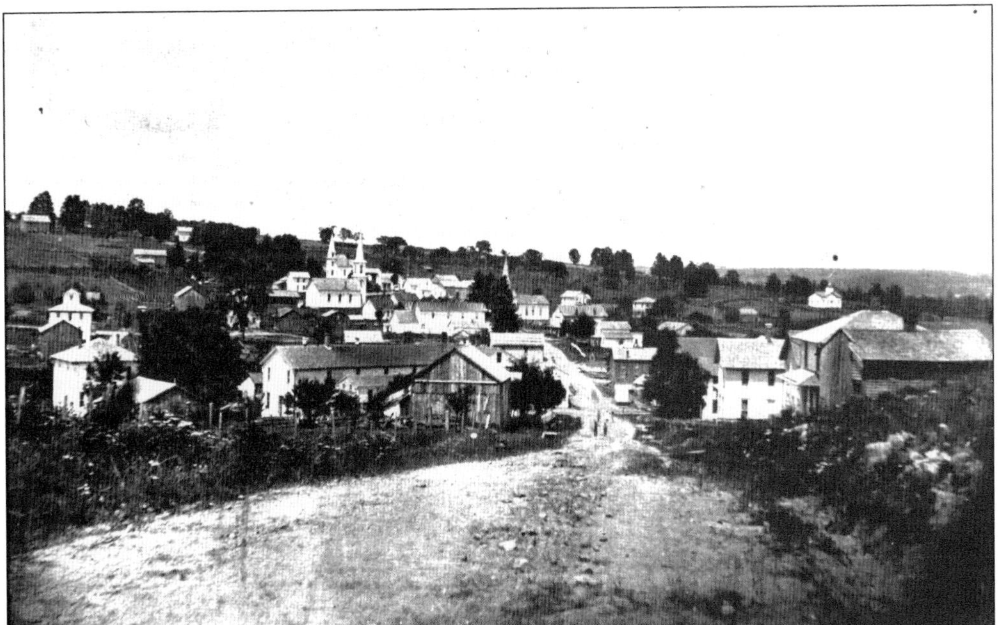

This faded photograph, looking north, provides the history of Guys Mills at a glance. All the roads were dirt, and there were no electric or telephone poles, dating this photograph before 1905. In the far right distance, the Guys Mills School stands sentinel. The dark building on the right past the intersection is Guy's Saw (and later) Grist Mill. The Covenant Baptist Church proudly stood on Ashley Hill, visible here beyond the Methodist church. (Author's collection.)

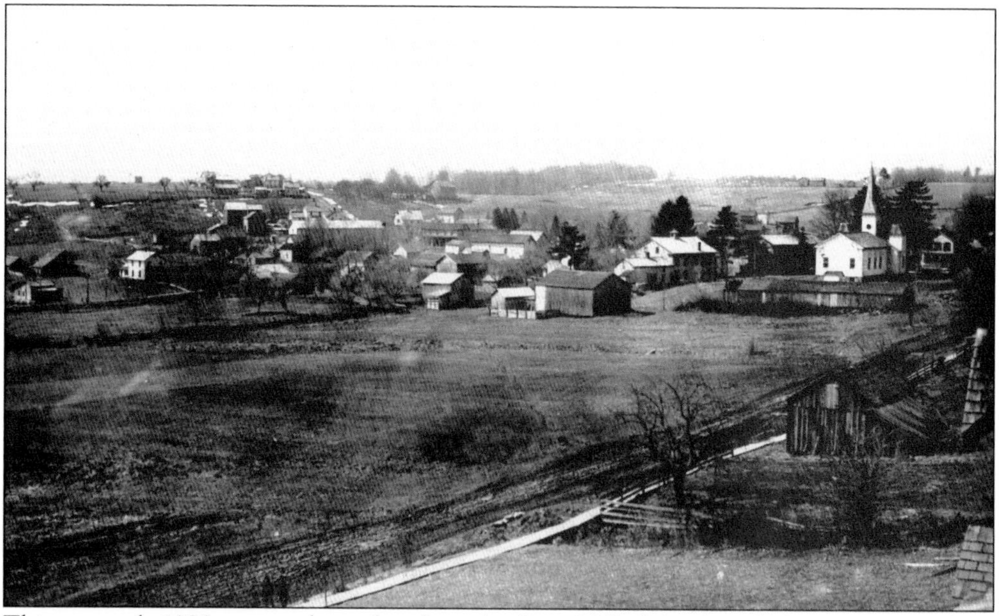

This rare early 1900s postcard was shot from the Guys Mills School roof. Notice corners of the first and second grade belfry in the extreme far right foreground. The Congregational carriage shed and Guy House Hotel livery stables give insight as to the mode of transportation of the day. The mill is in the center of the photograph and the 120-foot-long roof on the left is Bannister's Store. (Author's collection.)

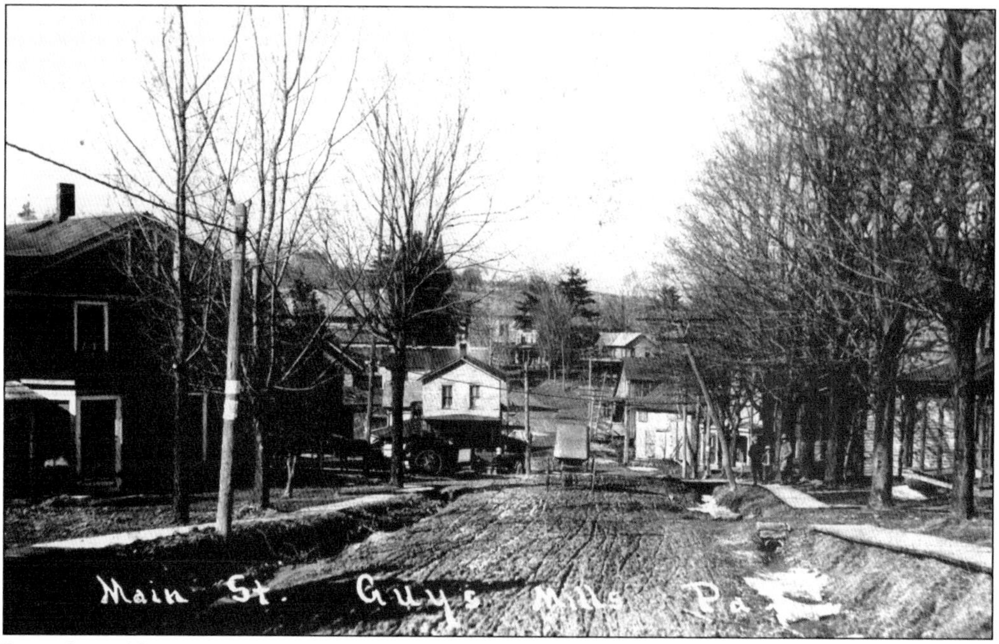

Rutted muddy springtime roads were a perennial problem, even in 1912. Plank sidewalks alleviated the nuisance for those on foot. Nonetheless, to the left is Cutler's Department Store, with several customers' buggies parked outside. The porch of Jacob Guy's mill is visible as well as the porch of the Guy House Hotel. In left foreground, three young men seem curious about the rare sight of a camera. (Author's collection.)

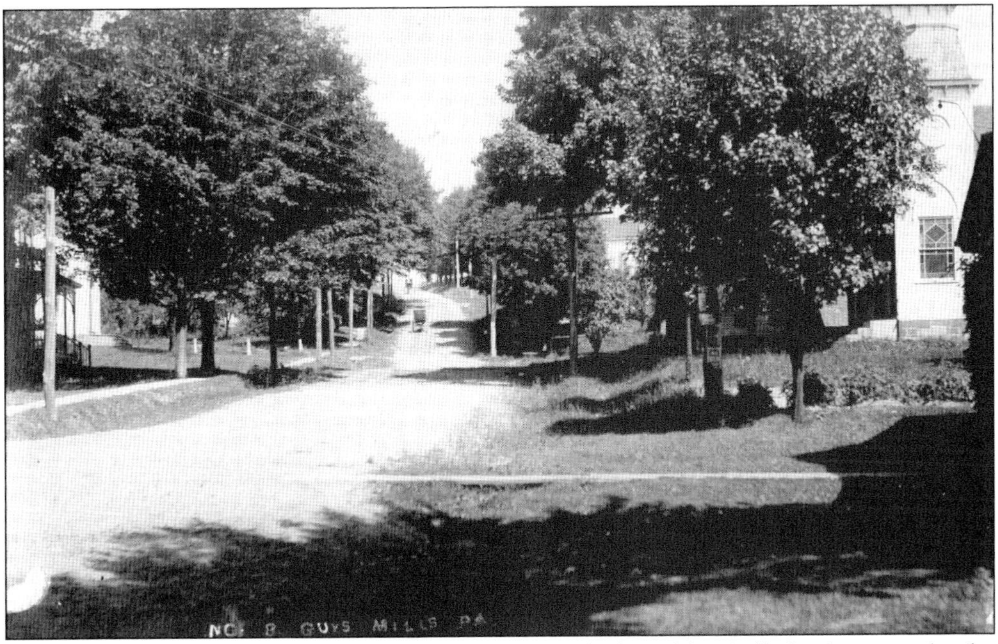

In the photograph above, two horse-drawn buggies climb Ashley Hill. Looking north, the photographer is flanked by the Congregational church on the right and the Methodist church on the left. A tip of an arch-topped Baptist window is visible through the trees. The photograph below was taken from the top of Ashley Hill looking down into Guys Mills. A shy young couple sits in the grass, protecting themselves from the sun with a black parasol or umbrella. These two postcards were probably taken on the same day between 1903 and 1910. (Author's collection.)

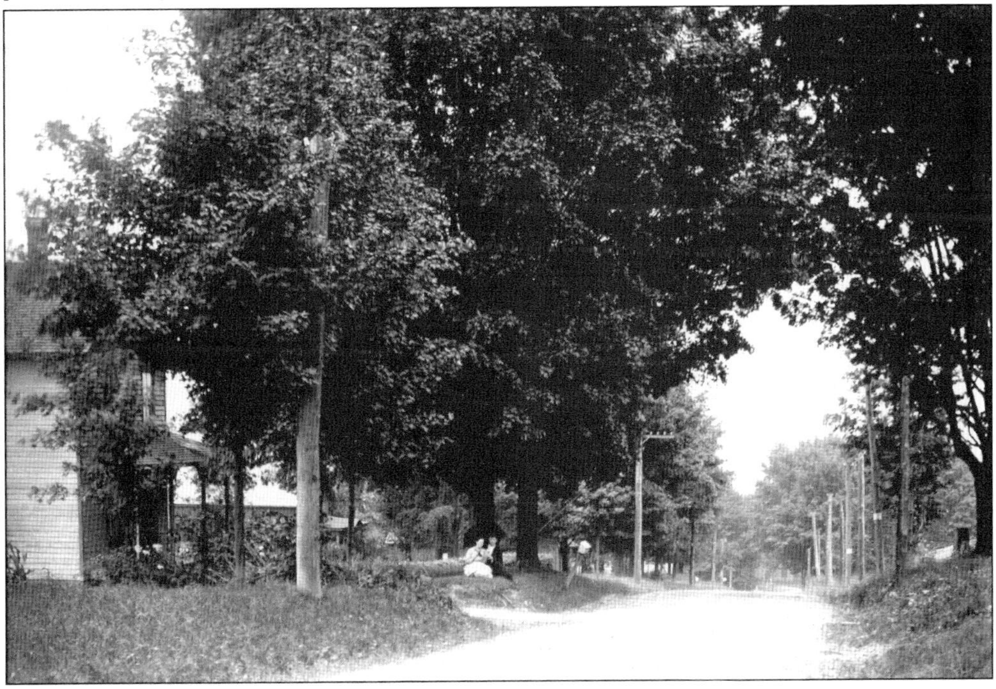

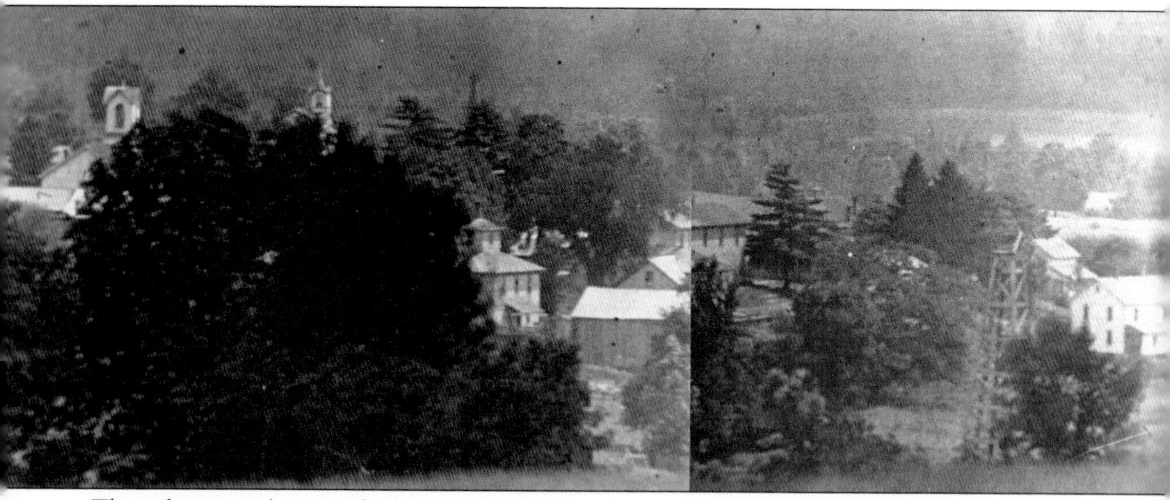

These four rare photographs form a connected panoramic view of Guys Mills looking northeast prior to 1907. They were developed from glass negatives found in a local attic. The middle of the three steeples is the school belfry. An oil well stands in the foreground. The mill appears to be in operation because there is smoke coming out of the chimney. A congested corner included

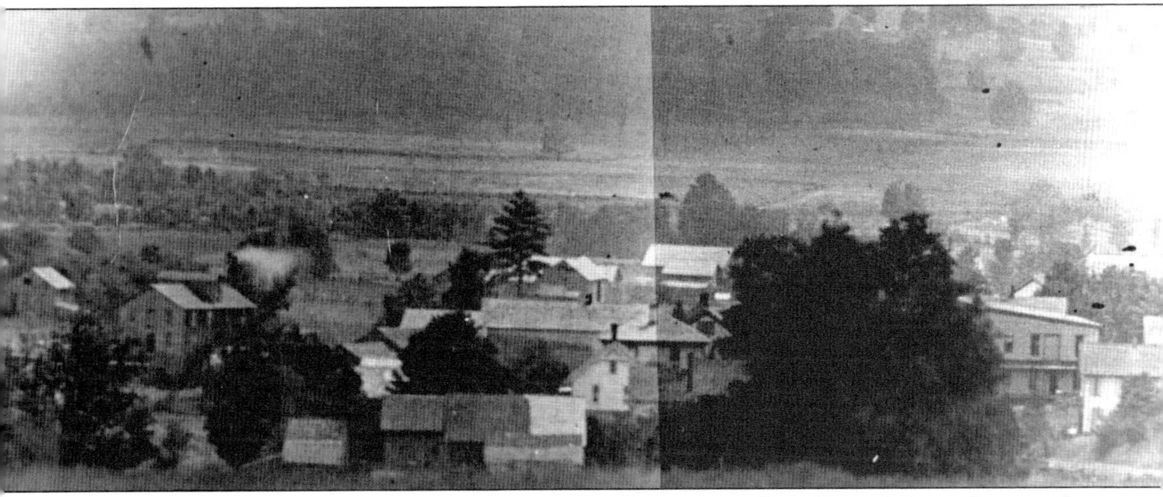

rooftops of the harness shop, Wygant's Blacksmith Shop, Dr. William Roueche's residence and office, and the back of Cutler's Department Store, displaying a self-reliant community. At the far right, the side of Waid's Funeral Home is visible. (Author's collection.)

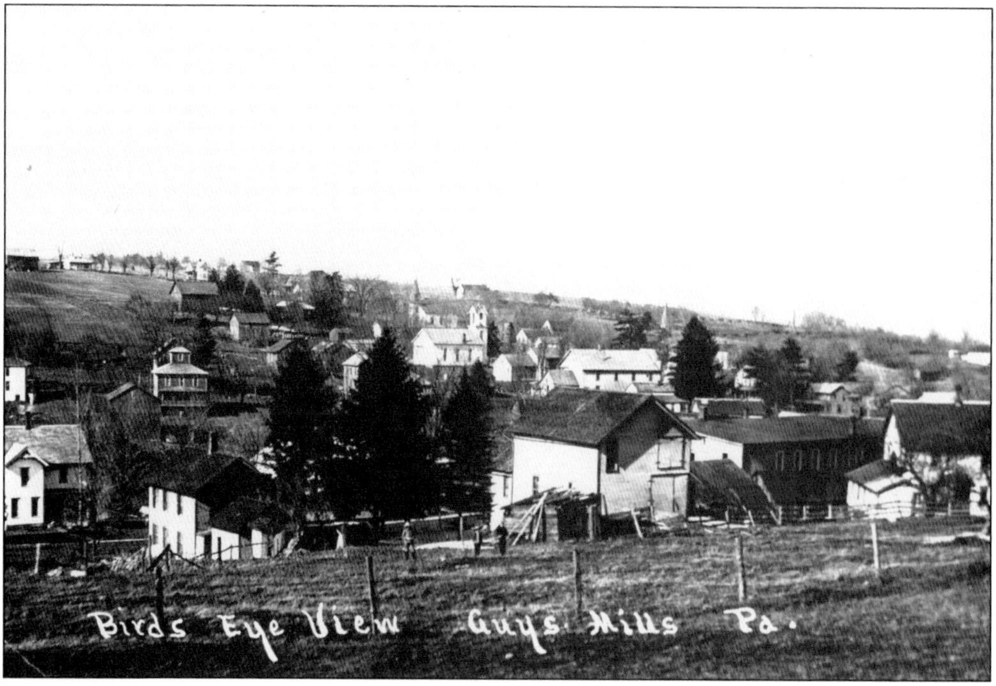

In 1912, Guys Mills was guarded by three churches. Further down, the Odd Fellows building (now Norma's Store) had two stories before the fire in March 1933. To the far right is the Cutler residence and the rear of Cutler's Department Store. The immediate foreground shows Waid's barn, which was rolled up the hill on logs with a horse-and-winch system in the 1930s, remodeled for a home, and bought by John L. Seber in 1947. (Author's collection.)

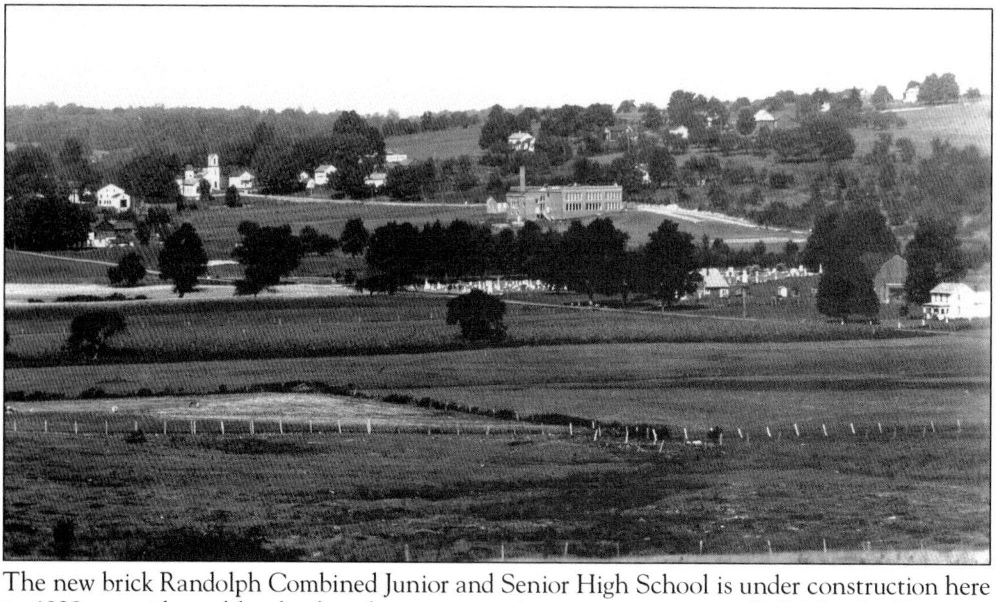

The new brick Randolph Combined Junior and Senior High School is under construction here in 1928, as evidenced by the fact that some windows are not yet installed. This building was built in 1927 and 1928, and dedicated in 1929. The Methodist Aid Building stands beside the Methodist church, and the Guy House Hotel is being renovated by new owners, Frank and Alice Childs. (Courtesy of Sharon Hayes and Leatha Humes.)

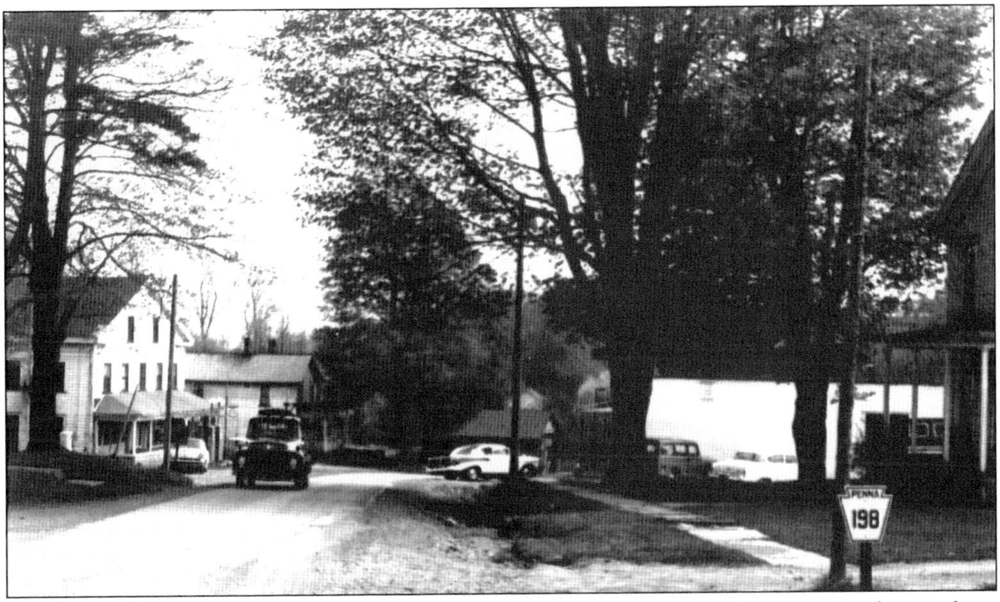

The photograph above shows Main Street in 1956 looking south. Below, an aerial view from 1947 shows a bustling town of about 400 residents despite a past of devastating fires. It has always been, and still remains, the hub of Randolph Township. Notice the empty lot on the intersection where a fire in May 1945 destroyed many buildings. Later, in 1956, the town would celebrate the Fourth of July with the new Randolph Volunteer Fire Department on this lot. (Above, courtesy of Leatha Humes; below, courtesy of Carolyn Miller, photograph by McCaskey for the Meadville Tribune.)

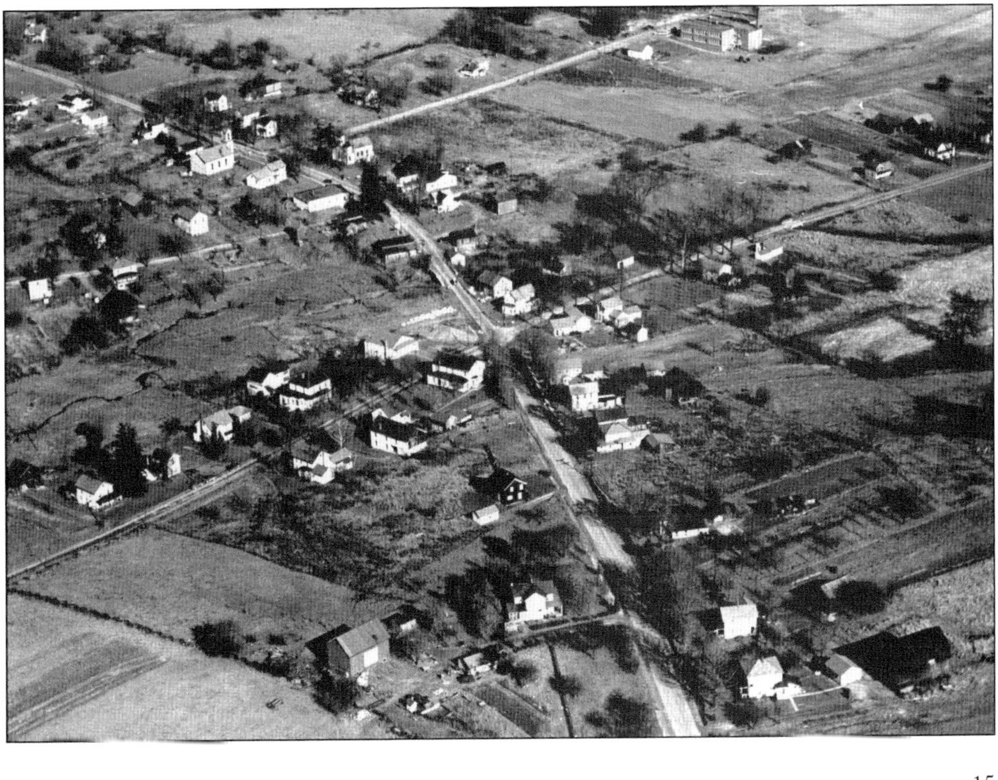

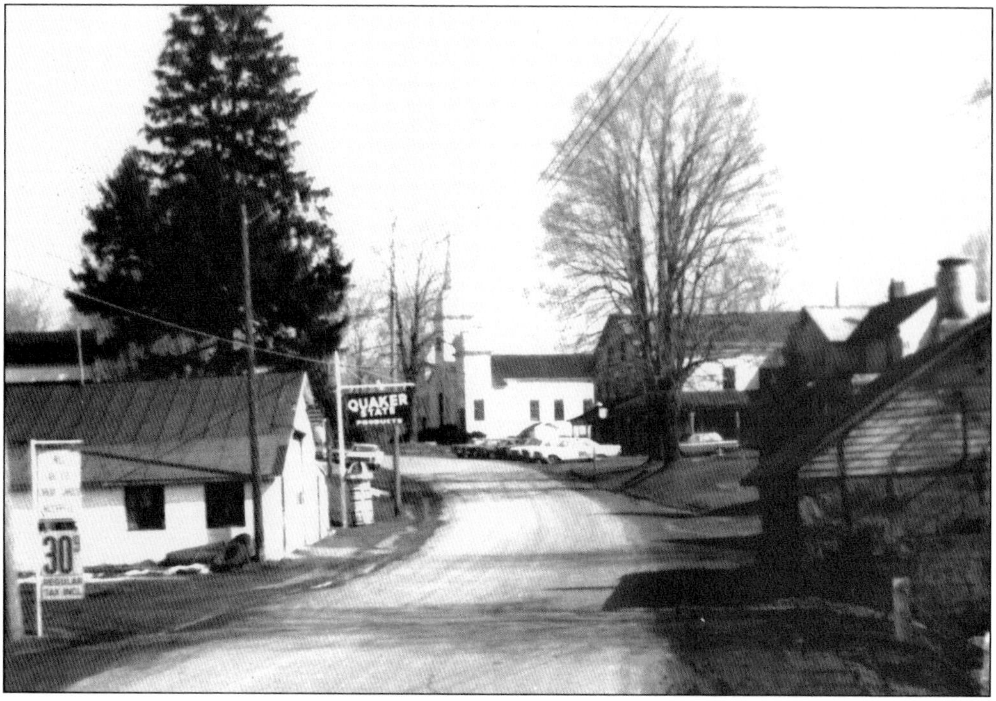

This photograph shows Main Street in 1967 looking north. On the left, Merton Terrill's Garage is selling gas for 30.9¢ per gallon. At right, the small stone building, originally built as the powerhouse for the Randolph Light and Electric Company, is now occupied by the Olde Grist Mill, a gift shop named in honor of the mill that once stood there. (Courtesy of Brian and Judy Kirberger.)

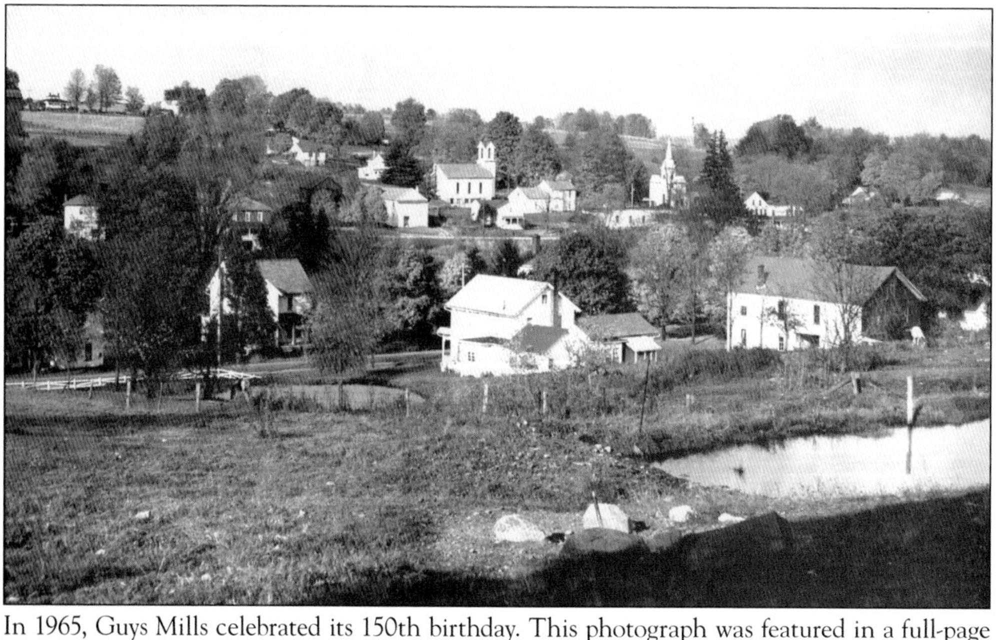

In 1965, Guys Mills celebrated its 150th birthday. This photograph was featured in a full-page *Meadville Tribune* article titled "Guys Mills Wears 150 Years Gracefully." (Courtesy of Brian and Judy Kirberger, photograph by Robert Pease for the Meadville Tribune.)

Two

They Nurtured
Families and Homes

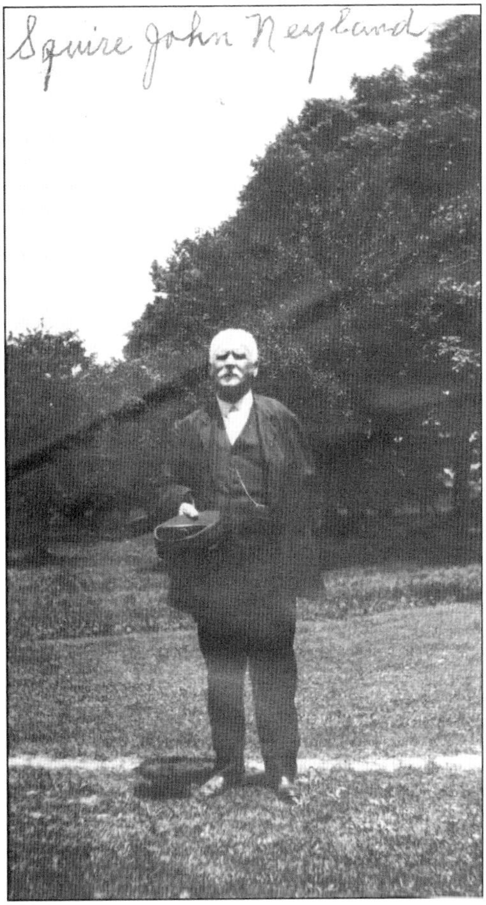

Squire John A. Neyland was a mere boy when he enlisted as a Union soldier in the Civil War. He lost his left arm on June 16, 1864, the day he turned 19 years old. He practiced law in Guys Mills. In 1925, then over 80 years old, he presented a public address for Guys Mills Old Home Week, declaring that "Randolph Township has never been found wanting when men were needed to stand up in defense of their country." (Courtesy of CCHS.)

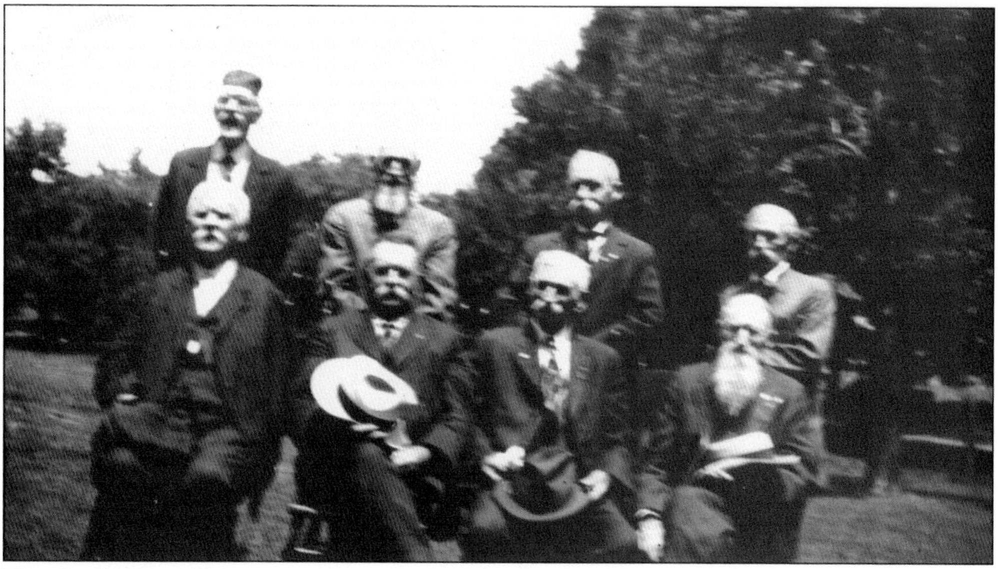

The Civil War soldiers reunion was held at the home of John W. Chapin sometime prior to 1919. Pictured are, from left to right, (first row) John A. Neyland, Charles Wygant. T. Jeff Shorts, and Don F. Stewart; (second row) Ted Radle, John W. Chapin, Stephen Maryott, and Ammi Johnson. (Courtesy of CCHS.)

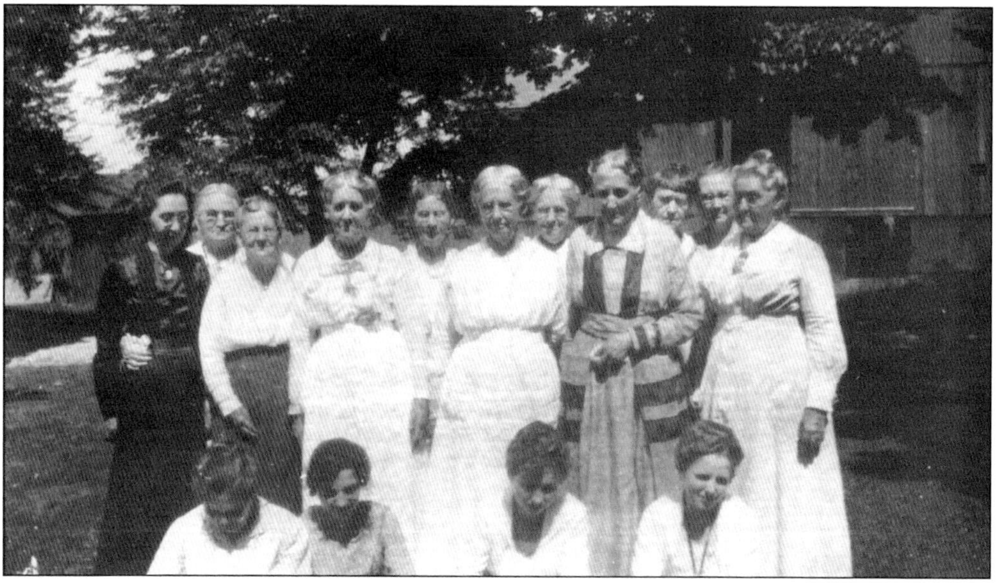

Many women were present at this Civil War soldiers reunion at the Chapin-Warner Farm sometime prior to 1905. Pictured from left to right are: (first row) Edith Warner, Sadie Hall, Rachel Lavely, and Katherine Lavely; (second row) Etta McElhenney, Matilda (Little) Blackmer, Carolyn (Miller) Hodge, Nancy (Harroun) Bogardus (Mrs. Timothy Bogardus), Ann Roueche, Phoebe Wood, Millie Sykes, Mary Neyland, Rebecca Radle, Mrs. Lavely, and Mrs. Wygant. (Courtesy of CCHS.)

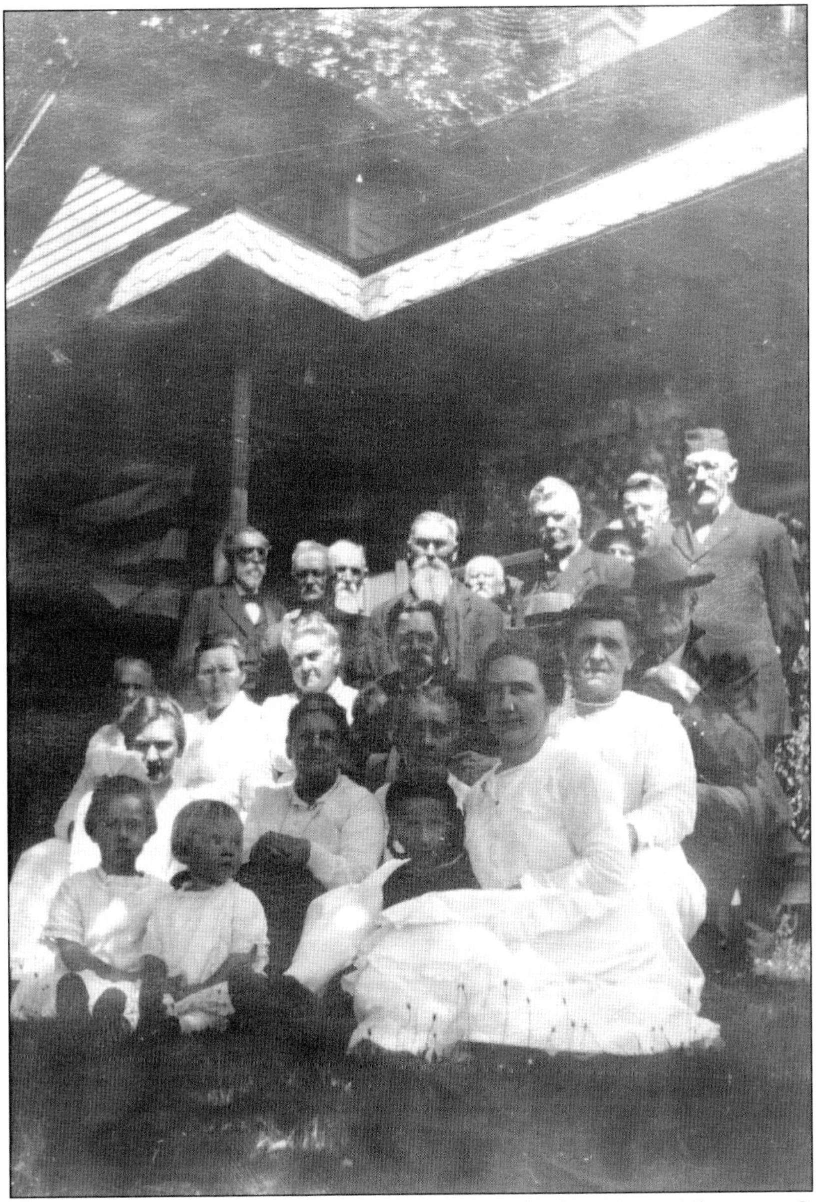

Families enjoyed the Civil War soldiers reunion held at Charles Wygant's home in Guys Mills sometime prior to 1905. Pictured are, from left to right, (first row) Mildred Hoyt, Mary Warner, Florence Hoyt, Carolyn Hodge, Mrs. Harroun, unidentified child, Alice Hoyt, and Rebecca Radle; (second row) Ella Holmes, Mrs. Ross, Mrs. Wygant, Charles Wygant, Don Stewart, and Mr. Harroun; (third row) Seth Waid III, Mr. Hodge, John W. Chapin, Jesse Hodge, John A. Neyland, Walter C. Holmes, Ammi Johnson, Rev. W. H. Garnett of the Methodist church, and Ted Radle. Ella Holmes, wife of Walter C., was a young girl living near Appomattox Court House when Gen. Robert E. Lee surrendered in 1865. He surrendered under an apple tree that she and her sister used to climb to gather apples. She is quoted as saying, "No one but those who were present can tell what the horrors of a battlefield looked like. I have stood and looked on at a distance and heard the sounds of cannons roar all around me, not knowing what minute would be my last." (Courtesy of CCHS.)

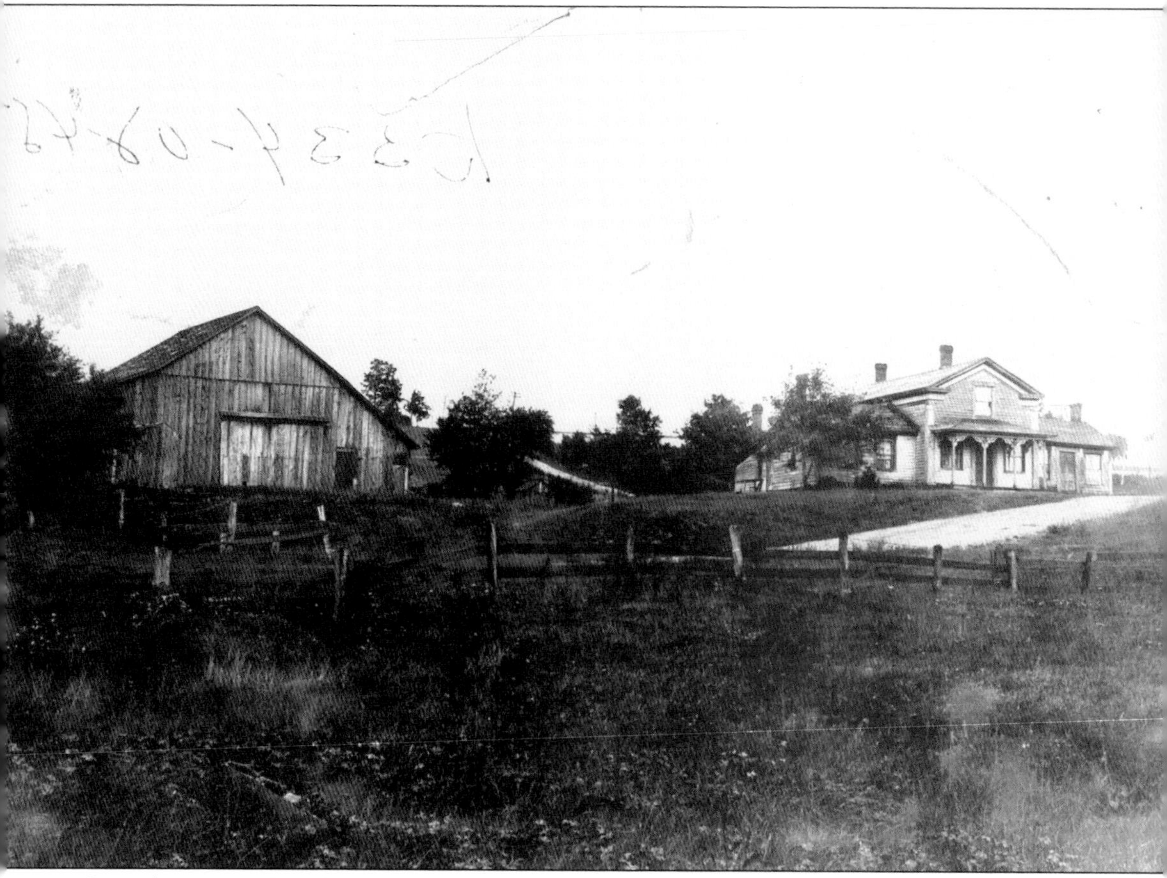

Long known as "Brawley Stand," the foot of Beuchat Road where Oil Creek Road and Route 27 converge was the hub of the original Brawley settlement and is older than Guys Mills. This is a rare photograph of the old Brawley Stand, a residence where overnight lodging and meals could be obtained. These "stands," including the Kane Stand and the Halfway House east of Black Ash, were important in the days of carriage, horseback, and travel afoot. These stopping-off points served as stagecoach stops, taverns, mail drop off and delivery points, public meeting places, and watering holes for both man and beast. In the excitement of the great oil boom, these stands flourished as traffic was heavy on Oil Creek Road (prior to Route 27) between the Titusville Oil Fields and the county seat in Meadville. Anyone with a team of oxen and a sturdy wagon could haul barrels of oil and make good money. Travelers wishing more amenities were willing to travel a bit north to the Guy House Hotel. (Courtesy of Wenna Bean.)

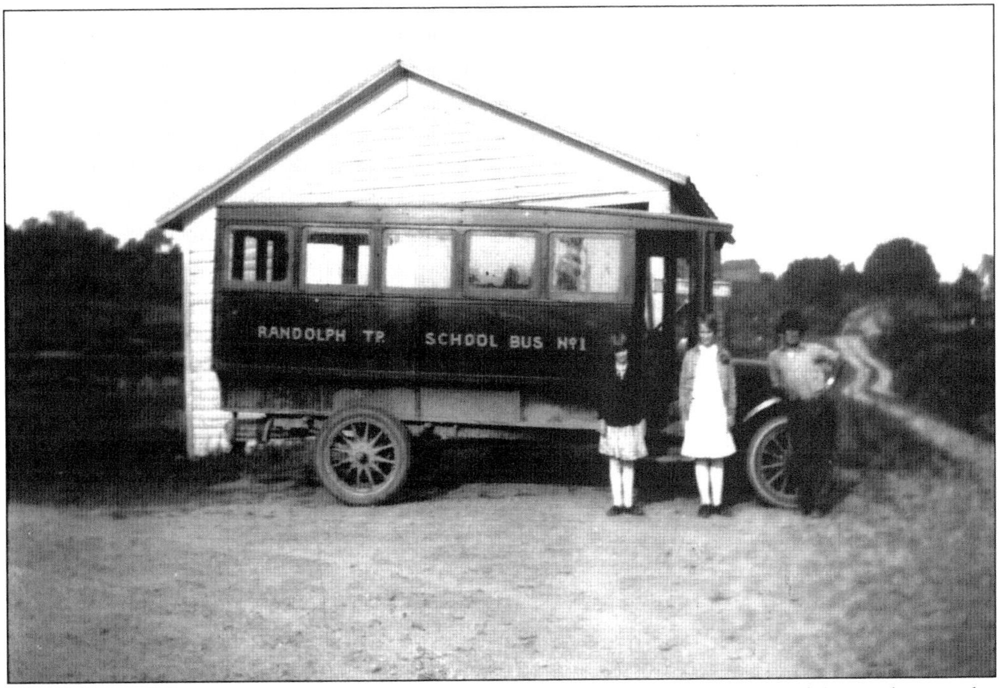

The former one-room Brawley Schoolhouse was moved down the hill and located near the Brawley Stand where it was used as a garage. Pictured are Kathryn and Mary Lang, with their school bus driver John Smith, in the 1920s. The lane to the right was part of Oil Creek Road, now abandoned. (Courtesy of Wenna Bean.)

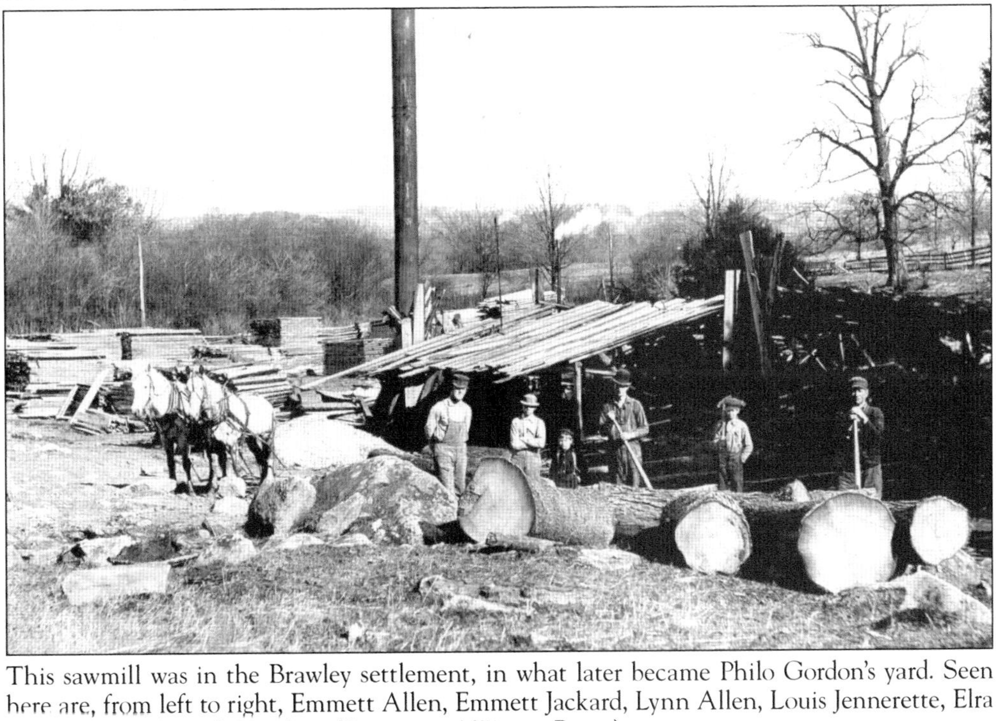

This sawmill was in the Brawley settlement, in what later became Philo Gordon's yard. Seen here are, from left to right, Emmett Allen, Emmett Jackard, Lynn Allen, Louis Jennerette, Elra Jeanerette, and Frank Beuchat. (Courtesy of Wenna Bean.)

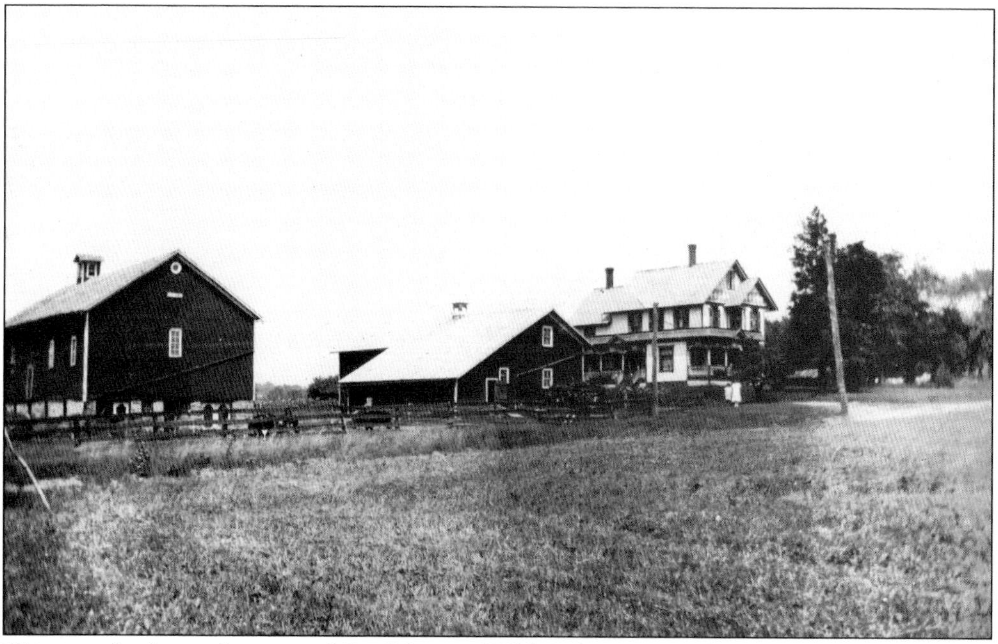

This was the former location of Dr. Sylvester Wilder's farm, west of Guys Mills on the road to Meadville. The esteemed doctor practiced medicine for 28 years while also carrying out an extensive farming business. Dr. Wilder was a staunch Congregationalist, generous with his support to the church, and active in the anti-slavery movement, reportedly hiding runaway slaves in a hidden room under his pantry. Later this stately Victorian was the home and farm of the Berley family, the Vance Collins family, Carl Wilkey, Frances Rogers, and is presently the home of Joseph and Elli Tinko. In the image below, the Collins family enjoy a break from farm work to drink an imaginary brew for the camera. Nellie Collins married Jim Welsh and ran Welsh's Garage in Guys Mills until it burned in 1944. (Courtesy of Barbara White.)

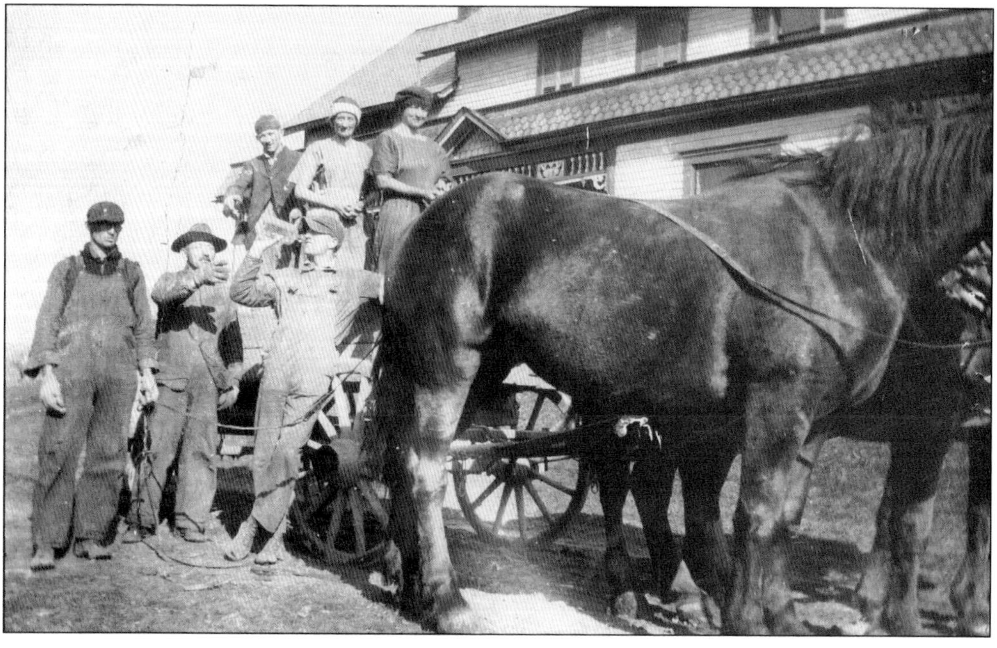

Dr. Jacob Wilson, physician and surgeon, lived near Hickory Corners and had an extensive practice throughout the territory. He entered Allegheny College at the age of 17, studied under two doctors in Iowa for four years, and subsequently completed studies at Ann Arbor College, Michigan, and Western Reserve College in Ohio. (Courtesy of Barbara Anderson.)

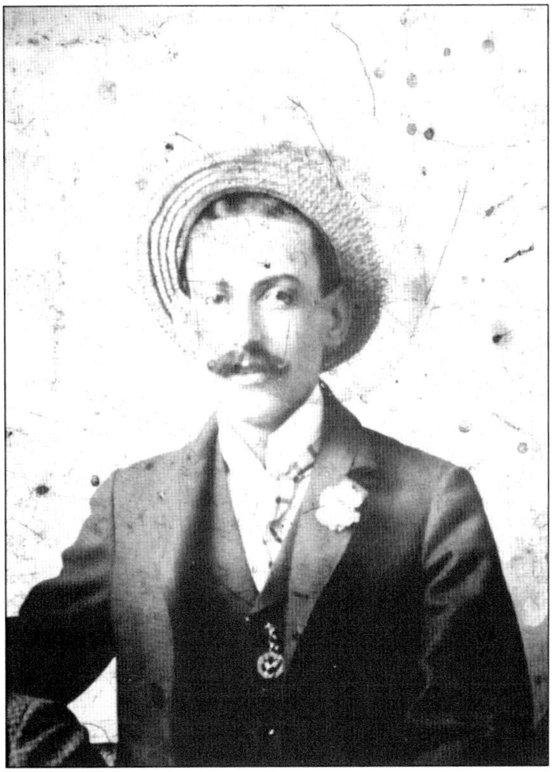

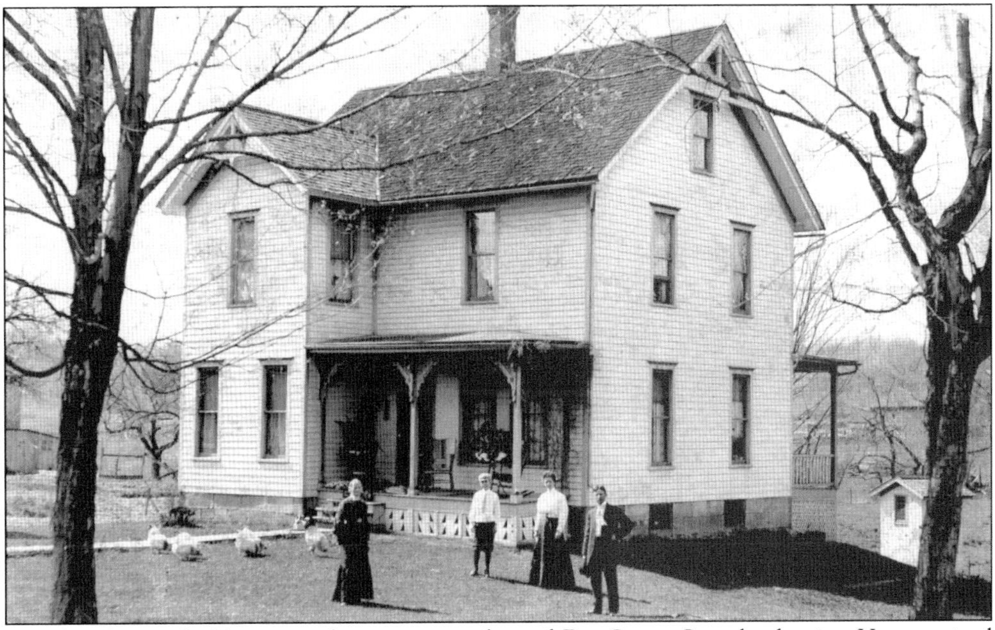

Another home doubling as a business was that of Dr. Grant Smock, dentist. He practiced dentistry in the left front room. Judd and Mabel (Bentley) Lingo lived there next, shown here with son Chester, possibly Judd's mother, and a flock of prize hens around 1908. Later as the Methodist parsonage, many weddings were solemnized in the parlor, and then schoolteacher Phoebe Humes and her daughter Leatha resided there. (Courtesy of Leatha Humes.)

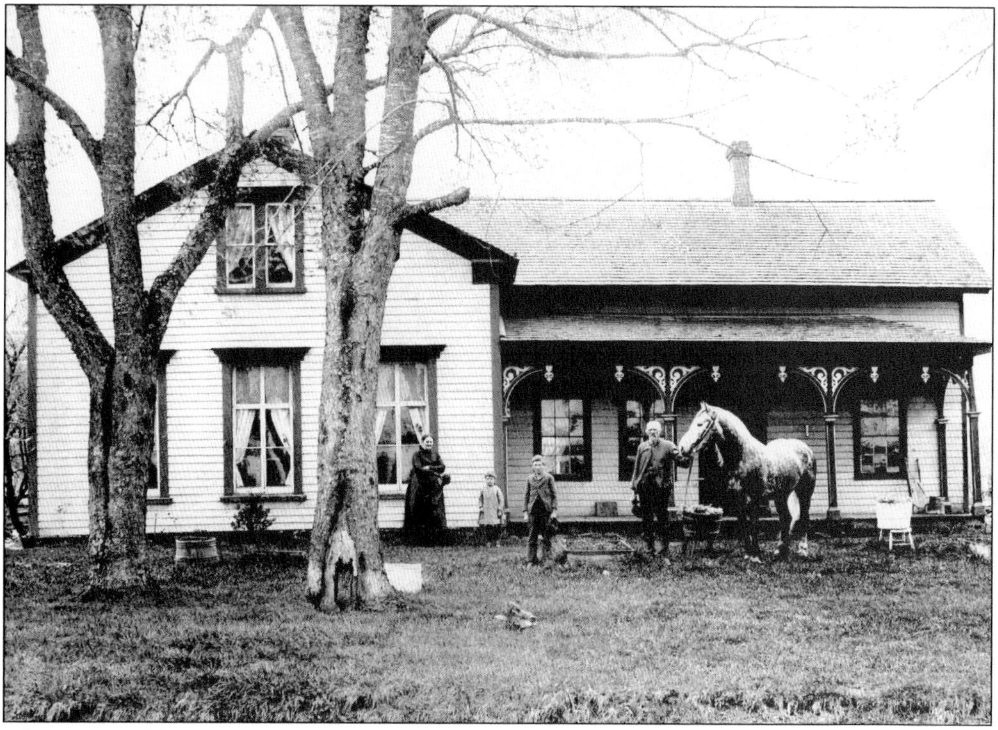

John H. Hotchkiss (1835–1906) was a two-term Crawford County commissioner, serving from 1897 through 1902. He is shown here with his wife, Sarah Irene, and their children Bessie and Charles at the old Hotchkiss Homestead (the current site of Sharon Hayes's home) at the end of Cooper Road. (Courtesy of Gary and Joyce Sliter.)

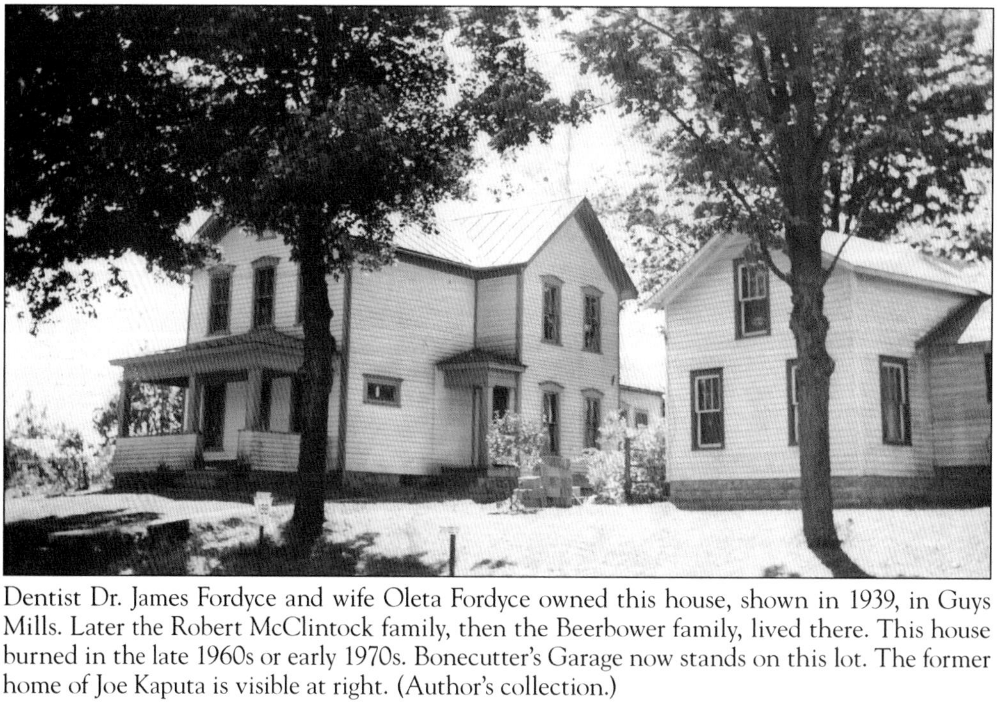

Dentist Dr. James Fordyce and wife Oleta Fordyce owned this house, shown in 1939, in Guys Mills. Later the Robert McClintock family, then the Beerbower family, lived there. This house burned in the late 1960s or early 1970s. Bonecutter's Garage now stands on this lot. The former home of Joe Kaputa is visible at right. (Author's collection.)

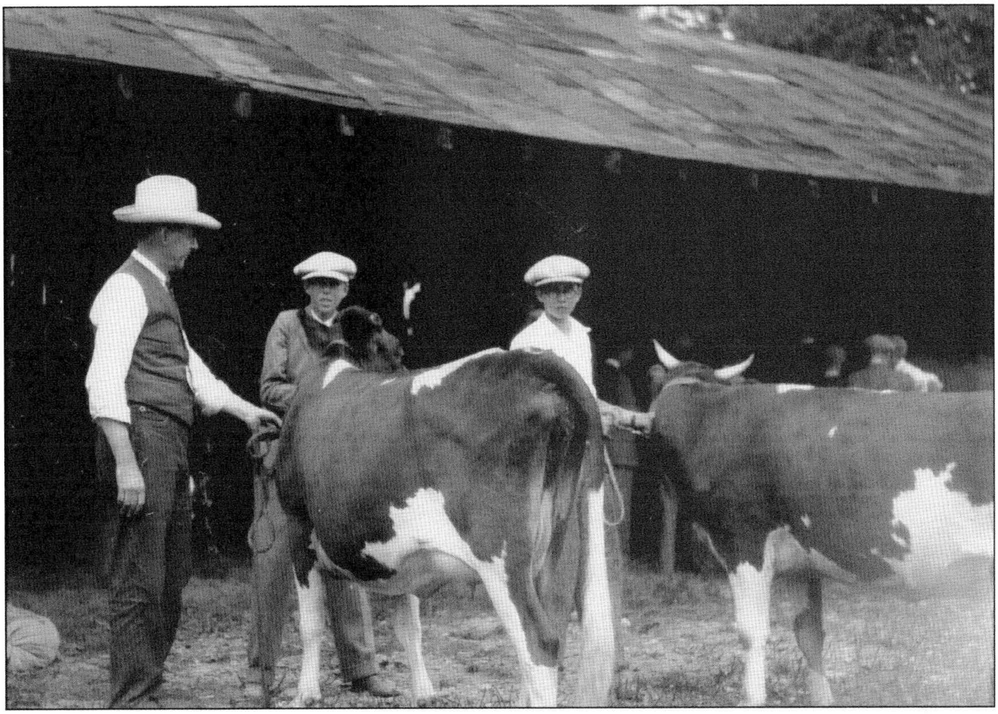

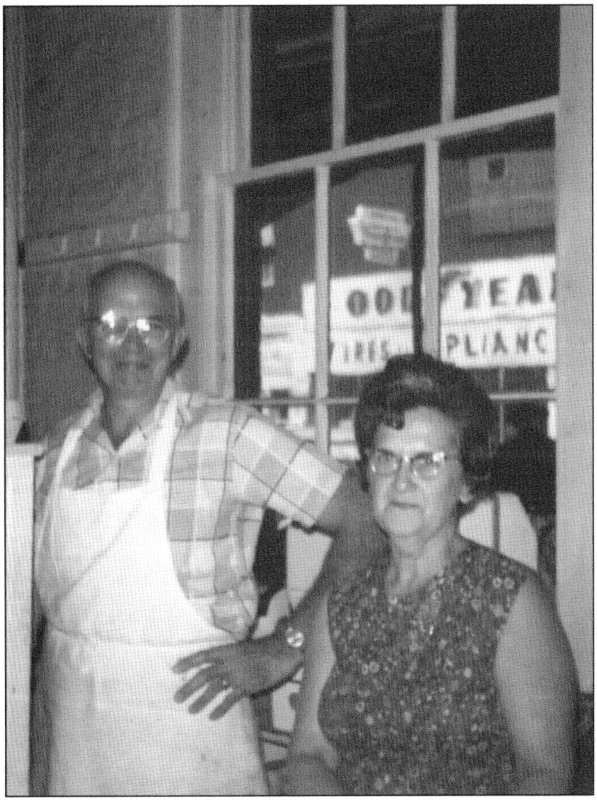

Moses Gilbert, Karl Gilbert's great, great grandfather, settled in Randolph near a large spring in 1818, just a couple years after Jacob Guy. Karl was just 14 when he built his first chicken coop near that spring. Above, David (Gerald) Bird Jr. (center) and Karl Gilbert (right) have their school Vo-Ag Course project animals judged by David (Gerald) Bird Sr. Gilbert tried his hand at pigs and ducks, but turkeys and chickens would be his life ambition. Gilbert married Virginia Cutshall in 1940 and brought her to Cool Spring Farm where they raised five sons and thousands of birds. They were regulars at Meadville Markethouse (right) for nearly 40 years, selling fresh poultry and 600 to 900 dozen eggs each Saturday. They also supplied stores and institutions. Doug Gilbert still farms the original family tract. (Above, courtesy of Doug Gilbert; right, courtesy of CCHS.)

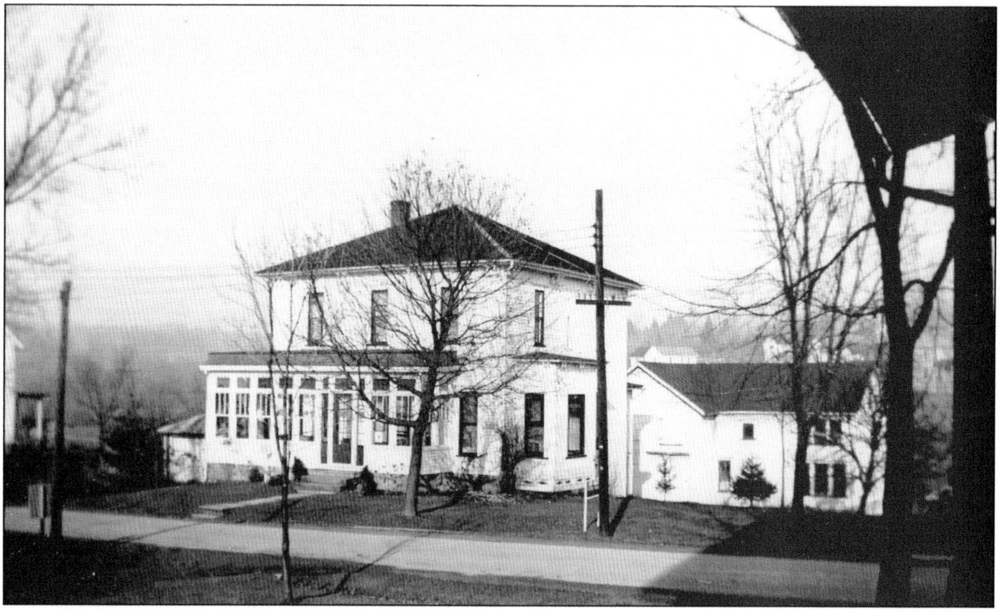

Dr. Charles W. Burgwin arrived in Guys Mills in 1909, bought this home and office from Dr. William Roueche, and practiced medicine here for 37 years. This is the current home of Russell Boyd. In 1920, he built a stone powerhouse and formed the Randolph Light and Power Company. An enterprising visionary, he bought the old Hall Store building and converted it into Egg-win Poultry Plant. When the price of eggs did not cover the feed, he converted it into Burgwin Apartments. Government controls pushed him out of that business. He then started a community woodworking shop manufacturing folding chairs. He had just completed 300 chairs when the building was swept by fire in May 1945. Yet his most valuable mission was the consolidation of Randolph Schools. Effie and he remained beloved residents for many years. (Above, courtesy of Leatha Humes; below, courtesy of Janet Marvin.)

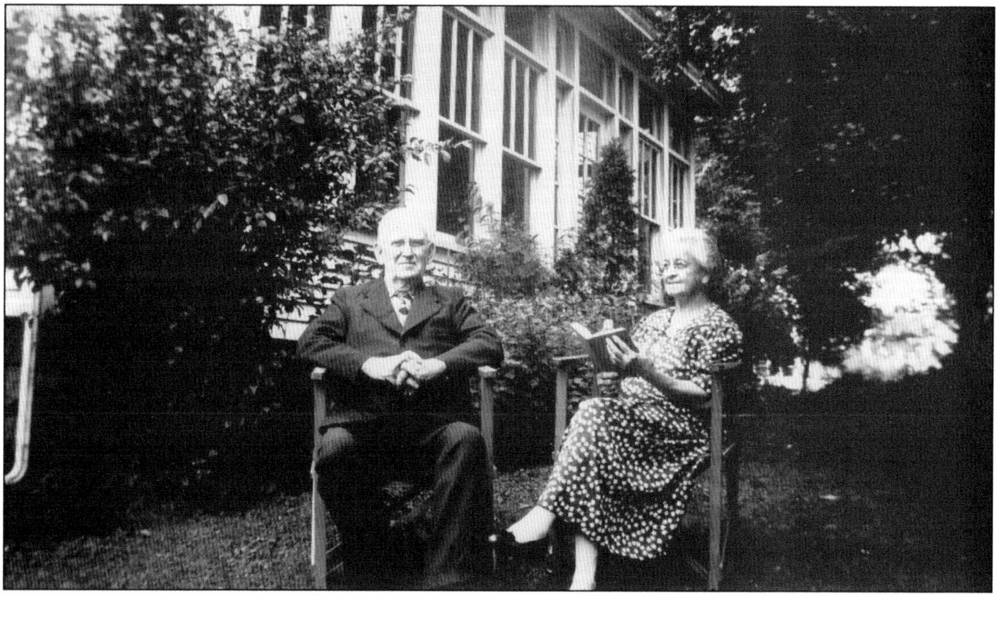

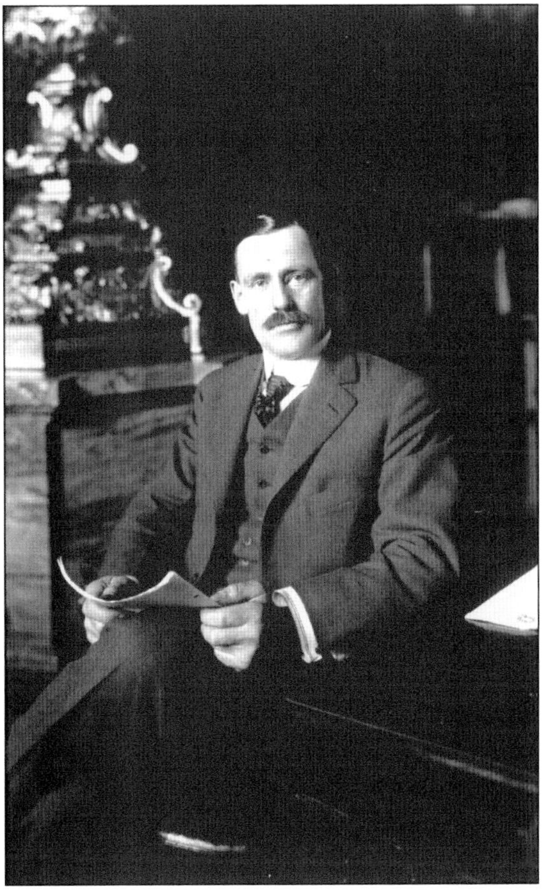

Raymond E. Smith was elected as Pennsylvania senator in 1914 and served Mercer and Crawford Counties for four years. Smith was born in 1878 in Guys Mills and was educated in local schools, Edinboro Normal School and Allegheny College. His Allegheny education was interrupted to enlist in the Spanish-American War, returning in 1899. He was a member of the Randolph School Board for 10 years and Randolph Township auditor for 15 years. He served as secretary-treasurer of the Crawford Telephone Company and president of the Crawford-Venango Dairymen's Association. He was president of trustees of the Mount Hope Methodist Church, a member of the John Brown Memorial Association, and a past master of Mount Hope Grange. He and wife Caroline (Graham) had five daughters. Their former home, pictured below, still stands on the intersection of Shaffer and McFadden Roads. (Right, courtesy of CCHS; below, courtesy of U.S. Fish and Wildlife Service, Erie National Wildlife Refuge, photograph by Dale Coggeshall.)

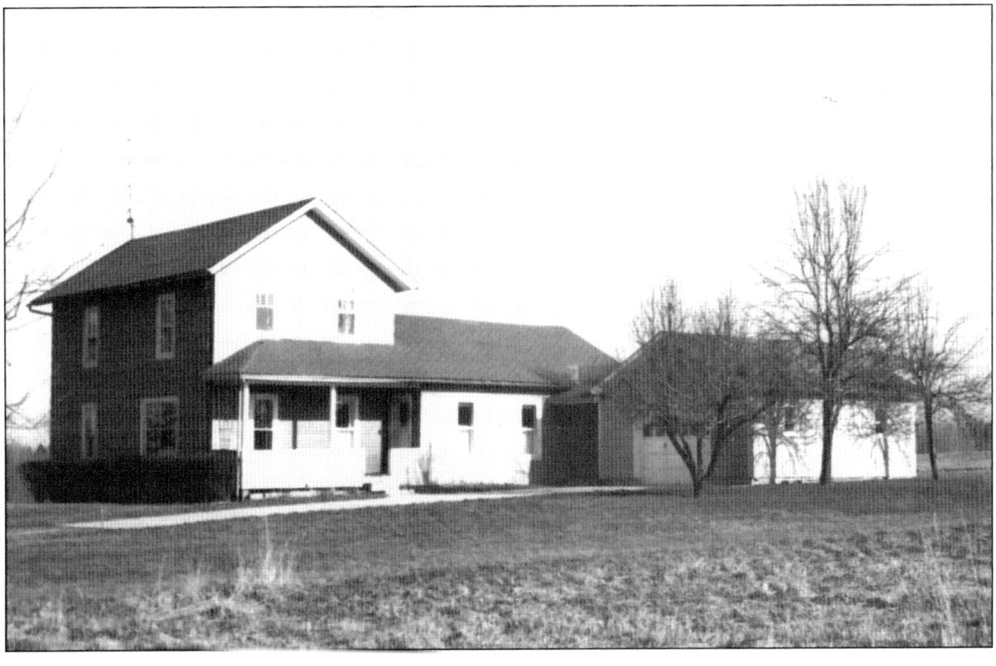

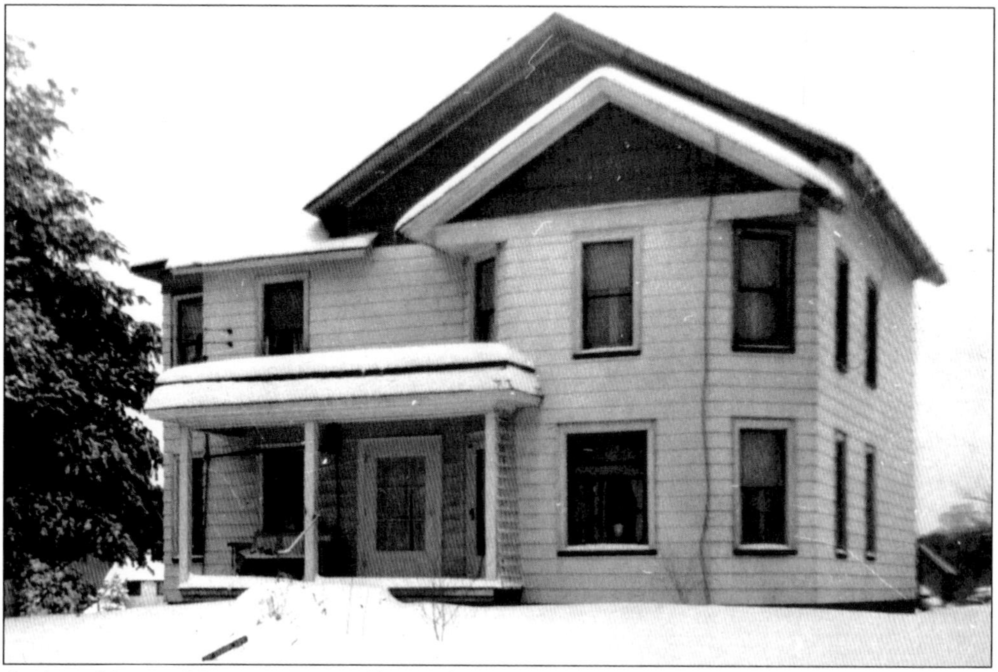

Graham Nursing Home on Townville Road was founded by Howard and Mae (Luzier) Graham in the early 1930s. Full capacity was 14 elderly. The Graham family lived upstairs along with a few residents who could manage the stairs. All food was grown there on Minnowbrook Farm. The meat was canned in one-gallon jars, and many bushels of fruits and vegetables were canned each year. Water for bathing, cooking, and laundry was carried from the outdoor pump until indoor plumbing was added in the 1950s. Mae was a practical nurse. Alelia Hanson, their daughter who lived next door, was a registered nurse, and Dr. Paul T. Poux served as the attending doctor. Seen below, residents enjoyed ice cream and cake in the dining room on New Year's Eve 1961. Velma Lenhart, a nurse's aid, is standing in the center. (Courtesy of the Childs family.)

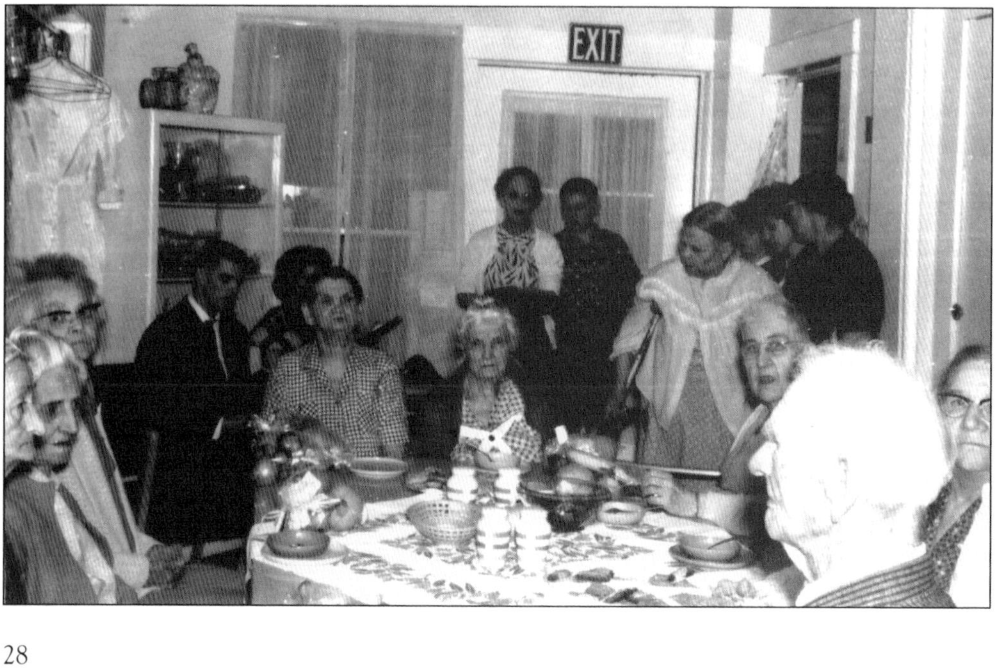

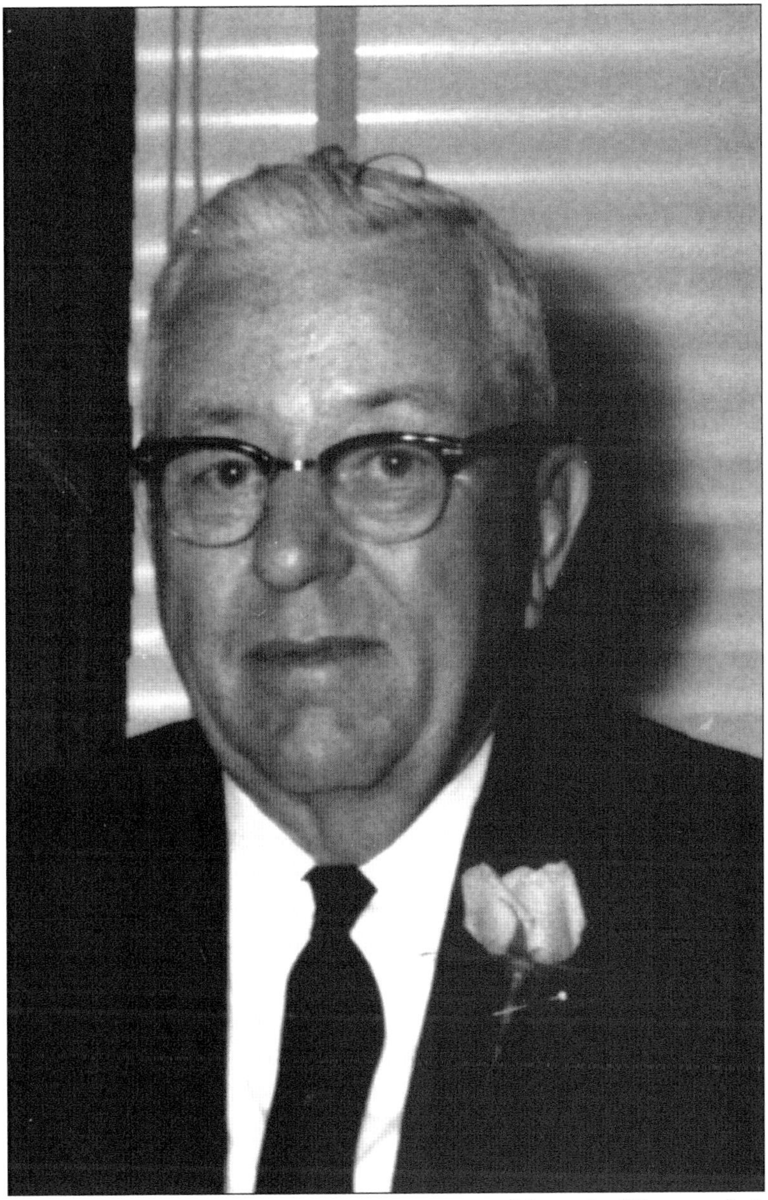

Prior to his tenure as Crawford County commissioner, Harry L. Wentworth had been a Randolph Township dairy farmer and raised draft horses. He founded Wentworth Auto Sales at Mount Hope in 1930 and remained involved for 33 years. During his four terms as Crawford County commissioner, 1940 to 1956, a sizable county debt was eliminated, the County Home was modernized, and in 1954, the courthouse was fully renovated. All of this was accomplished without impairing the county's financial security. Yet he is best remembered as the main thrust behind the establishment of the Crawford County Fair in 1946. He was instrumental in the purchase of 67 acres of land for the fairgrounds and remained president of the fair board for many years. His intense convictions guided him to advocate Crawford County's best interests. He was elected to the GOP State Committee in 1958 and was a member at his death. He passed away in 1963 at the age of 72 following a stroke. He and his wife, Kerna (Oakes), had a daughter and two sons. (Courtesy of Sally Wentworth.)

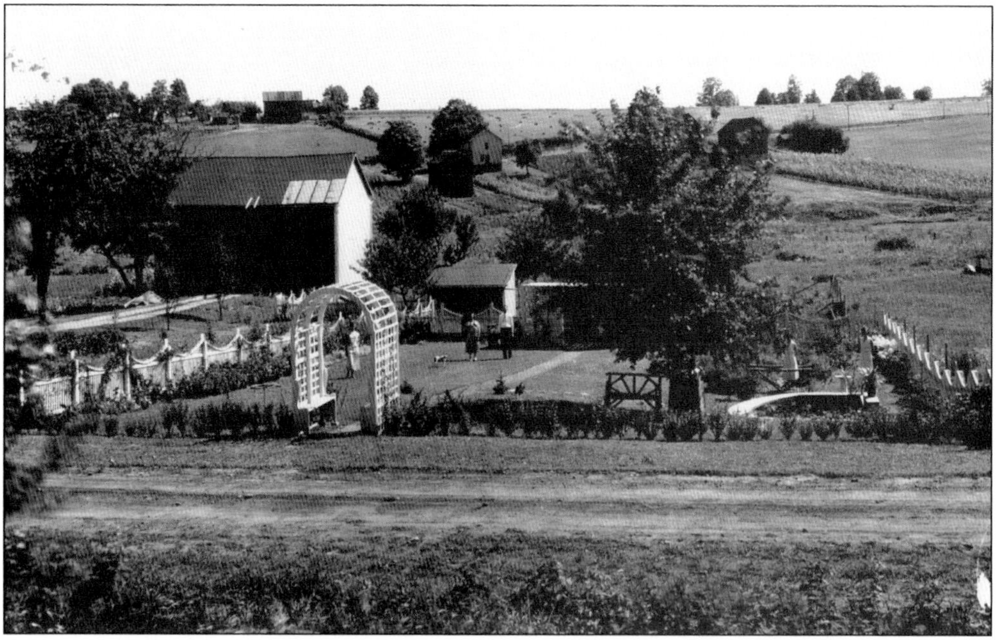

Bert and Nellie (Loper) Brown had a lovely home with beautiful gardens and a spring-fed goldfish pond on Plank Road. Bert was a mail carrier for the Guys Mills Post Office. (Courtesy of Bonnie Murphy.)

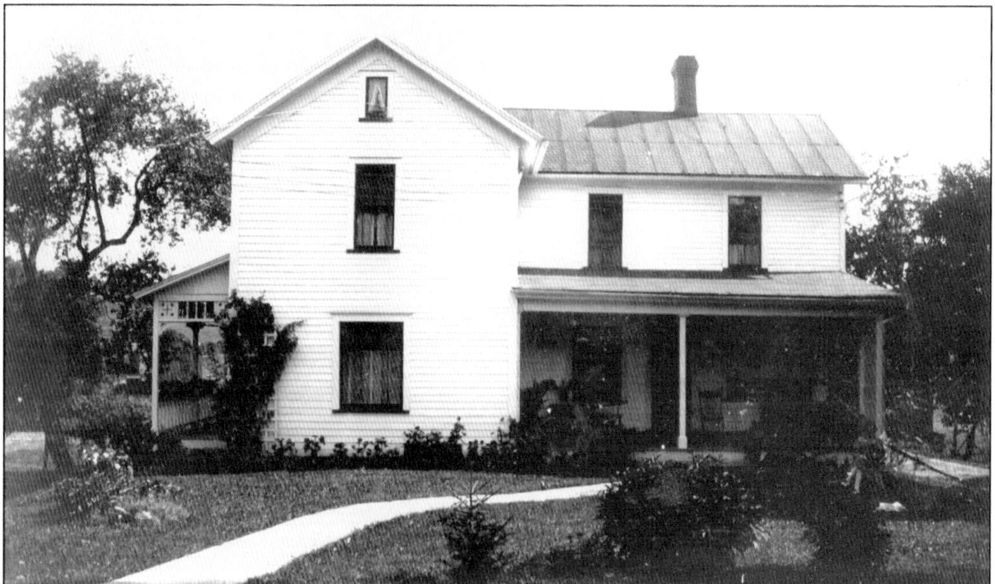

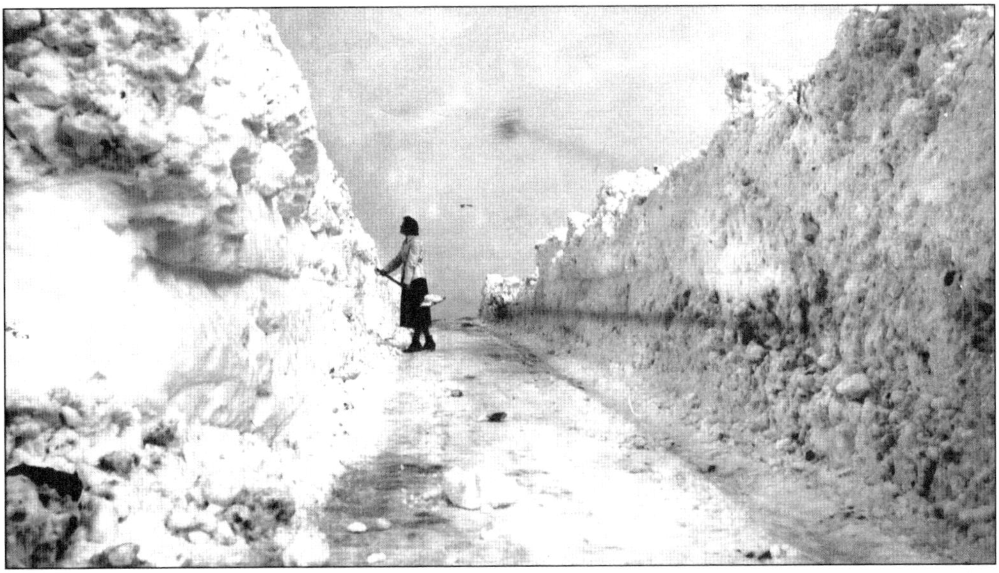

The blizzard of February 1958 isolated the area for a full week, creating 16-foot snow piles, sometimes reaching the tops of the telephone poles. The Guys Mills Water Company's six-foot-deep water lines froze, and Walter Kent thawed them with his welder. Ruth Armstrong, above, gives perspective to the walls of snow opened for one lane of traffic. (Courtesy of Brian and Judy Kirberger, photograph by Photo-Graphic Arts for the Meadville Tribune.)

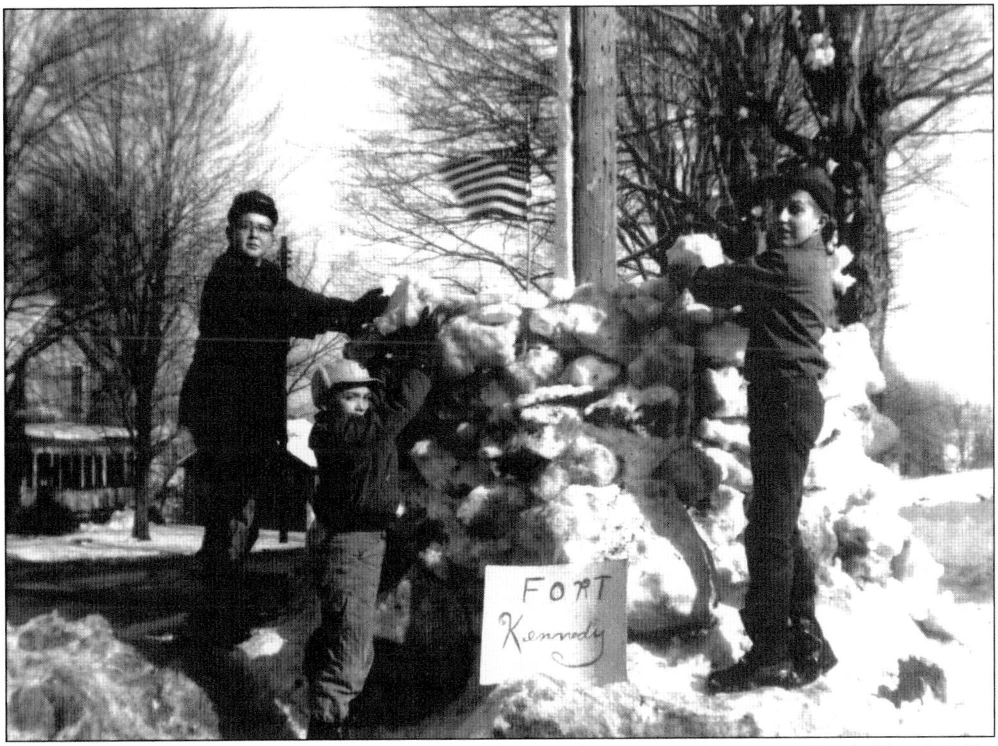

Taking full advantage of heavy snow and school cancellations, neighbors Lyle Bird, Chuck Lilly, and Jim Kaputa made their own fun by building elaborate snow forts. Any passersby in the line of fire were fair game for a friendly snowball. (Courtesy of Darlene Jablon and Dorothy Anthony.)

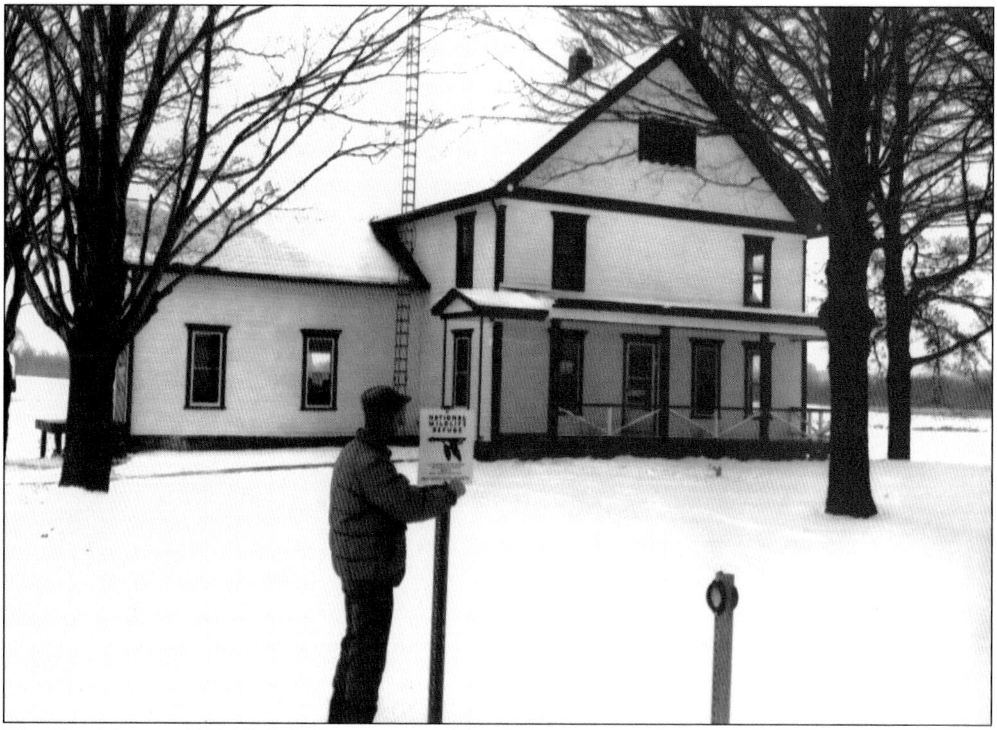

The Erie National Wildlife Refuge was established in 1959. The primary objective of the refuge is to provide waterfowl and other migratory birds with a nesting, feeding, brooding, and resting habitat. The first offices were housed in the former Glenn Woodcock home, shown here in 1966, and are now on Wood Duck Lane. (Courtesy of Janet Marvin.)

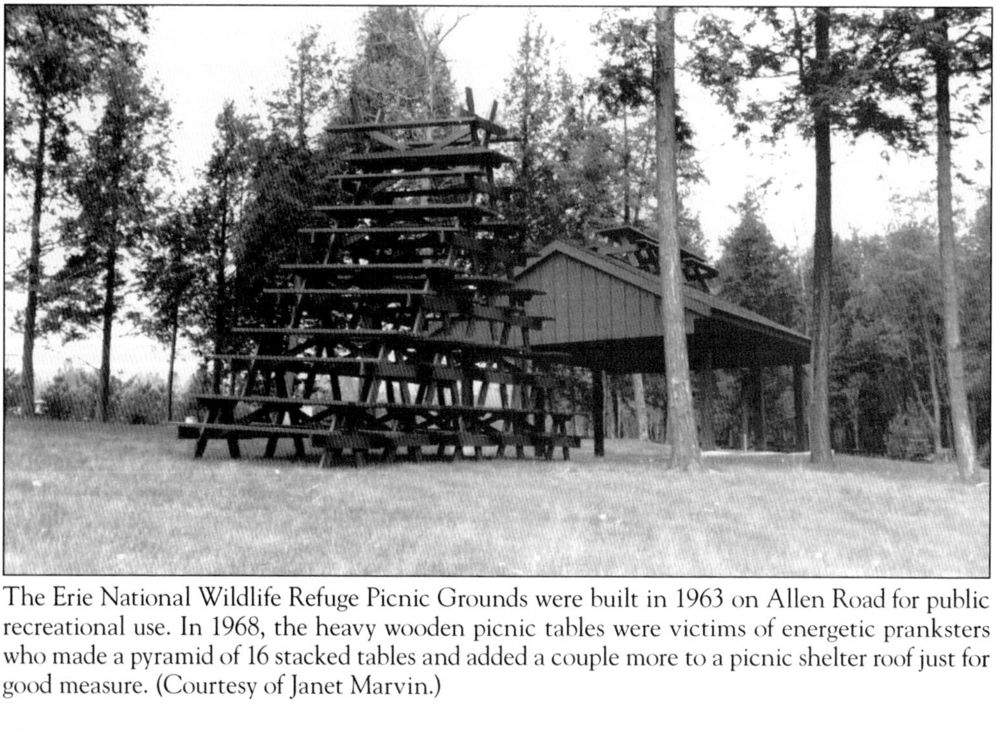

The Erie National Wildlife Refuge Picnic Grounds were built in 1963 on Allen Road for public recreational use. In 1968, the heavy wooden picnic tables were victims of energetic pranksters who made a pyramid of 16 stacked tables and added a couple more to a picnic shelter roof just for good measure. (Courtesy of Janet Marvin.)

Three

They Worshipped
Church History

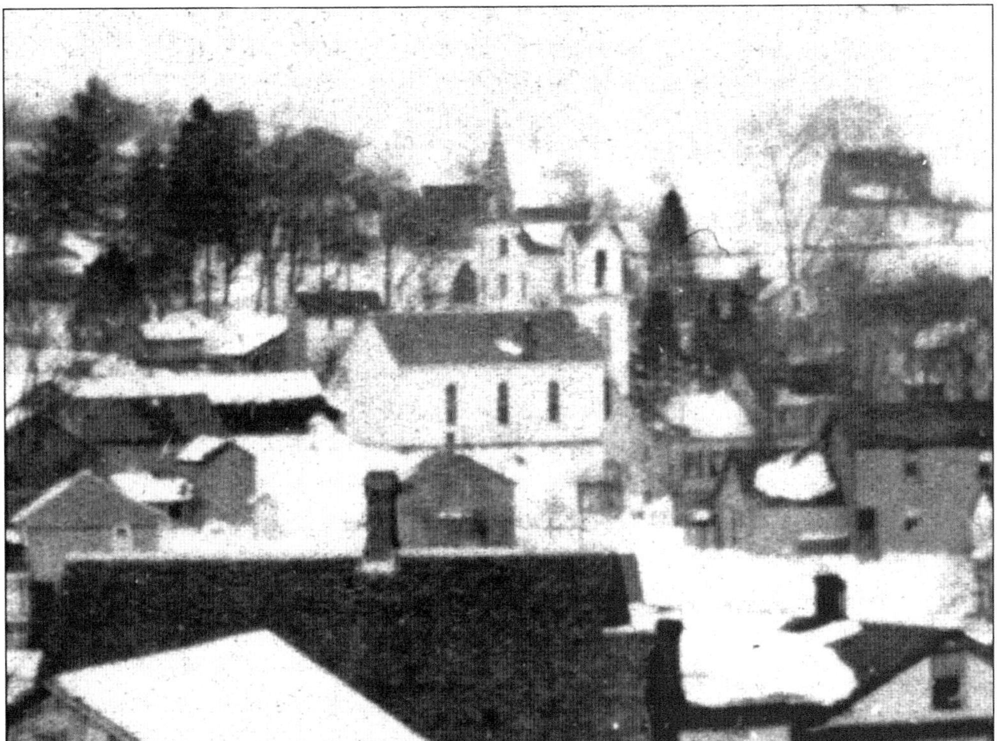

The Covenant Baptist Church on the north hill in Guys Mills is shown here beyond the Methodist Church about 1906 or 1907. This body of believers was the first Baptist congregation organized in Crawford County east of French Creek. By the time this photograph was taken, the building was no longer in use. It was eventually torn down by Brice Walker for used lumber. (Author's collection.)

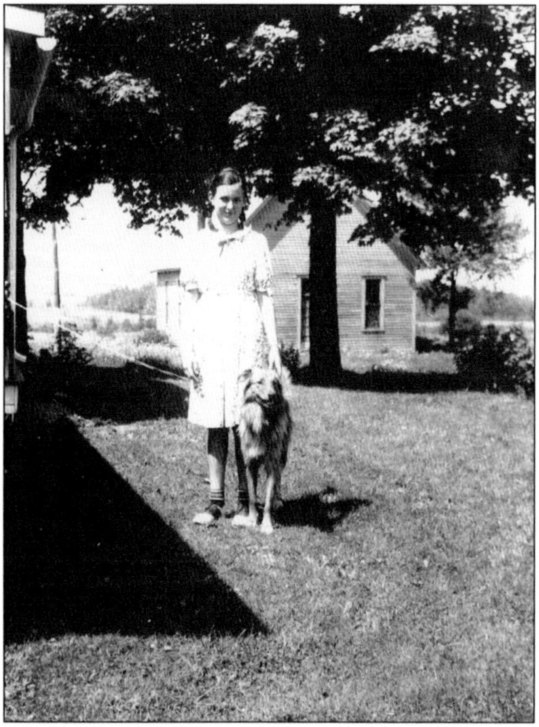

An unidentified girl and dog stand in front of the old church at Hickory Corners in the northern part of Randolph Township. (Courtesy of Brian and Judy Kirberger.)

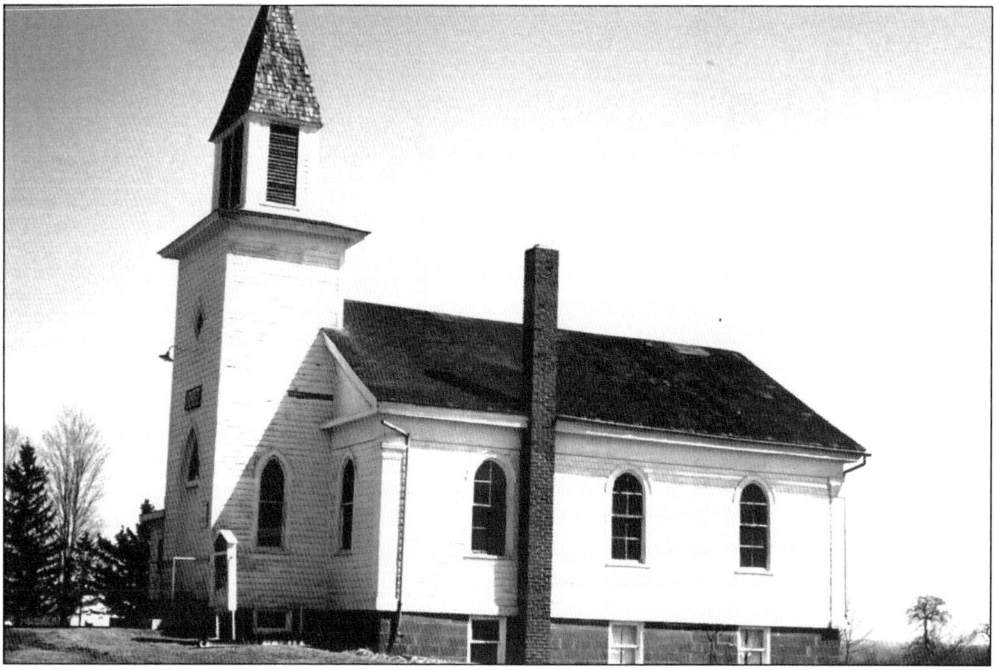

The Black Ash Methodist Church, shown here in 1971, was erected in the 1860s at a cost of $1,275 on land donated by the Bogardus family. Until the church was built, members met in a schoolhouse across the road. Mr. and Mrs. Mark Bogardus, Mr. and Mrs. Nicholas Bogardus, and Mr. Loveless were early members, with Rev. Edwin Hull as their first pastor. The church was closed in 1977 and the building was remodeled for a residence. (Courtesy of Dorothy Wilson.)

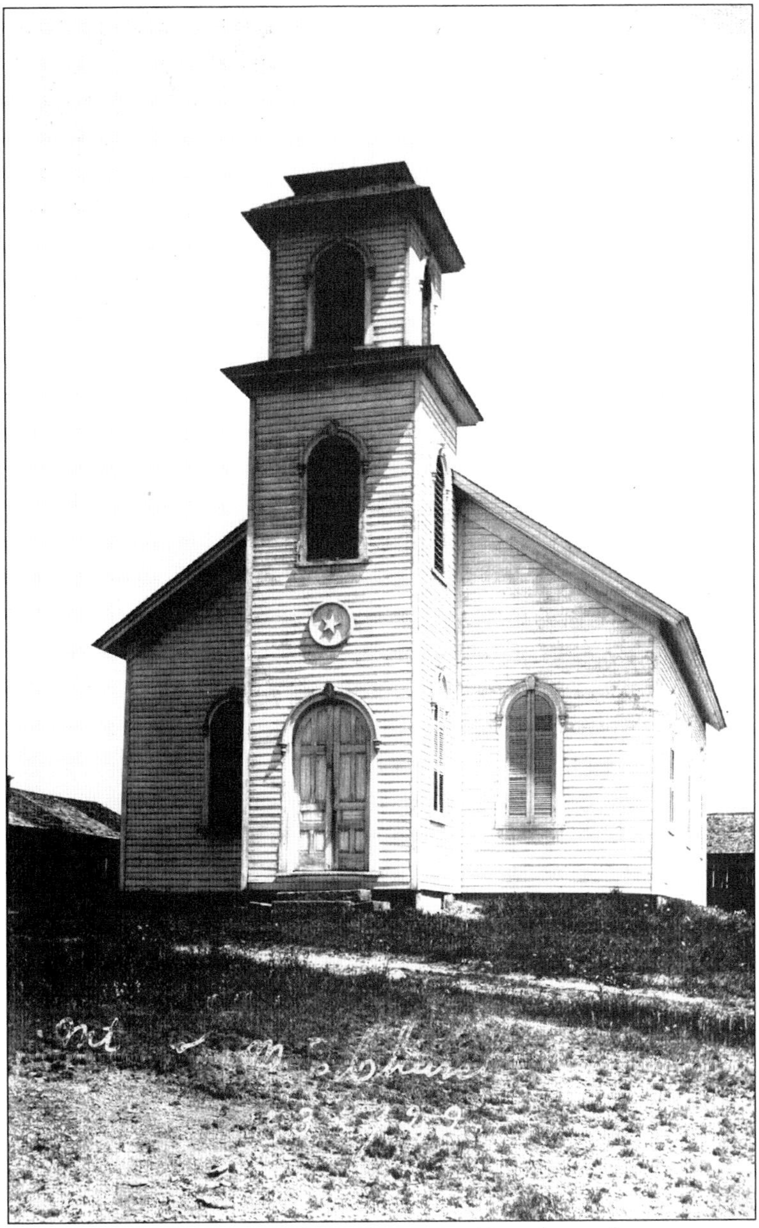

The Mount Hope Methodist Church, shown here in 1922 with its adjacent carriage shed, was founded on faith in God and a desire to enhance the spiritual welfare of the Mount Hope community. This building was built on land donated by Levi Oakes in 1858, at a cost of $900 and seated 300. The Methodists of that era took their religion very seriously. Religious fervor ran high at the old camp meetings, and many new converts were added to the rolls. The Mount Hope Methodist Church declined the invitation to join the Guys Mills Methodist Church in the 1965 merger with Congregational church. Church historians have been Raymond E. Smith, Howard Byham, Joanne Burchard, and Mae Sutley. This congregation has been attached to several different charges, has seen many pastors come and go, and has updated and remodeled several times. Through all these changes in the past century and a half, their zeal for the Lord has never wavered. (Courtesy of Mae Sutley.)

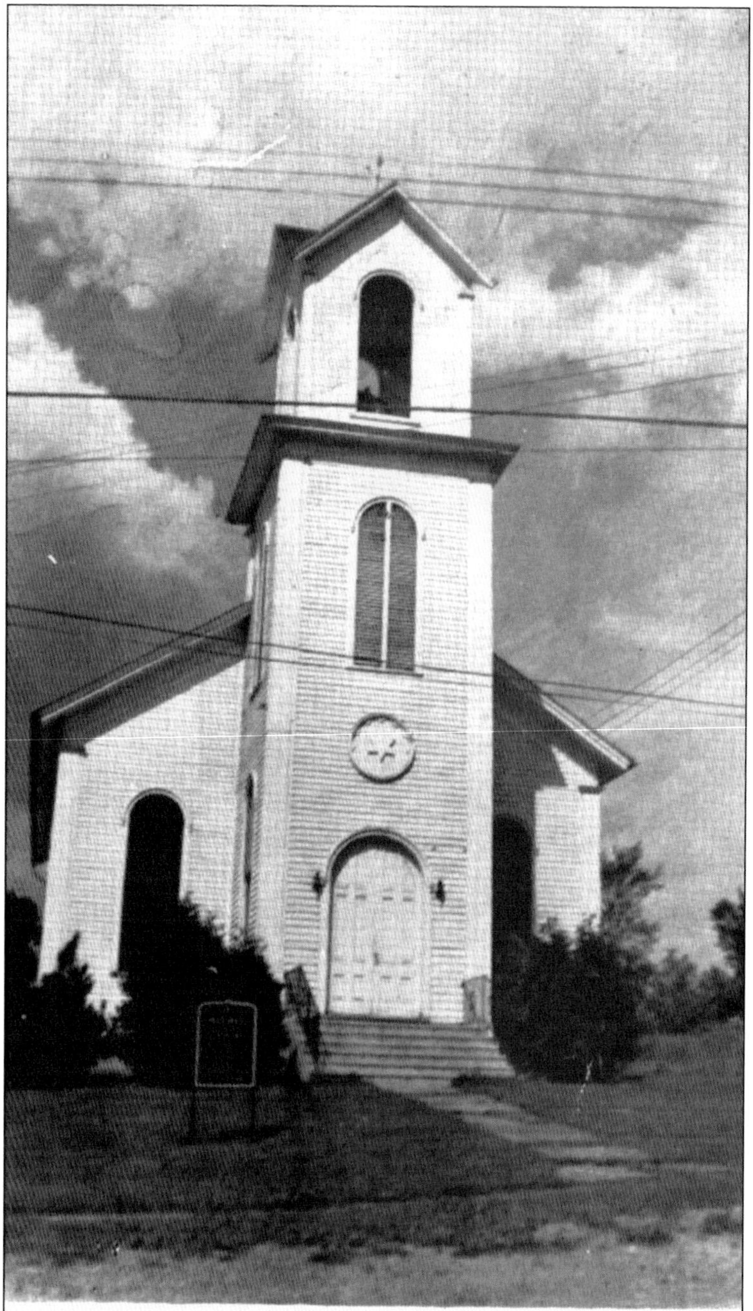

Guys Mills Methodist Church

The first pastor of the Guys Mills Methodist Church was Rev. John W. Blasdell with 55 members. This handsome frame edifice was erected in 1871 at a cost of $3,500 with a seating capacity of 350 people. Timbers were donated by the Virtue family. Nearly a century later, in 1965, the Guys Mills Methodist Church merged with the Guys Mills Congregational Church to form the United Church of Guys Mills, United Church of Christ. This building is still standing and is used as the United Evangelical Free Church Youth Complex. (Author's collection.)

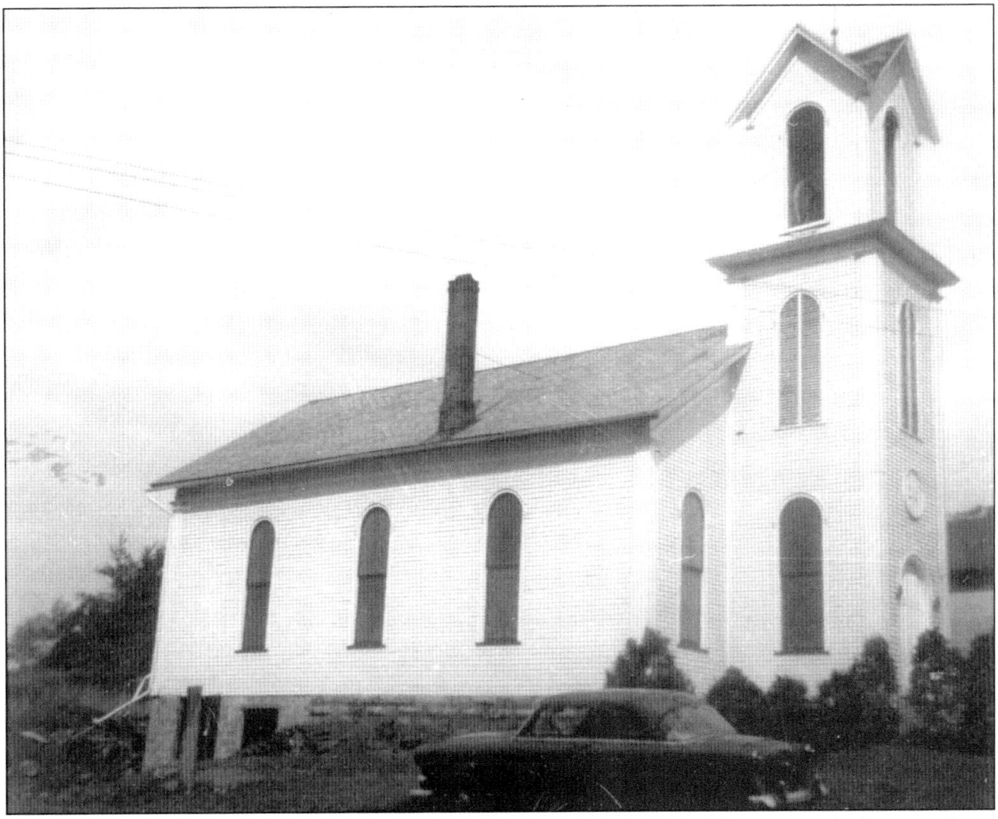

The side view of the Guys Mills Methodist Church, above, shows the original chimney from the wood stove that warmed the sanctuary. In the photograph below, pretty young ladies and two young men pose on the church steps for a Sunday school class portrait in the 1940s. Their Sunday school teacher was Ruth Graham. (Courtesy of Leatha Humes.)

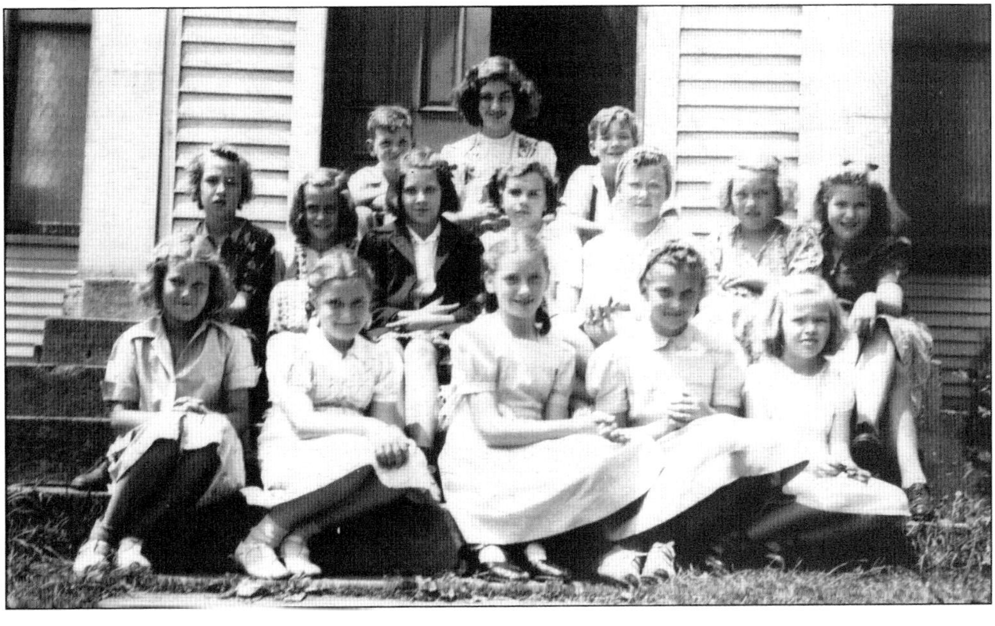

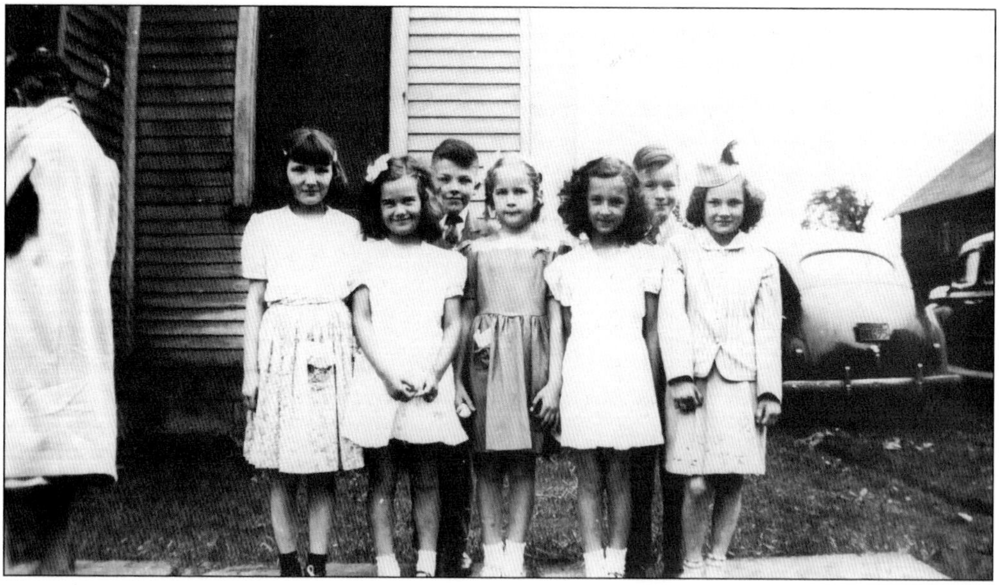

Seen above, a young Sunday school class in June 1947 poses in front of the Guys Mills Methodist Church. Students are, from left to right, Sue Hickernell, Jane Carpenter, Paul Minelley, Carol Virtue, Gertrude Carpenter, Gordon Kent, and Ramona Fairman. In the image below, the entire adult and youth Sunday school poses in front of the Guys Mills Methodist Church in June 1947. (Author's collection.)

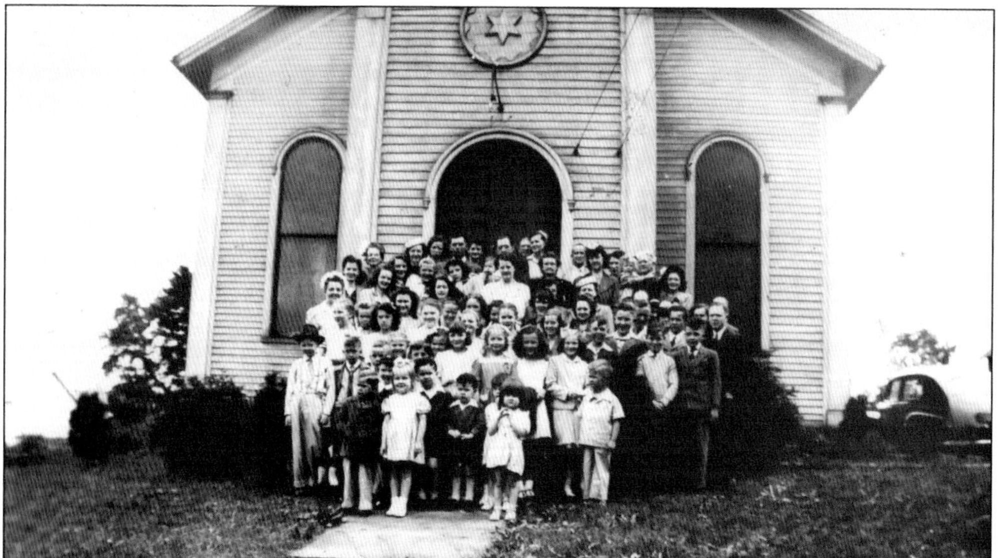

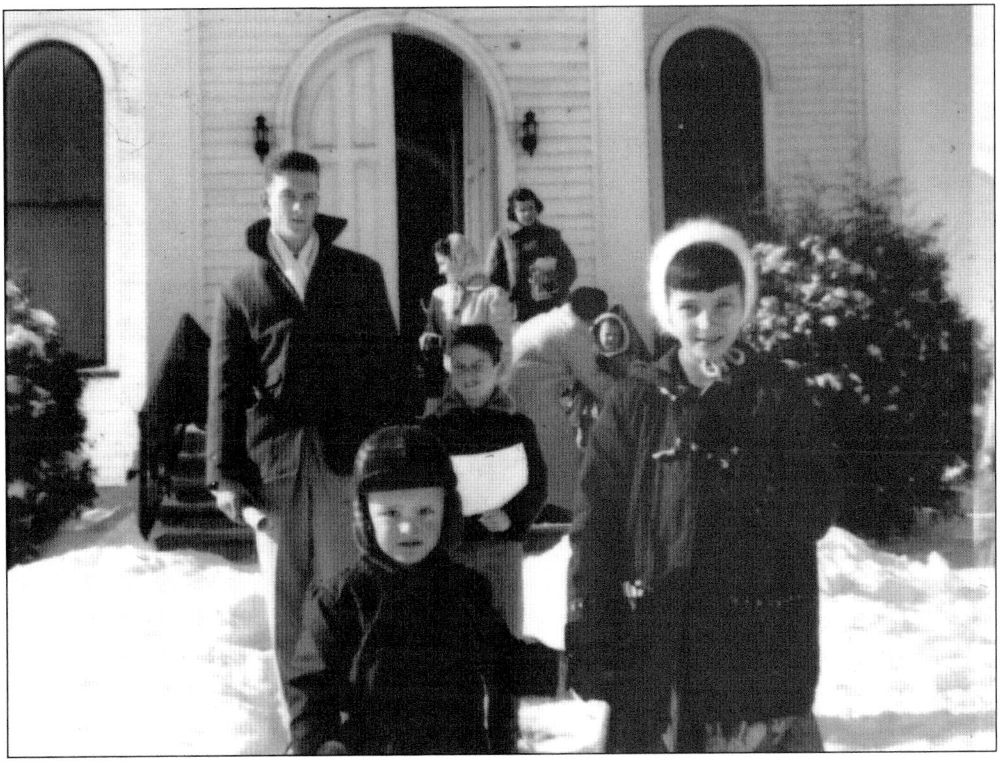

Following the benediction, with Sunday school papers and bulletins in hand, members of the Guys Mills Methodist Church headed home. Anne Stewart holds her brother Randy's hand with Alan and Gordon Carpenter close behind them. At right is a 1940s view of the Methodist Aid Hall that stood just north of the church. Ladies Aid served lunches here every Wednesday (10¢ for school children) and then spent the afternoon quilting to raise money for the church. The Sunday school rooms for the children's division, led by Effie Burgwin, were upstairs. This building was torn down around 1956 or 1957. (Above, courtesy of Leatha Humes; right, courtesy of the Childs family.)

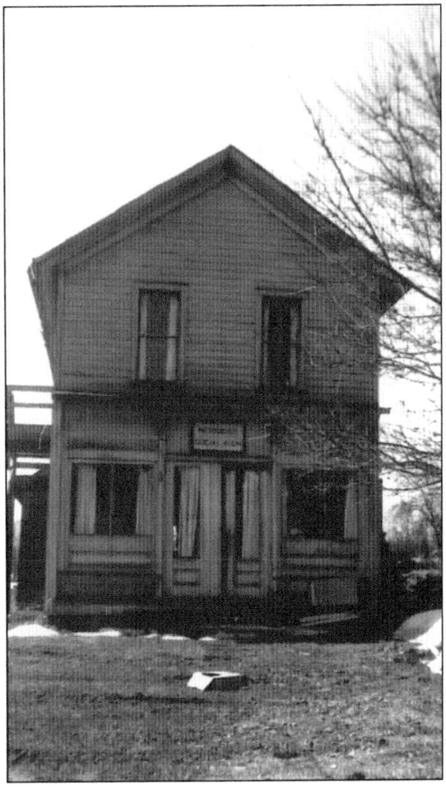

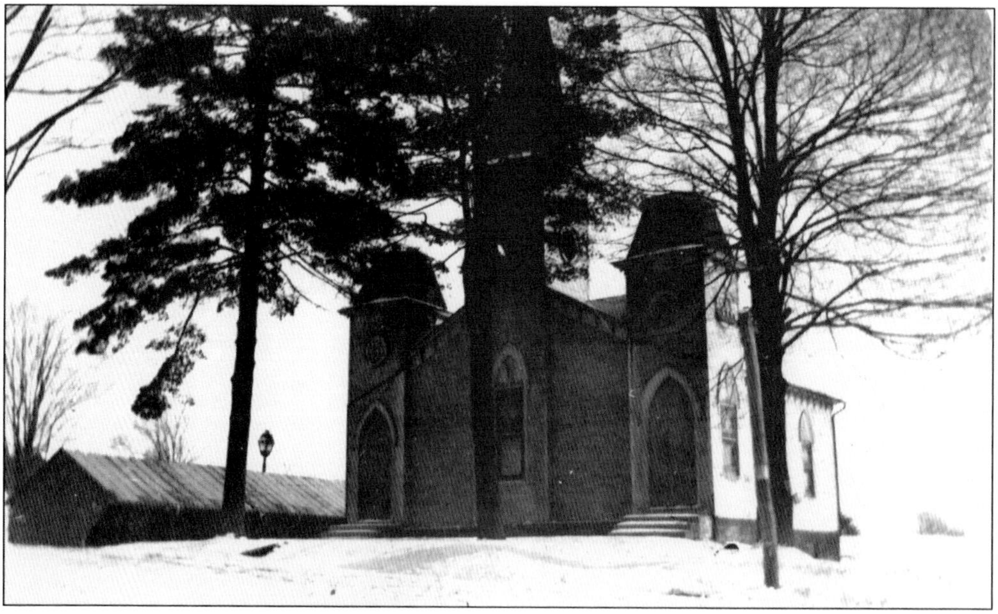

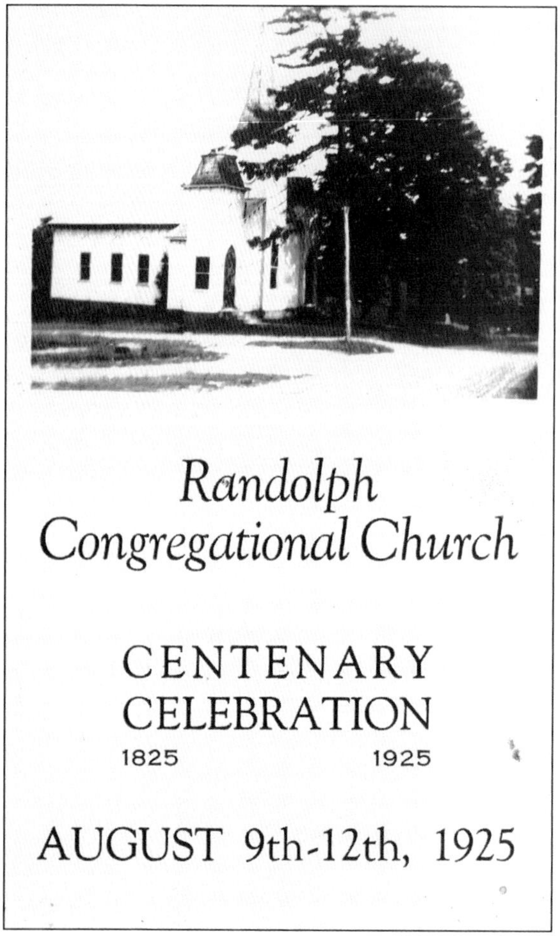

Randolph
Congregational Church

CENTENARY
CELEBRATION
1825 1925

AUGUST 9th-12th, 1925

The First Congregational Church of Randolph in Guys Mills was organized as a Presbyterian and Congregational society in 1825 and a Congregational society in 1839. Rev. Timothy Alden, founder of Allegheny College, conducted early services as a supply pastor before the church was built. Jacob and Susanna Guy were early members. Meetings were held in the schoolhouse until 1845, when a frame church was built on land donated by the Guy family. The original design had one set of double doors in front and stairs in the vestibule leading to a choir loft. Remodeled and enlarged in 1871, the church is shown here about 1912. The Congregational Church Centenary Celebration in 1925 was a four-day grand jubilee of sermons, elocution, tableaux, visiting speakers, basket dinners, a baseball game, choirs, and orchestras. Rev. Walter S. Percy was pastor at the time. (Above, courtesy of Robert W. Waid; left, courtesy of Leatha Humes.)

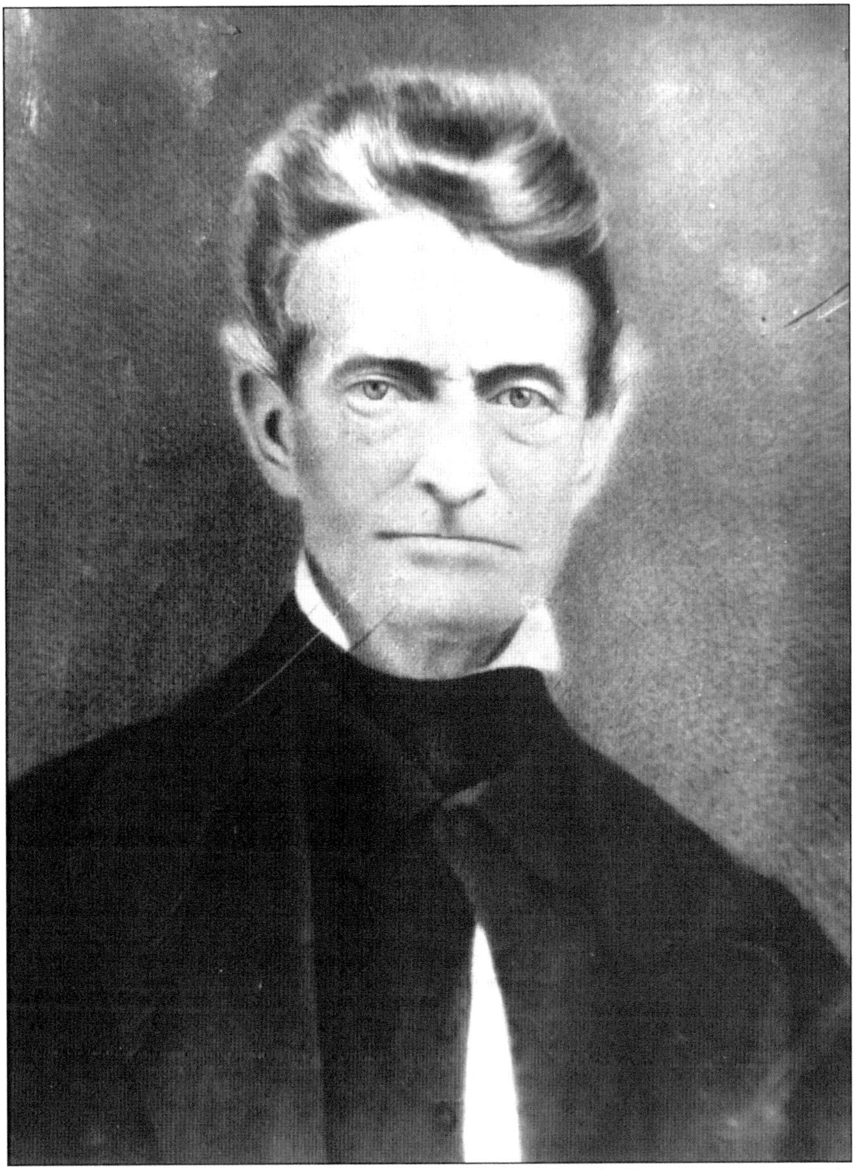

The famed abolitionist John Brown has been long associated with the Congregational church in Guys Mills. He may have attended sometime between 1825 and 1831, when he started his own Independent Congregational Society above his tannery. This was before the Guys Mills church building was erected in 1845, so he would have joined the temporary schoolhouse meetings. However, dates do not support an oft-quoted legend that John Brown was choirmaster two winters there. A letter by Estelle Thomson (1846–1941) written in 1938 states that a John Brown was her music teacher when she was 15 years old and that they met in the Congregational church. She stated, "I wonder that any roof timbers remained after our singing of anthems. I have longed for John Brown's anthems ever since." However, Thomson was not born yet when John Brown the abolitionist moved from Pennsylvania in 1835. He was hanged in 1859, before Thomson turned 15 years old in 1861. And in fact, several men by the name of "John Brown" (using their middle initials) lived here when these singing classes took place. One of these men was a well-known singing teacher. (Courtesy of CCHS.)

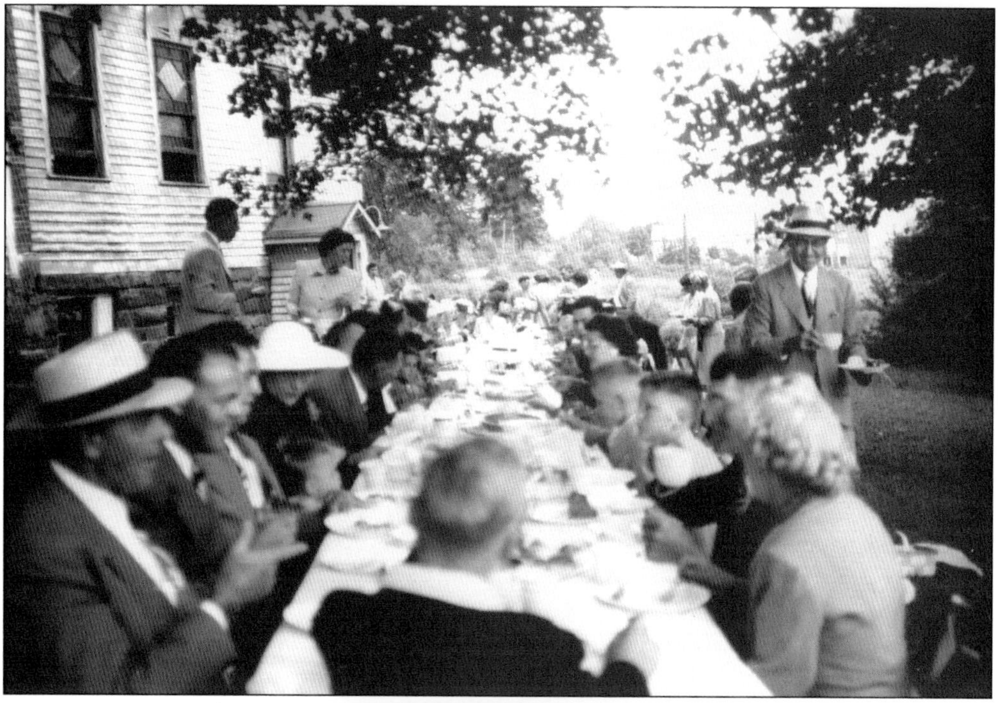

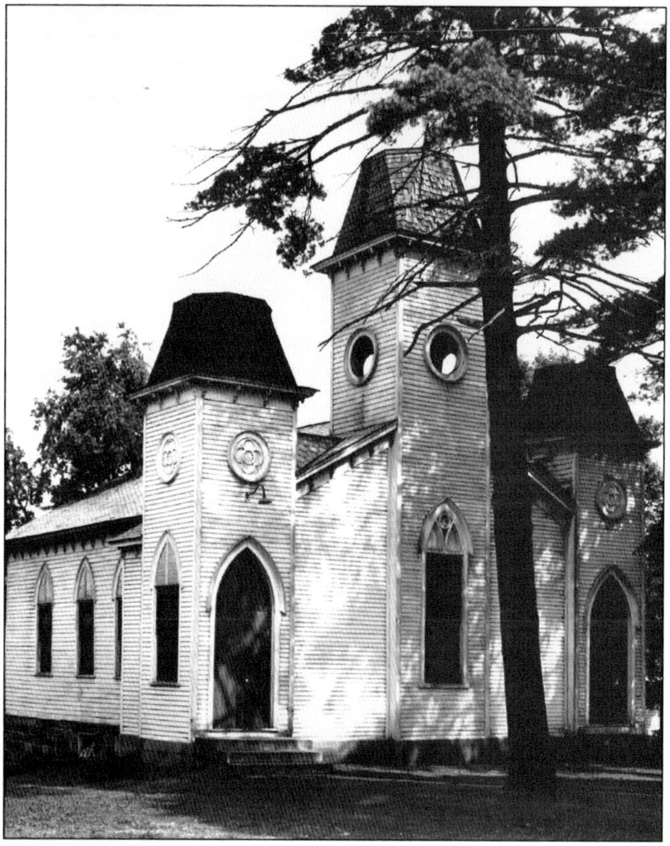

A picnic lunch was attended by over 60 guests on the church lawn as part of the festivities for the 125th anniversary celebration in 1950. Notice the new brick school in the background. The photograph at left is the Congregational church's portrait for the 125th anniversary celebration. The original cut stone foundation, visible here, was replaced along with the base timbers in 1953 and 1954. (Courtesy of Leatha Humes.)

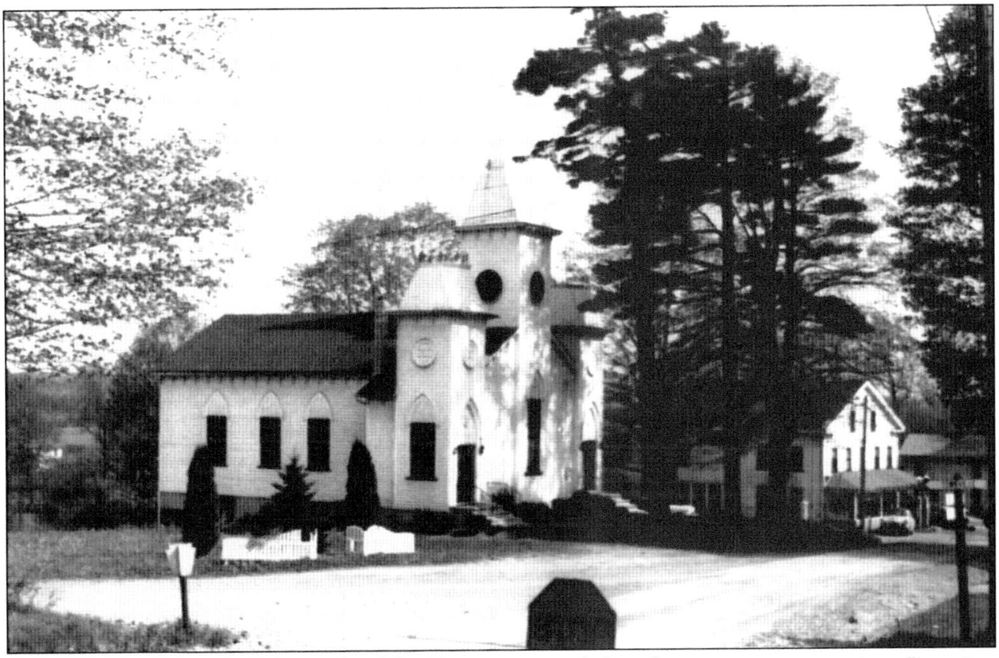

Remodeling the inside and outside of the Congregational church was a two-year project. Boasting a brand-new block foundation, pews, communion table, pulpit chairs, brass collection plates, organ, spire, and landscaping, the Congregational church was ready for rededication services in 1955. In 1965, 10 years later, the Methodist and Congregational churches merged and formed the United Church of Guys Mills, United Church of Christ. (Courtesy of Leatha Humes.)

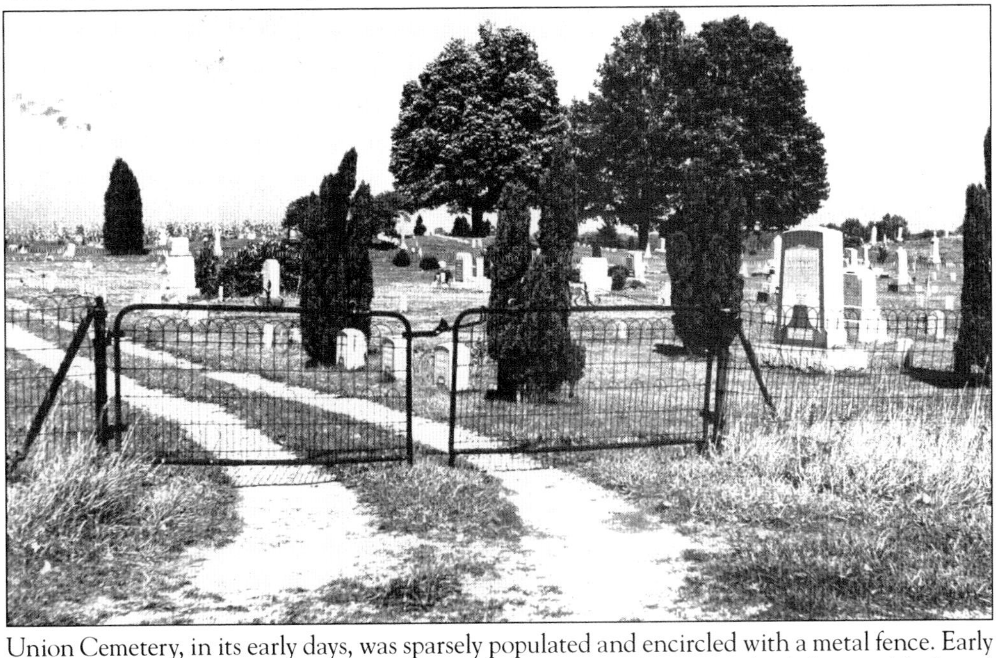

Union Cemetery, in its early days, was sparsely populated and encircled with a metal fence. Early sextons received 25¢ for digging a grave by hand. The original acre was deeded as a public burial ground in June 1857, and since then, many loved ones from all denominations and walks of life have been laid to rest there. (Courtesy of Wilford and Carolyn Miller.)

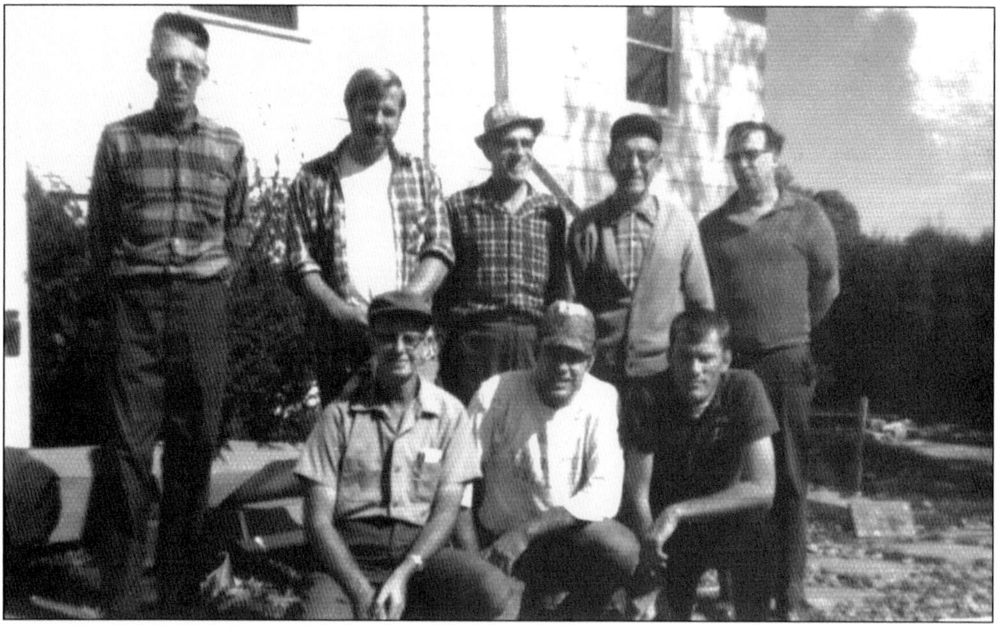

Congregational church members take a break from installing eaves spouting. Pictured are, from left to right, (first row) Raleigh Marr, Rick Smith, and Bill Houck; (second row) Arthur Smith, Tom Radecki, Francis Groshner, Steven Heme, and Wilford Miller. Seen below, participants in the 150th anniversary service are, from left to right, Rev. Jay Metzler, former pastor, called in 1966; Rev. Walter Thoms, retired former pastor of this congregation and Park Congregational Church, Meadville; Rev. Paul Westcoat, Penn West Conference Minister, United Church of Christ; Rev. Donald Evans, former pastor, called in 1970; Rev. Wayne Sova, current pastor; Rev. Blair Ward, retired pastor of the Church of the Nazarene and resident of the community who served in the pulpit; and Norman Rough, lay preacher, who served faithfully. Now known as the United Evangelical Free Church, its motto is "To know Him and to make Him known." (Above, courtesy of Leatha Humes; below, courtesy of Russell and Virginia Boyd.)

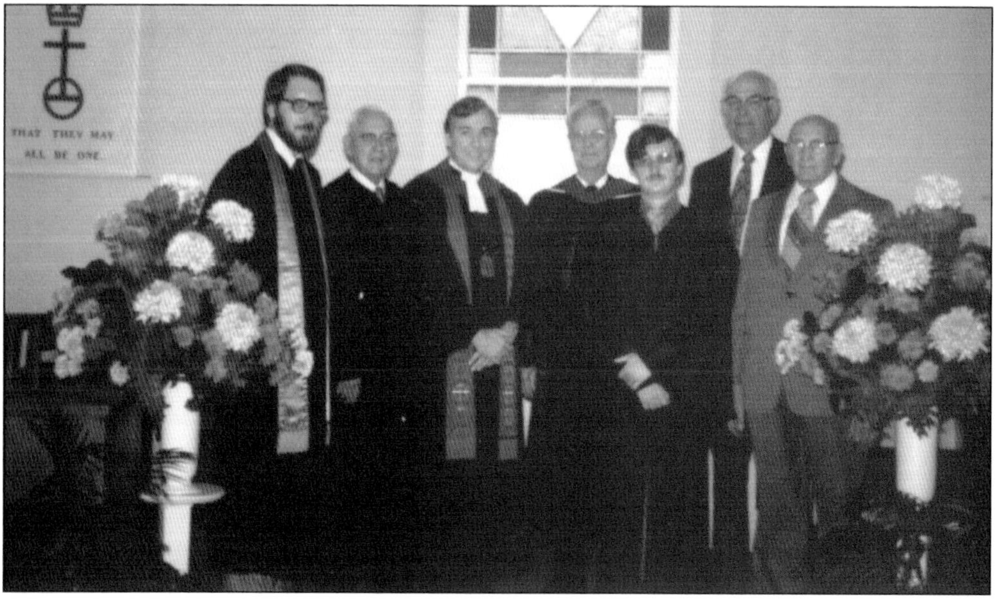

Four

THEY LEARNED
SCHOOL HISTORY

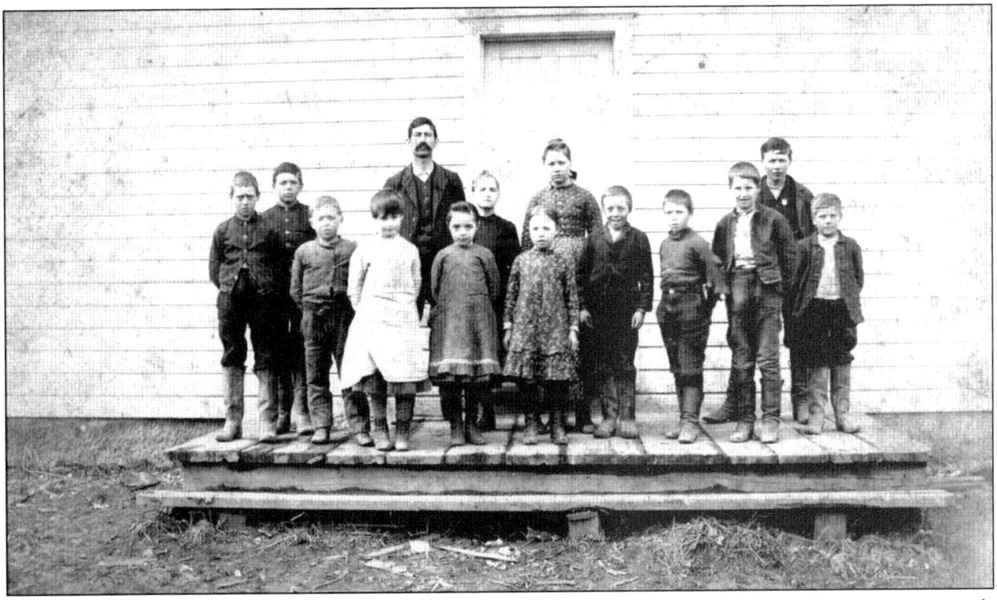

By 1896, there were 17 one-room and two-room schools in Randolph with a seven-month school year. The Forest Grove School near Black Ash closed around 1920. This rare 1890 photograph shows, from left to right, (first row) Alva Noel, Lee Luce, Daisy Walker, Mabel Hall, Cora Kightlinger, George Hall, Arthur Webster, Brice Walker, and Warren Noel; (second row) Clarence Noel, teacher Ellsworth "Worthy" McDonald, Vinnie Luce, Daisy Kightlinger, and Verne Kightlinger. (Courtesy of CCHS.)

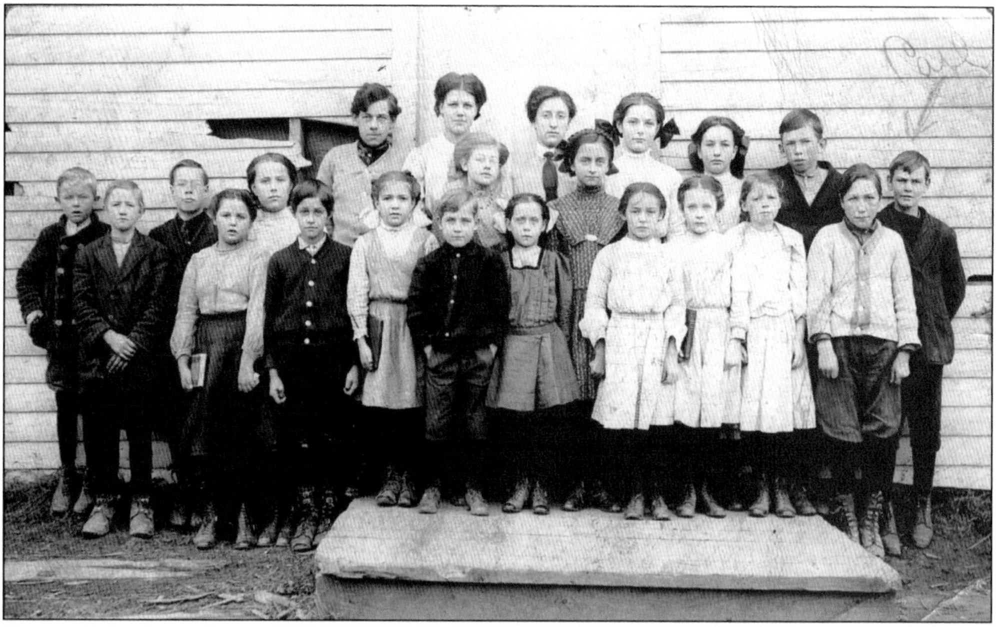

Centre School was located across from the present Maplewood High School, on the southeast part of the corners. The 1912 postcard above shows Dorinda Courtney as teacher. Below, the annual school souvenir folder for the 1906–1907 school year listed all the students of Centre School. Karl Russell was teacher at the time. In 1923, Chester Lingo was hired to teach the 41 students in eight grades at Centre School. He wrote, "To prepare myself for the job, I purchased a pair of rubber boots and an oilskin raincoat, as I walked three miles to school mostly through the woods, was my own janitor, carried in the wood, started the fire, and swept the floor. In order to soothe hunger pains, I made soup two times a week on the old wood stove, usually vegetable-beef. " (Courtesy of Betty Nelson.)

SOUVENIR

....CENTRE SCHOOL....

Randolph Township

Crawford County, Pennsylvania

1906—1907

KARL M. RUSSELL, Teacher

SCHOOL OFFICERS

Joseph Brunot, President
Raymond E. Smith, Secretary
Wm. H. Canfield, Treasurer
John D. Goodwin, County Superintendent

NAMES OF PUPILS

Alex Courtney	Ora Ross
Bertha Smith	Osa Smith
Flossie Smith	Lily Proper
Susie Cross	Tryphena Baker
Ermine Maryott	Don Wiltse
Luella Childs	Floyd Pennel
Pret Cross	Daisy Smith
Stanley Cutshall	Irene McLaughlin
Rosy Proper	Neva Wiltse
Clemmine Cutshall	Fanchion Gray
Claud Hunt	Freeman Gray
Revella McLaughlin	Carl Foulk
Don Barber	Elwood Cutshall
George Barber	Mable Courtney

Etta Baker

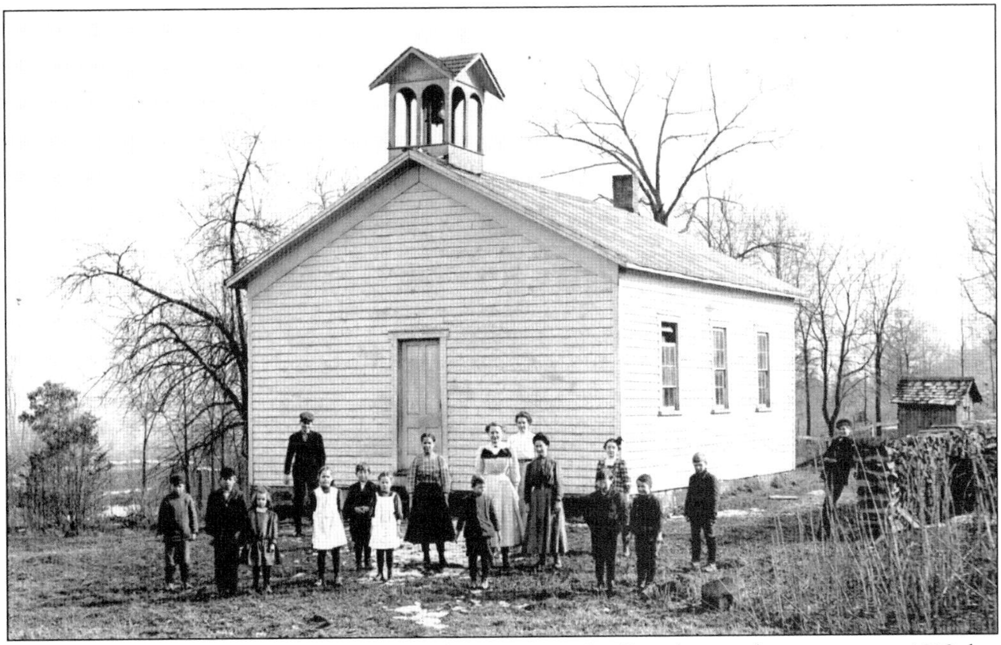

The first organized school in the township was in the Brawley settlement in an 1813 log schoolhouse. It was described as "a crude yet solid structure no better than the homes the children came from." The one-room, eight-grade Brawley School pictured here was located on Oil Creek Road in southern Randolph Township. It was built about 1820 after the log schoolhouse burned. When it closed in 1925, the building was moved down the road and used as a garage. Brawley pupils pictured below are, from left to right, (first row) Bill Beuchat, Wesley Brawley, Lynn Allen, Millard Smith, and a Lucas girl; (second row) Dorothy Oakes, Audrey Beuchat, Maude Brawley, Elsie Oakes, Marian Oakes, two Lucas girls, Mae Murdock, Lucas boy, Lewis Snyder, Oscar Brawley, Willard Smith, Elva Lang, and Lyle Smith. Brice Walker was the teacher. (Courtesy of Wenna Bean.)

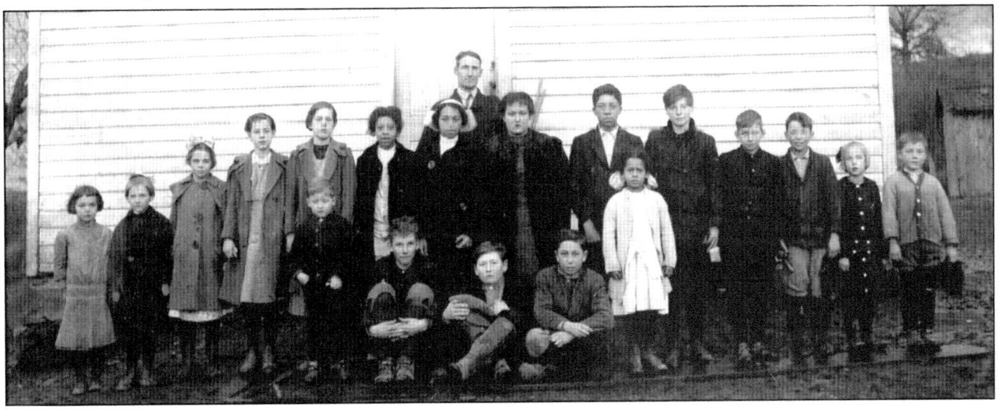

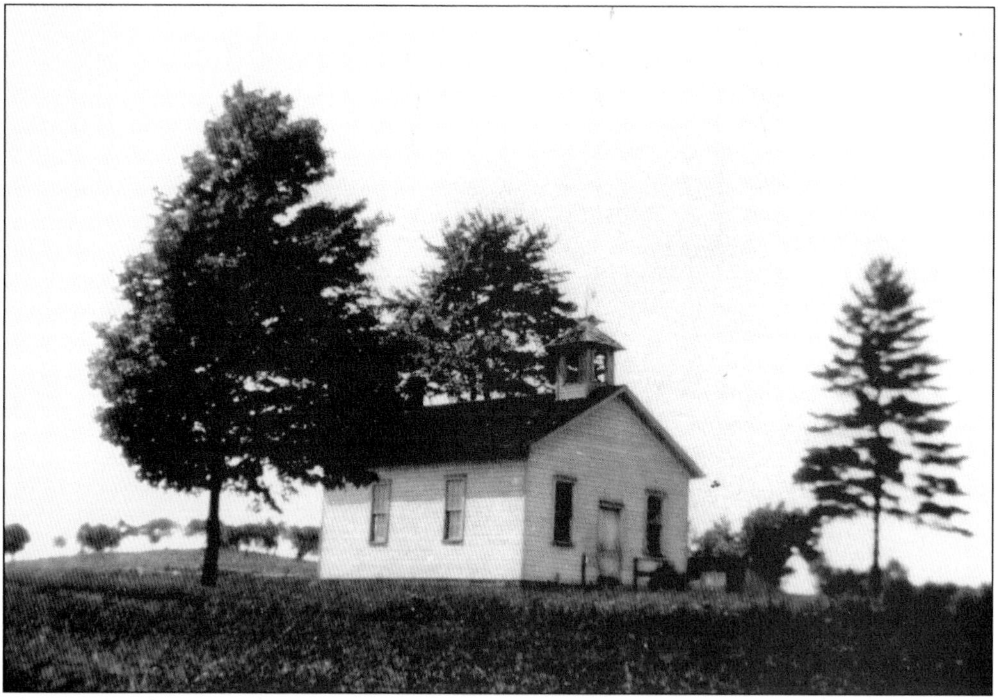

The Hatch School was located just south of Hatch Cemetery on the road to Hickory Corners. Seen below, former students attending the Second Hatch School reunion in August 1956 fondly reminisce about their early years at the Hatch School. (Above, courtesy of Wilford and Carolyn Miller; below, courtesy of Janet Marvin, photograph by Stanton Rand.)

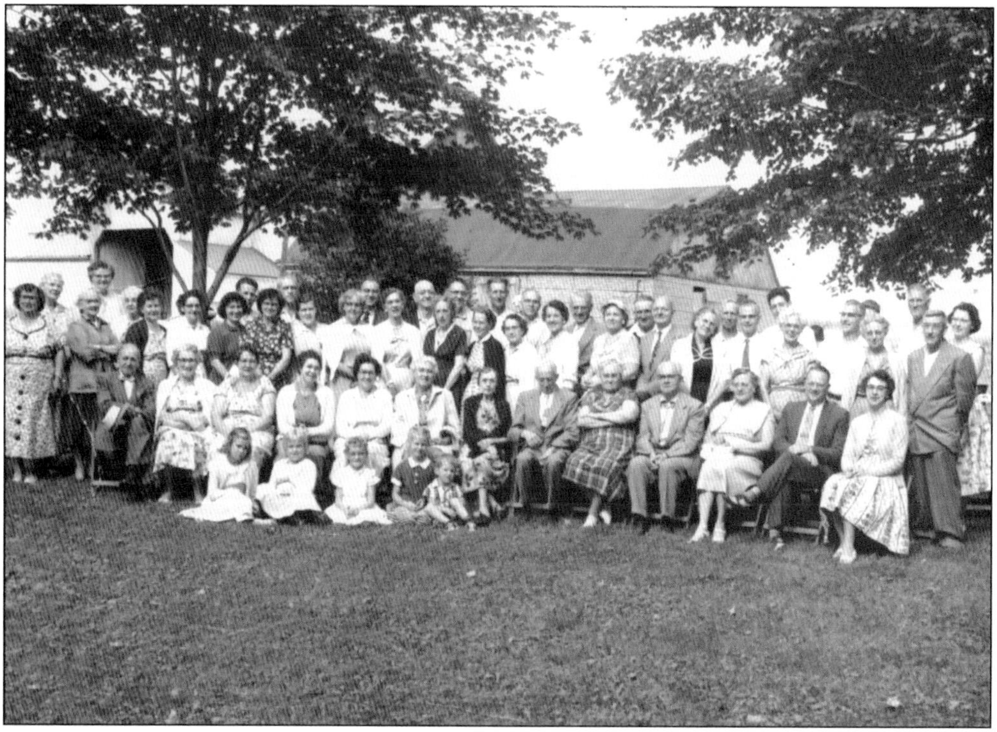

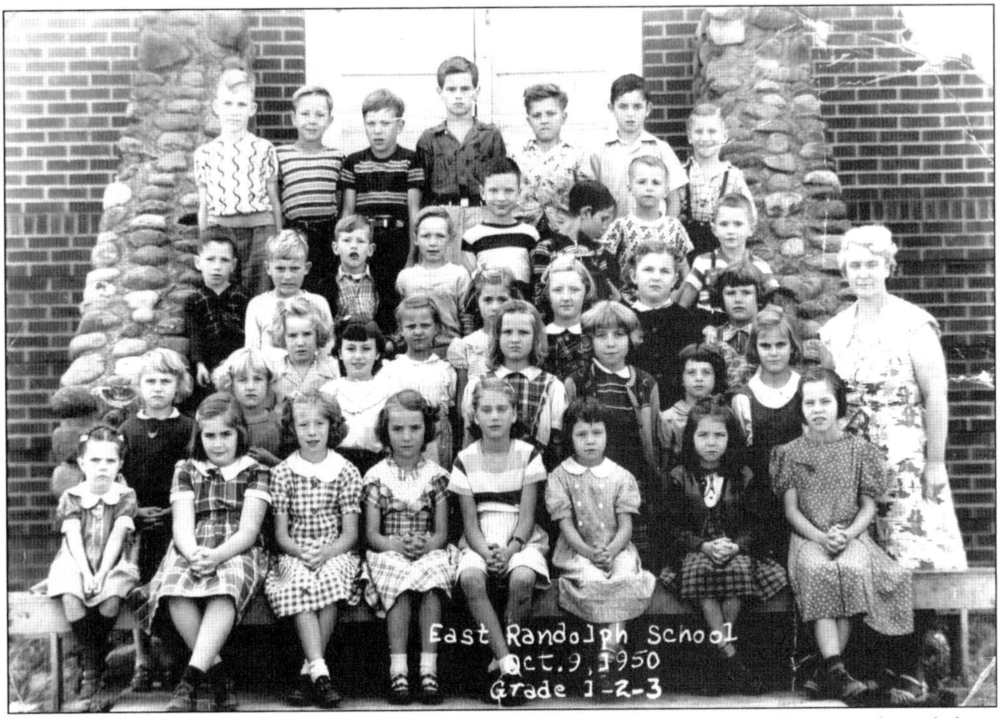

Students from the Black Ash School pose in the photograph above. They are, from left to right, (first row) Linda Mesarch, Dorothy Shaffer, Patty Lamey, Donna Crist, Elaine Wilson, ? Roberts, Sherry Williams, and Joyce Roberts; (second row) Hazel and Mary Mattocks, Joyce Shontz, Mildred Rath, Karin Williams, Karen Miller, and Sandy Allen; (third row) unidentified, Viola Rath, Carolyn Wilson, Nancy Rooney, Edna Lang, and Betty Snyder; (fourth row) Roger Greathouse, Larry Dennis, ? Fowler, Paul Rudy, Phil Wentworth, George Hollibaugh, John Greathouse, and Tom Wentworth; (fifth row) Pat Kelley, Bob Kircher, Roy Hunter, Ken Roberts, Delmar Rath, Burton Hollabaugh, and Larry Terrill. March Wheelock was the teacher. Below is the Black Ash School in the 1920s. Notice the many children with bare feet. (Above, courtesy of Dorothy White; below, courtesy of Brian and Judy Kirberger.)

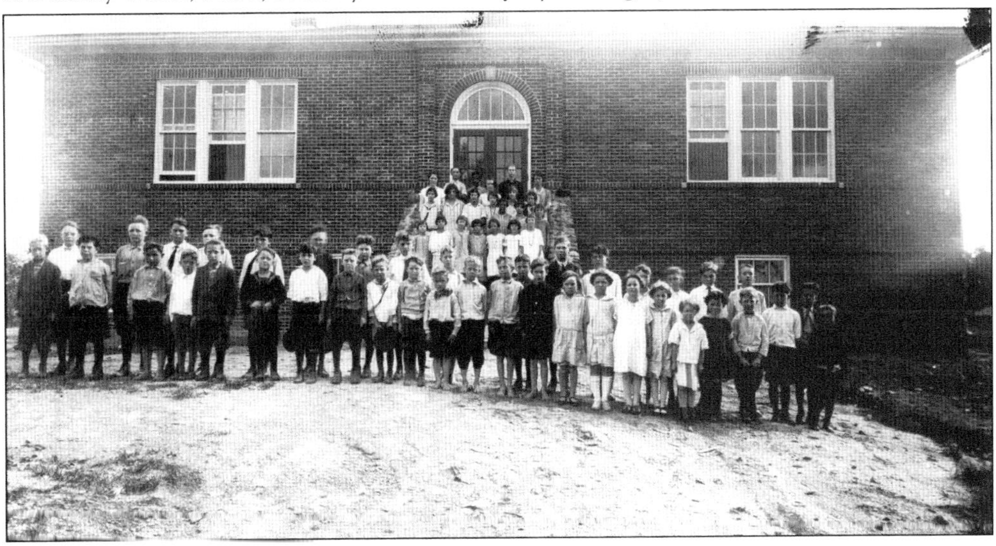

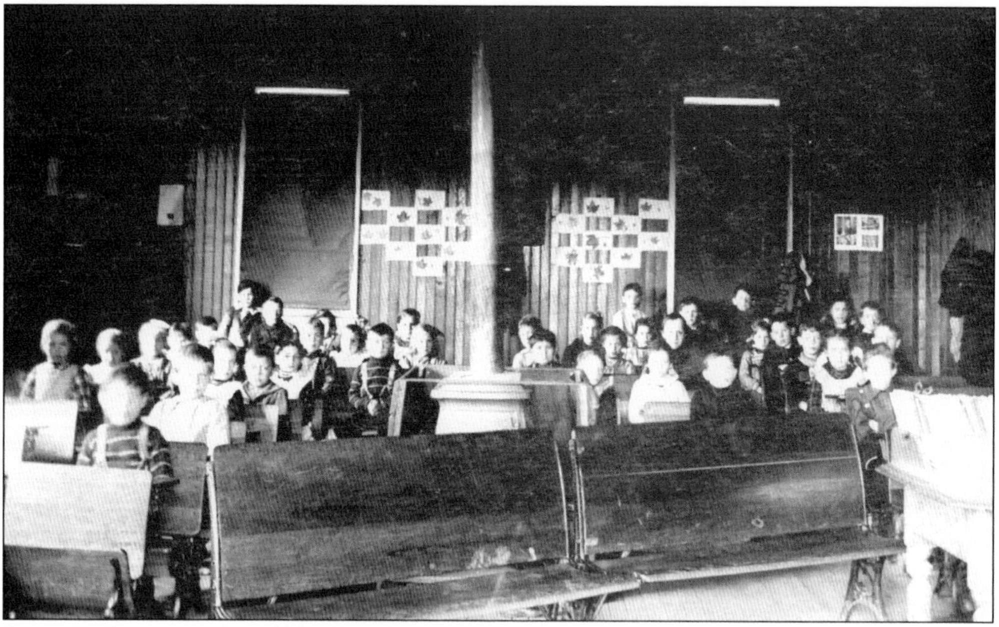

Some 38 first, second, and third graders were at attention in this rare 1906 view of the inside of the Guys Mills one-room schoolhouse. Notice the protective frame built around the wood-burning stove. Edna Coburn was the teacher, and Harry Ingraham was the photographer. (Courtesy of Wilford and Carolyn Miller.)

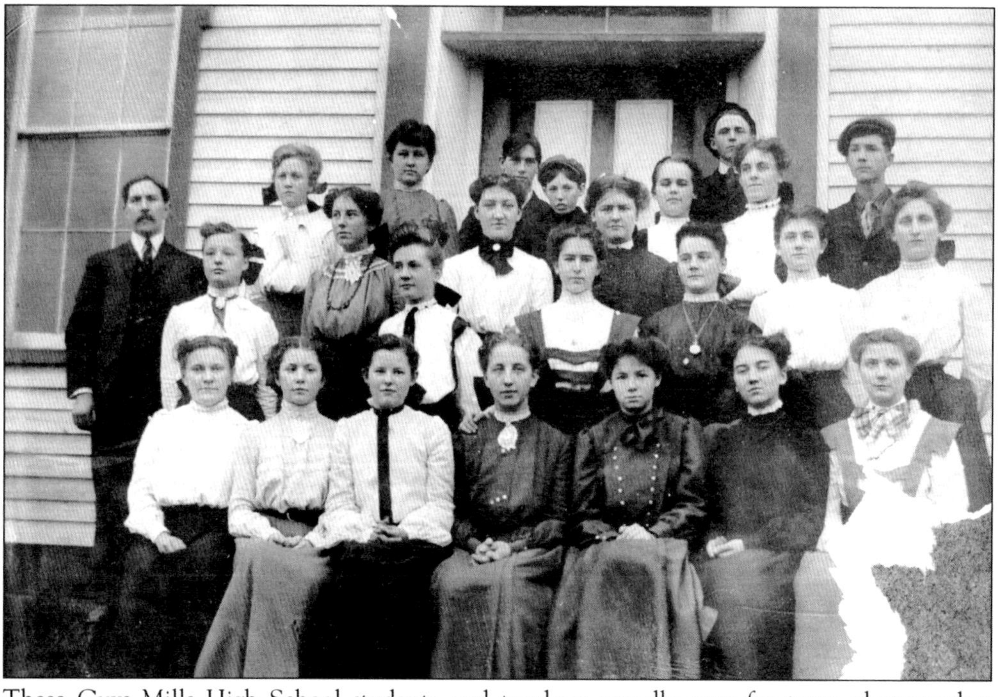

These Guys Mills High School students and teachers proudly pose for town photographer Harry Ingraham in front of the school in about 1906. These students would have walked, rode horses, or drove horse and buggies to school. Horses were tied in the carriage shed behind the Congregational church until school dismissal. (Author's collection.)

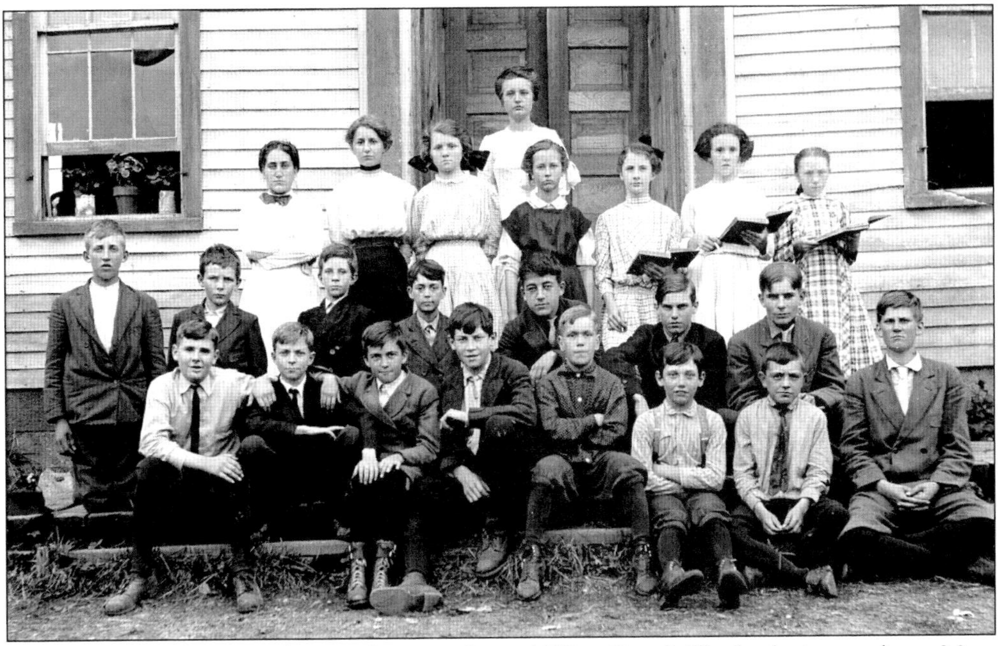

These photographs were taken on the same day in 1910 in Guys Mills. In the image above, Mary Smith is the teacher and the students are, from left to right, (first row) Stanley Smith, Harold Roueche, Hugh Bannister, Harold Hanks, Howard Boyd, Fern Hunter, unidentified, and Walter Burchard; (second row) Otto Schweitzer, Kenneth Virtue, Karl Hunter, Chester Lingo, Desire Poly, George Moore, and ? Pardee; (third row) Ileane Hodge, Ruth Bradley, Blanche Smith, Mabel Davison, Blanche Rodgers, Mildred Kennedy, and Jessie Brunot. Below the entire school (through 10th grade) is posed in front of the school. Many boys in the front row have bare feet. The principal was Alfred Foreman, and the teachers were Mae Hipple, Mary Smith, Dorinda Courtney, and Jessie Virtue. Eleventh grade was added in 1913, and 12th grade was added in 1919. (Author's collection.)

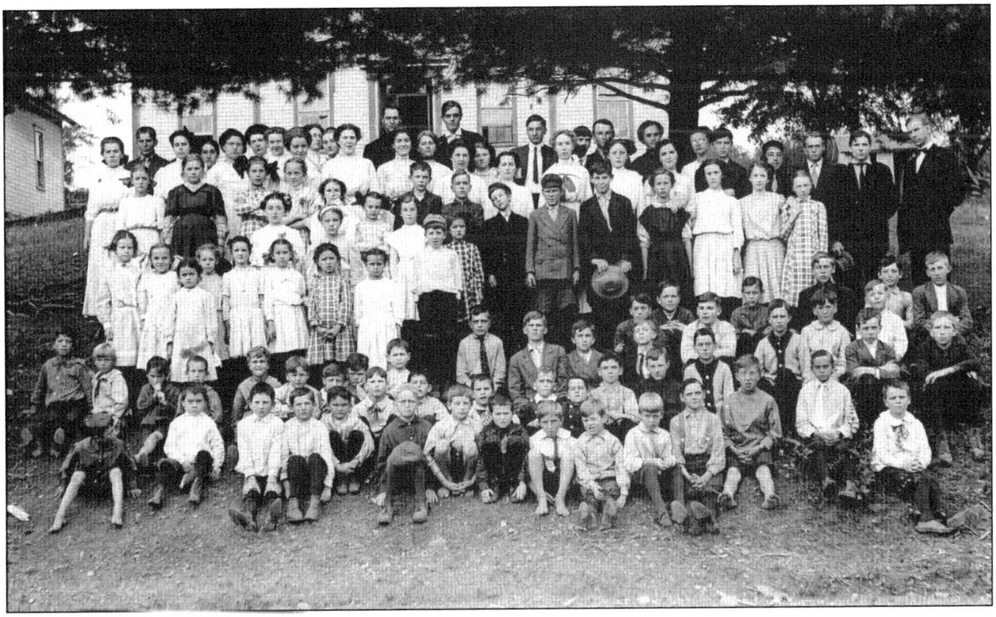

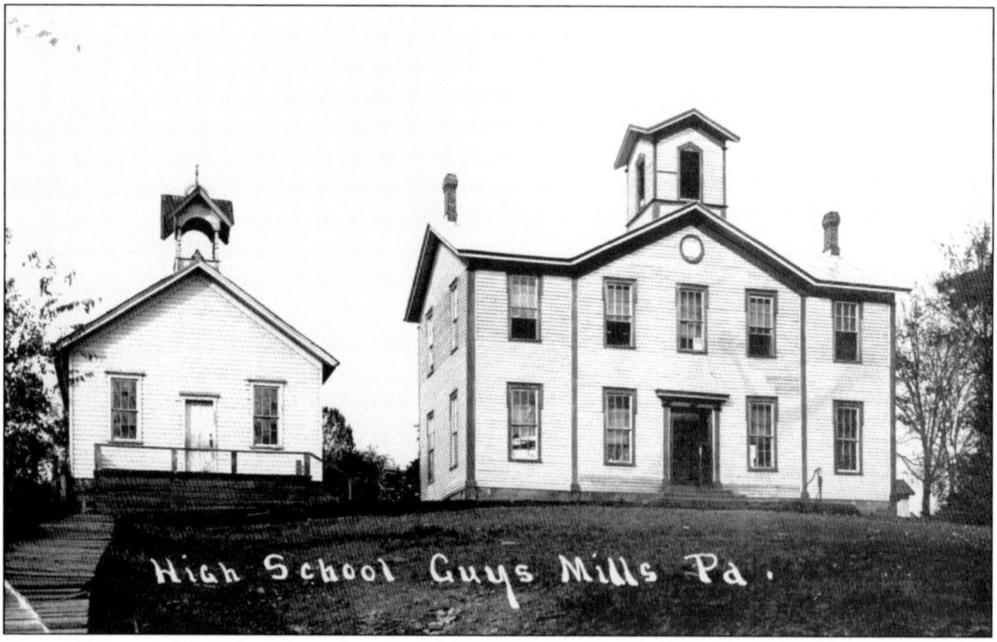

The old Guys Mills School stood across the road from the current school buildings (which are now the home of Faith Builders Educational Programs). The one-room building on the left housed the first, second, and third grades. The building on the right was originally a two-room schoolhouse and was enlarged about 1898. The fourth, fifth, and sixth grades occupied the downstairs on the left. The seventh and eighth grades were in the downstairs on the right. The upstairs housed grades 9 and 10 on the left and grades 11 and 12 on the right. Below, the entire Guys Mills High School is lined up in front of their Alma Mater in 1915. (Above, courtesy of Robert W. Waid; below, author's collection.)

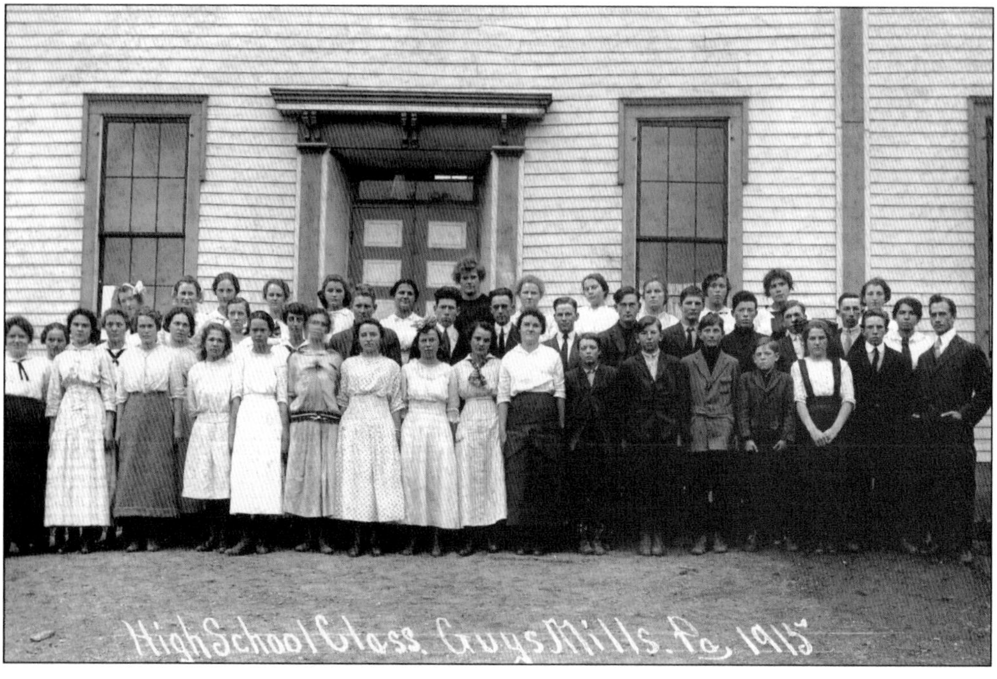

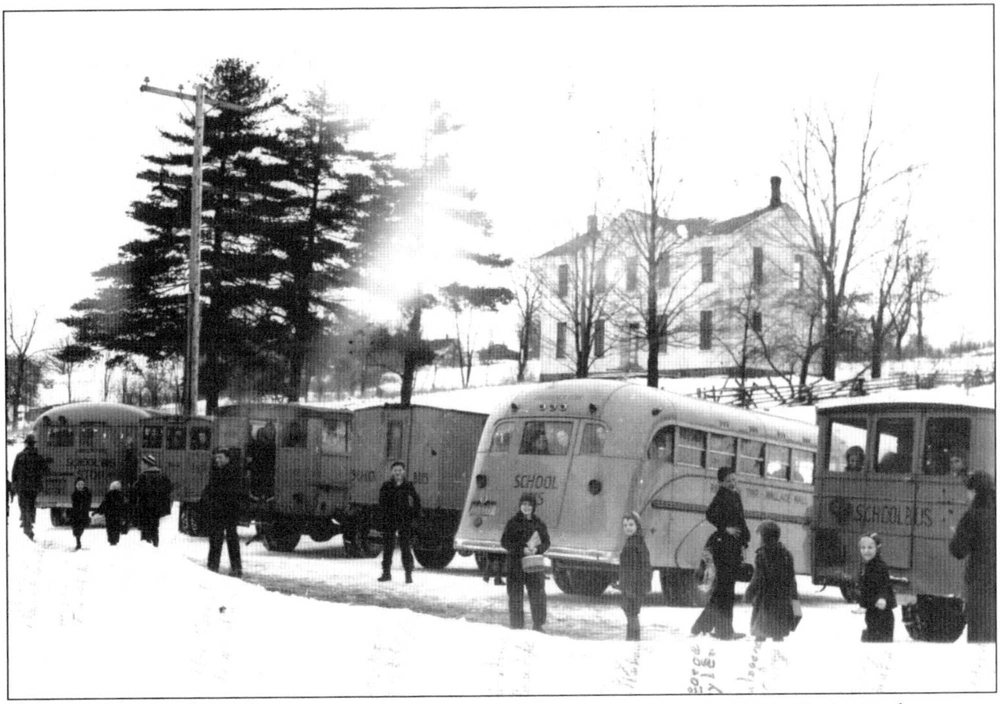

The first motorized school bus was purchased in 1924 and another in 1925. By 1928, there were three motorized busses, replacing the horse-drawn "kid wagons." (Courtesy of Leatha Humes.)

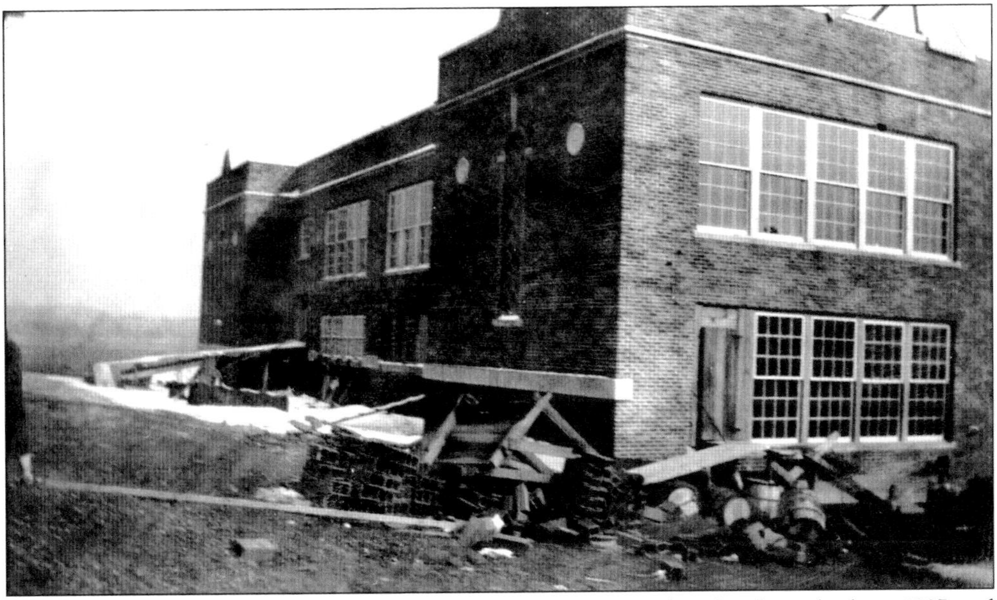

The modern brick Randolph Combined Junior and Senior High School was built in 1927 and 1928 and dedicated in 1929. Shown here under construction, it consolidated many of the rural one-room schoolhouses in the Randolph attendance area. The leaders in the "building movement" were Emmett Allen, David (Gerald) Bird Sr., Dr. Charles Burgwin, Parley Carpenter, Anell DeMaison, Clinton Gilbert, William Smith, Hampton Query, and Don Wright. (Courtesy of Bonnie Murphy.)

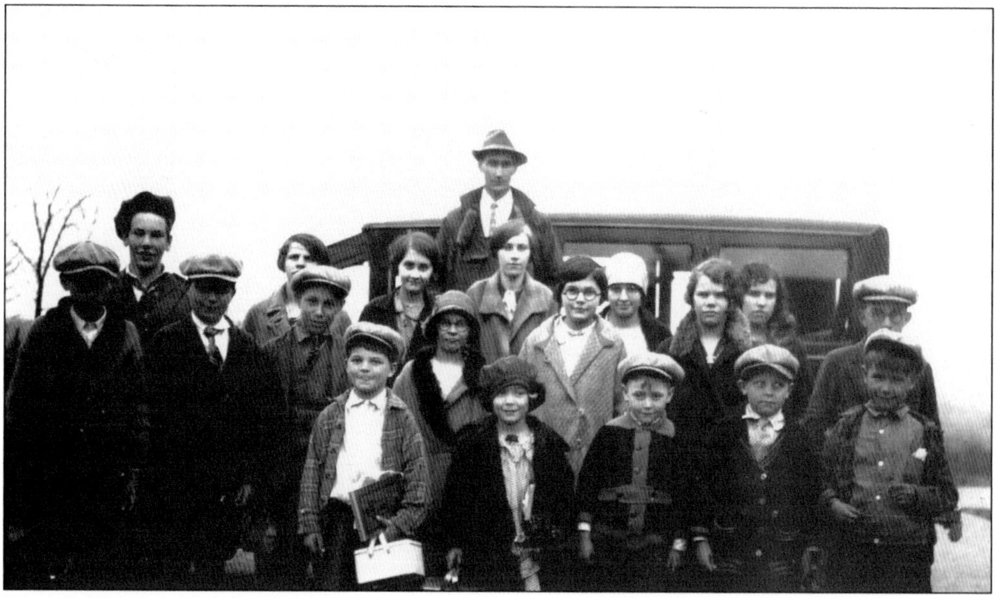

The children on Burdett Proper's 1930 bus run are, by grade, (first grade) Russell Woodcock, Virginia McFadden, George Proper, Fred Proper, and Wayne Jones; (third grade) Walter Jones; (fourth grade) Edith Woodcock; (fifth grade) Marian Longberry; (sixth grade) Richard Proper, Everett Woodcock, and Kenneth Jones; (seventh grade) Lucile Longberry and Ruth Gilbert; (eighth grade) Orlo Phillips and Ellen Proper; (ninth grade) Helen Proper and Dorothy Dingler. (Courtesy of Sharon Hayes.)

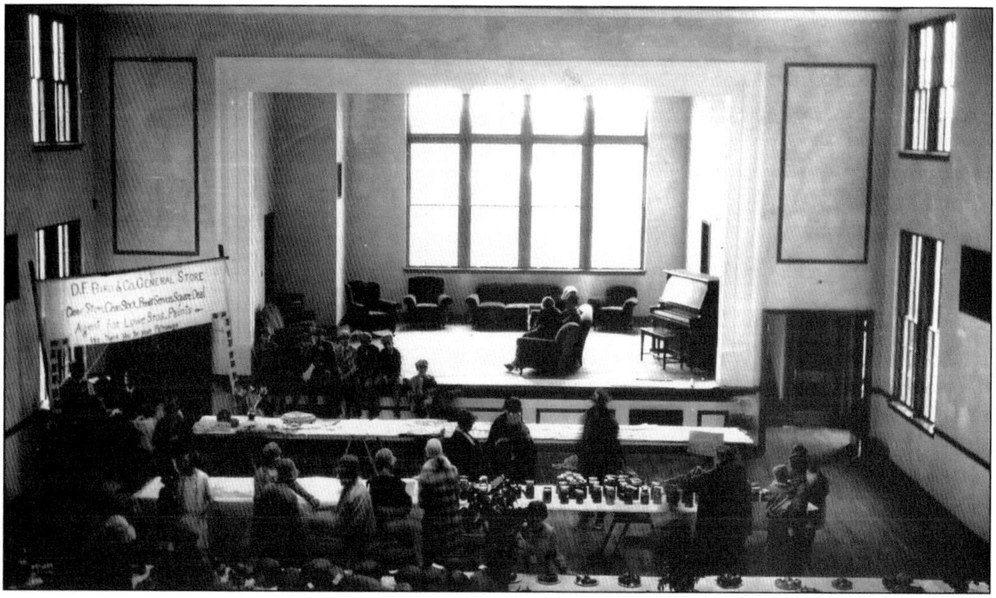

In the 1930s, school was dismissed for the community and school fair. Gardening and homemaking exhibits were displayed in the gym and the Congregational carriage sheds were used for cattle judging. Principal Chester Lingo and Harry L. Wentworth got mixed up while hauling cattle into the wee hours of the morning, sometimes hauling the wrong cattle from the pastures to the church shed. (Courtesy of Sharon Hayes.)

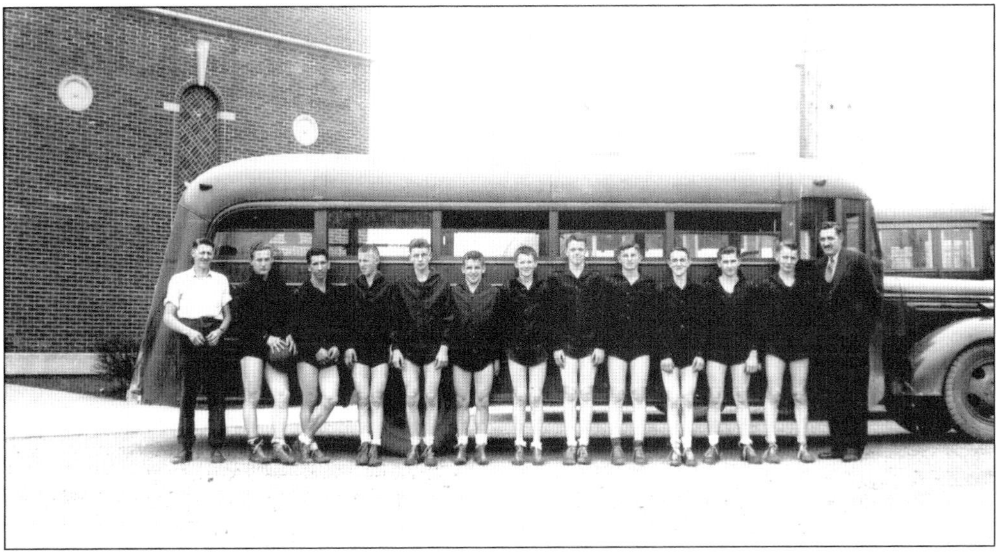

Perhaps ready to board the bus for an away game, the Randolph Boys Basketball Team was a handsome group of young men. This photograph was taken in 1944 or 1945 in front of the high school. Pictured are, from left to right, Elery Smith, manager; Jake Hill; Ed Mazza; Roger Schweitzer; Clarence Gordon; Russell Cutshall; Danny Richard; Bernard Hall; Clair Burchard; Frank Byham; Bob Cutshall; "Junior" Poux; and J. Paul Jones, coach and school principal. (Courtesy of Leatha Humes.)

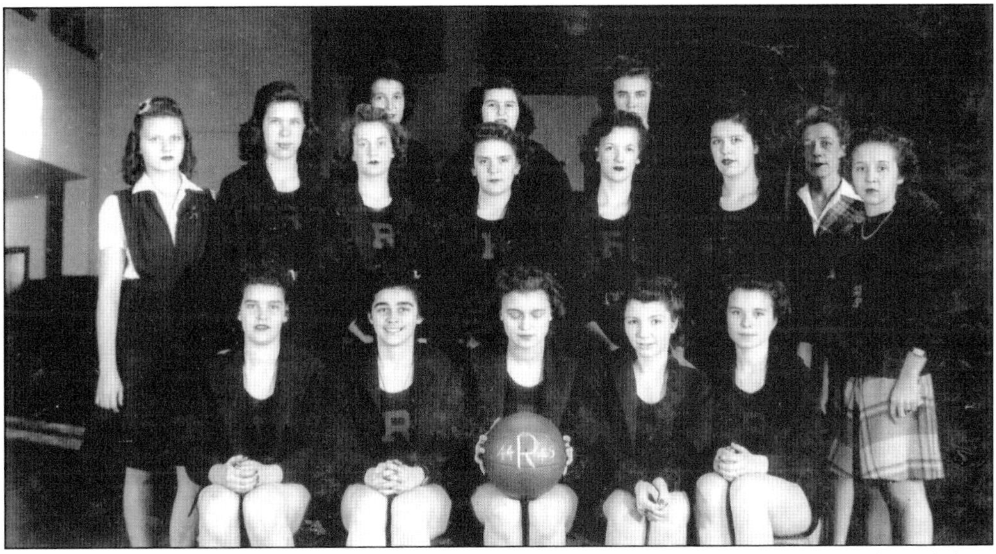

The 1944–1945 Randolph Girls Basketball Team poses in the gym. Pictured are, from left to right, (first row) Carolina Foulk, Cleo Furry, Phyllis Smith, Beverly Bidwell, and Dot Smith; (second row) Shirley Cutshall, Carolyn Boyd, Thelma Heath, Betty Smith, Harriet Woodruff, Jean Boyd, coach Rose Kinnear, and manager Joanne Cutshall; (third row) Norma McFadden, Helen Daniels, and Claire Footskulak. (Courtesy of Lucile Stallard.)

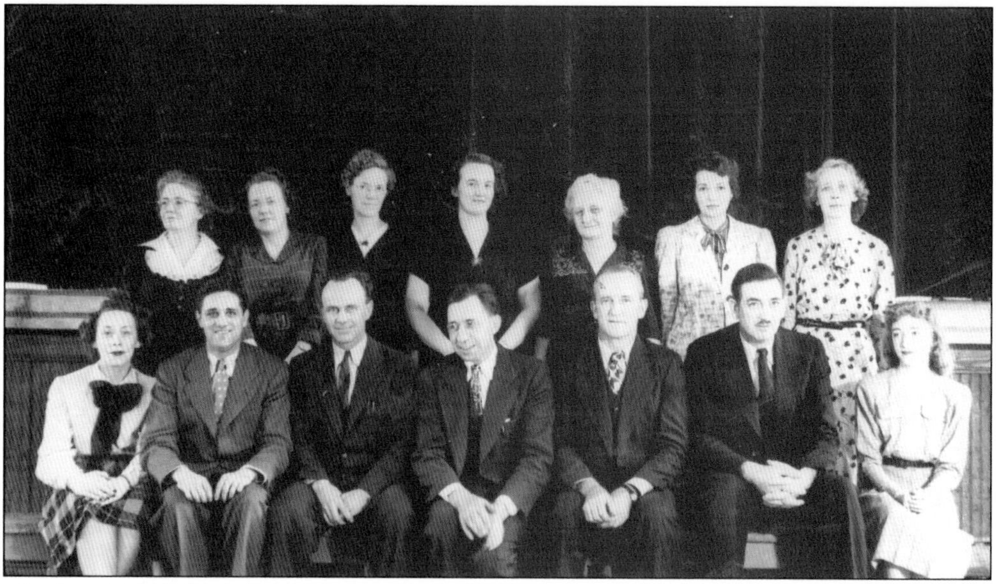

The Randolph School faculty for the 1948–1949 school year was a dedicated and hardworking team. Pictured are, from left to right, (first row) Bertha Blau, Leroy Brest, Raymond Bentley, Forrest Hollibaugh, Al Wheeling, J. Paul Jones, and Julia Nageotte McBride; (second row) Marian Gilbert, Ruth Shoemaker, Phoebe Humes, Bea Hanna Nicklas, Grace McElroy, Irene Doyle, and Rose Kinnear. (Courtesy of Janet Marvin.)

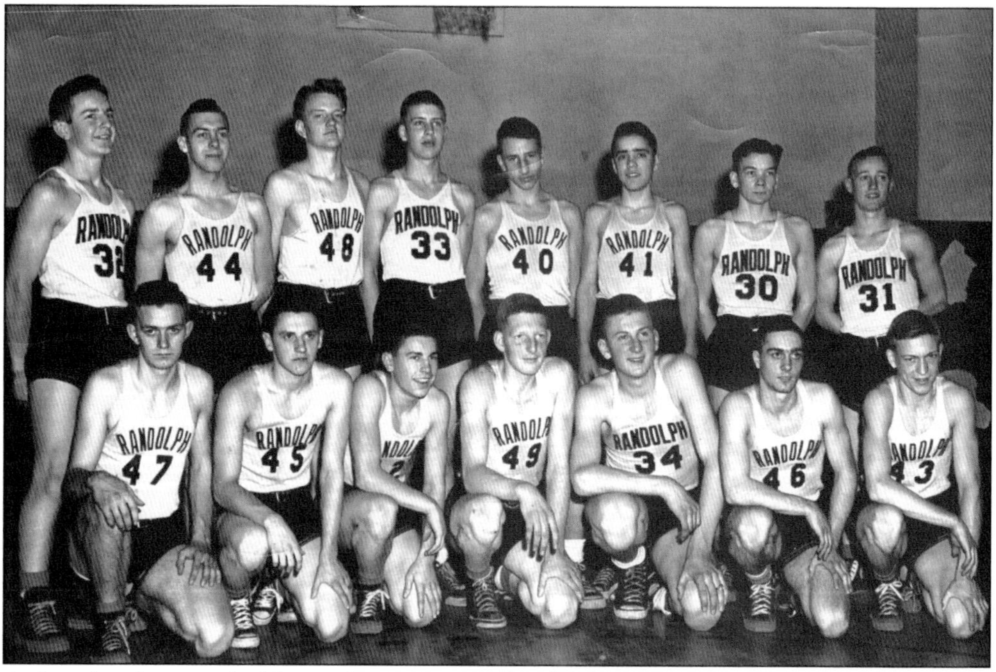

A disciplined team of athletes, the 1948–1949 Randolph Boys Basketball Team took a break for the camera. Pictured are, from left to right, (first row) Bob McCartney, Dick Cutshall, Bud Lang, Dick Heme, Ivan Virtue, Dick Stallard, and Bud Smith; (second row) Bob Lang, Dwight Stallard, Joe Caskey, Tom Terrill, Don Smith, Russell Boyd, Bill McFadden, and Warren Foulk. (Courtesy of Lucile Stallard.)

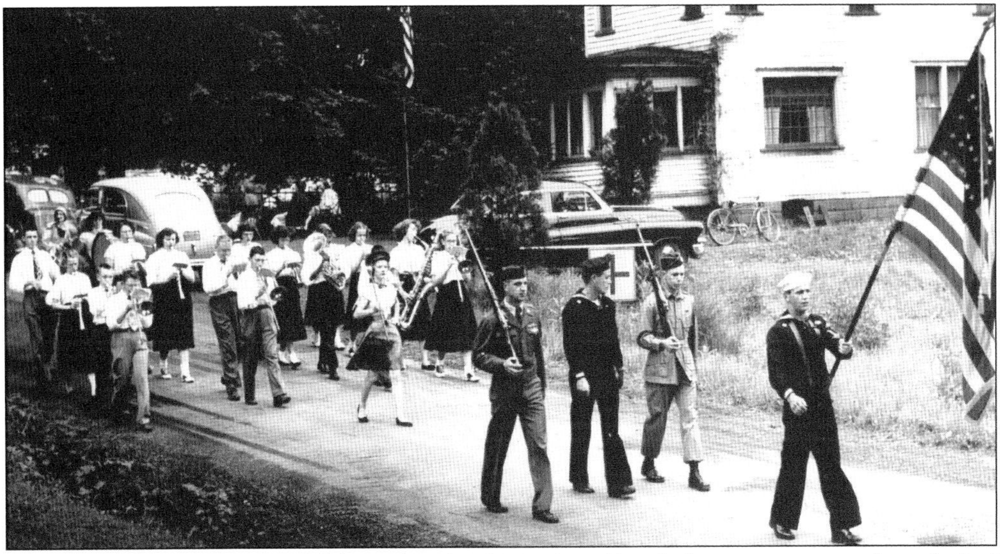

In the early days of the Randolph High School Marching Band, the musicians may have lacked uniforms, but they did not lack pride. They are shown in here in the early 1950s after just having turned at the intersection in Guys Mills, marching toward the back entrance of the school. (Courtesy of Lucile Stallard.)

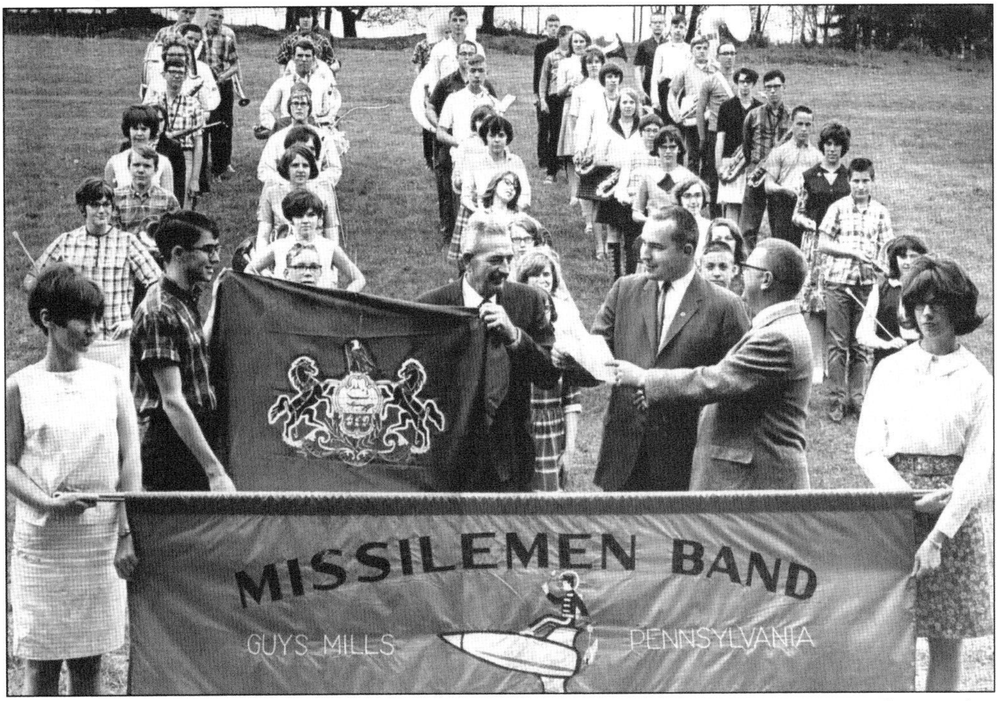

The 1966–1967 Randolph East Mead Missilemen Band proudly accepts a Pennsylvania flag from state representative R. Budd Dwyer from Blooming Valley. Dwyer served in the House of Representatives from 1965 to 1970, the state senate from 1970 to 1980, and as state treasurer from 1980 to 1987. Pictured are, from left to right, (first row) Linda Burchard, Tom Hunter, principal J. Paul Jones, R. Budd Dwyer, director George Menser, and Marie Johnston. (Courtesy of the Meadville Tribune and Brian and Judy Kirberger.)

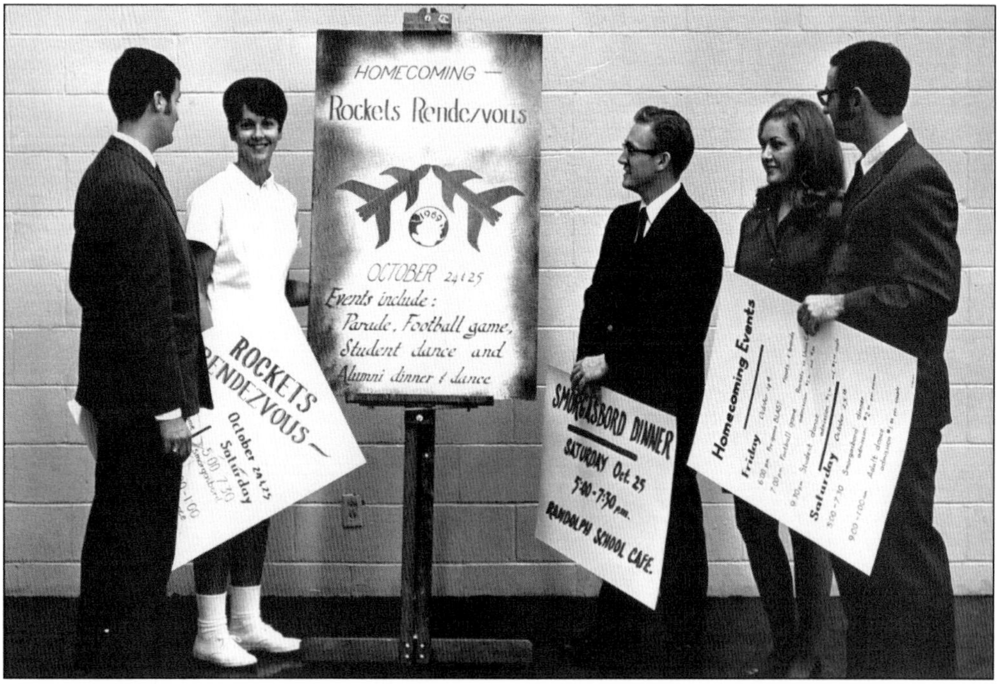

Drumming up support for the 1969 Randolph East Mead Homecoming, members of the faculty posted signs and made plans for a successful weekend of events. Pictured are, from left to right, Larry Guerrieri, Carol Turner, Larry Stevens, Lynette Rose, and John Battaglia. (Courtesy of Brian and Judy Kirberger, photograph by Pease for the Meadville Tribune.)

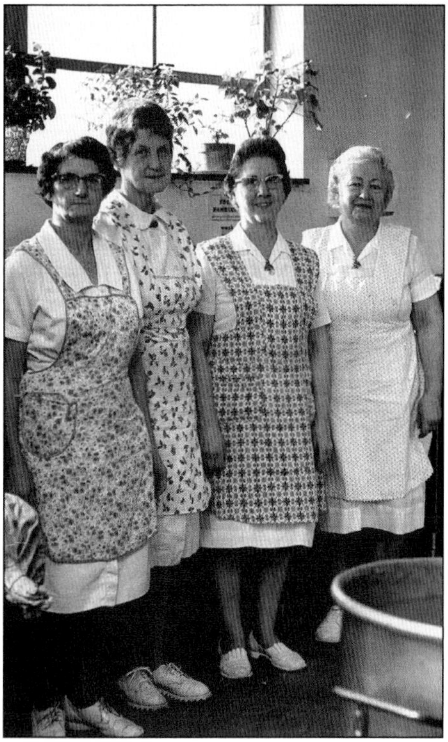

These ever-smiling school cooks were an important part of the Randolph students' days for many years. Pictured are, from left to right, Flossie Kent, Margot Sanner, Mildred Crago, and Ila Smith. (Courtesy of Lucile Stallard.)

Five

They Hosted
The Guy House Hotel

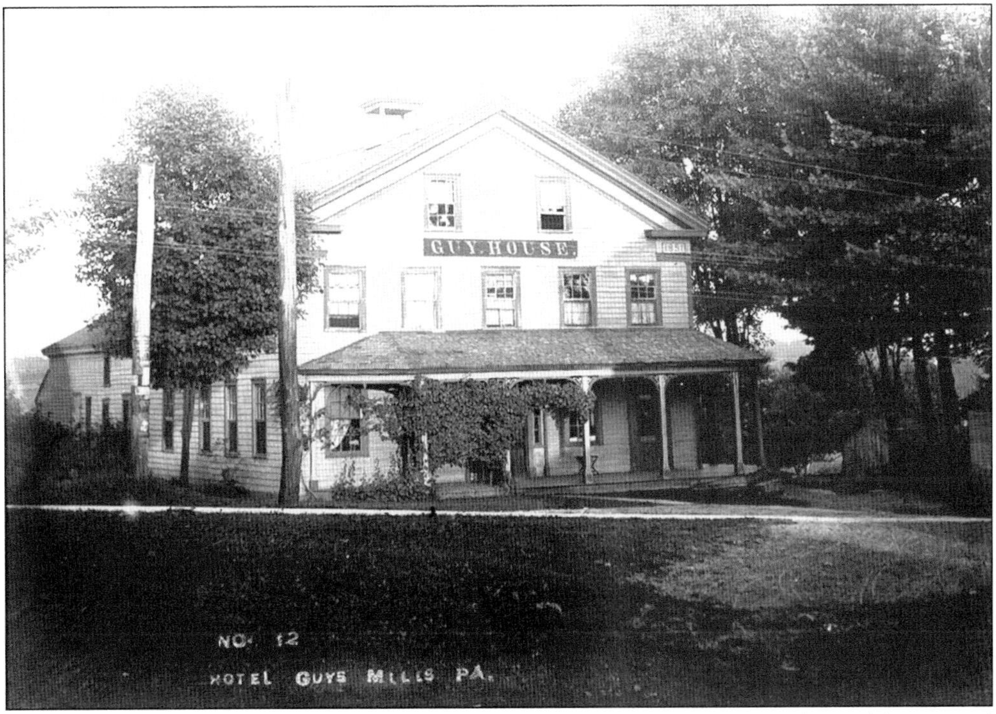

When the town's founder, Jacob Guy, died in 1850, his son Augustus Guy inherited his general store. Augustus sold the store and invested the proceeds to establish the stately Guy House Hotel in 1851. Just a few years later, Edwin Drake struck oil in Titusville and the resulting traffic filled the Guy House Hotel's 11 guest rooms. This "Grande Dame" was centrally located and soon became the hub of all community activity. (Author's collection.)

For the Benefit of the Congregational Church.

COLUMBIAN ART EXHIBITION

and Supper,

AT THE

GUY HOUSE,

Wednesday, January 30, 1895,

AT 7 O'CLOCK P. M.

SUPPER 20 CENTS.

Children under ten years of age free when accompanied by their parents.

EVERYBODY CORDIALLY INVITED.

Weddings were often solemnized in the parlor, and the third floor ballroom hosted dances and other parties. Itinerant dentists made weekly or monthly visits and set up temporary practice there, claiming "extraction without pain." Many cultural events also took place at the Guy House Hotel. This is a four-page program for an 1895 art exhibit to benefit the Guys Mills Congregational Church. Supper was 20¢, and 76 paintings were on display. (Courtesy of David and Marilyn Boyd.)

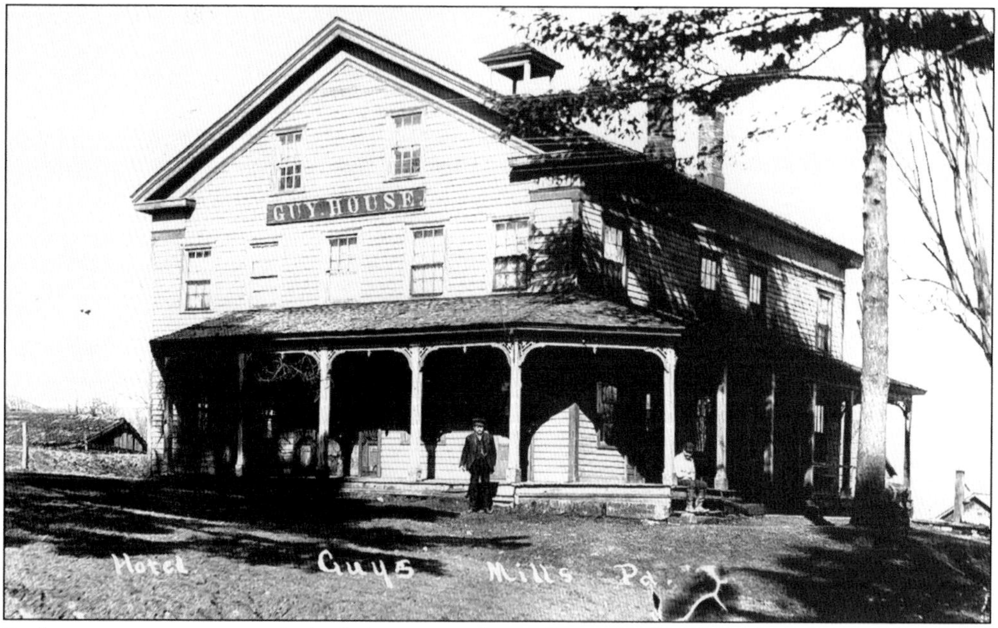

Each guest room contained a bed, dresser, washstand with bowl and pitcher, and a chamber pot under each bed. There was also a three-hole outhouse attached to the Guy House Hotel. The building was warmed by at least eight wood-burning stoves, including the cook stove. Shown here about 1912, some of the barns and livery stables are visible. There was also an icehouse. (Courtesy of Robert W. Waid.)

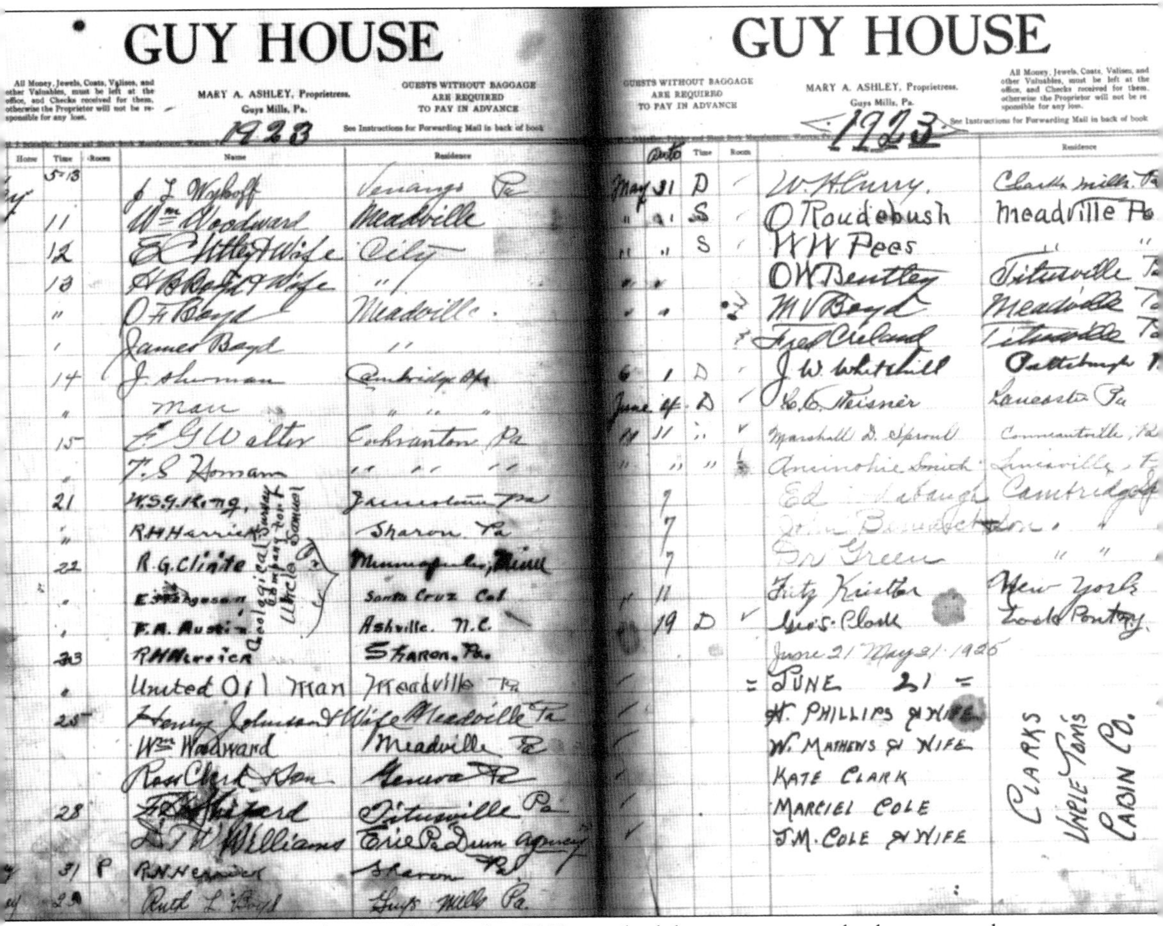

The Guy House Hotel guest ledger for 1923 tracked how many meals, horses, and rooms each guest was to be billed for. Many stopped for only a meal, so the Guy House Hotel served as the local restaurant. Notice the party in the lower right hand corner. This traveling vaudeville-style theater troupe appeared every June to entertain the villagers. This year's performance is a rendition of *Uncle Tom's Cabin*. (Courtesy of David and Marilyn Boyd.)

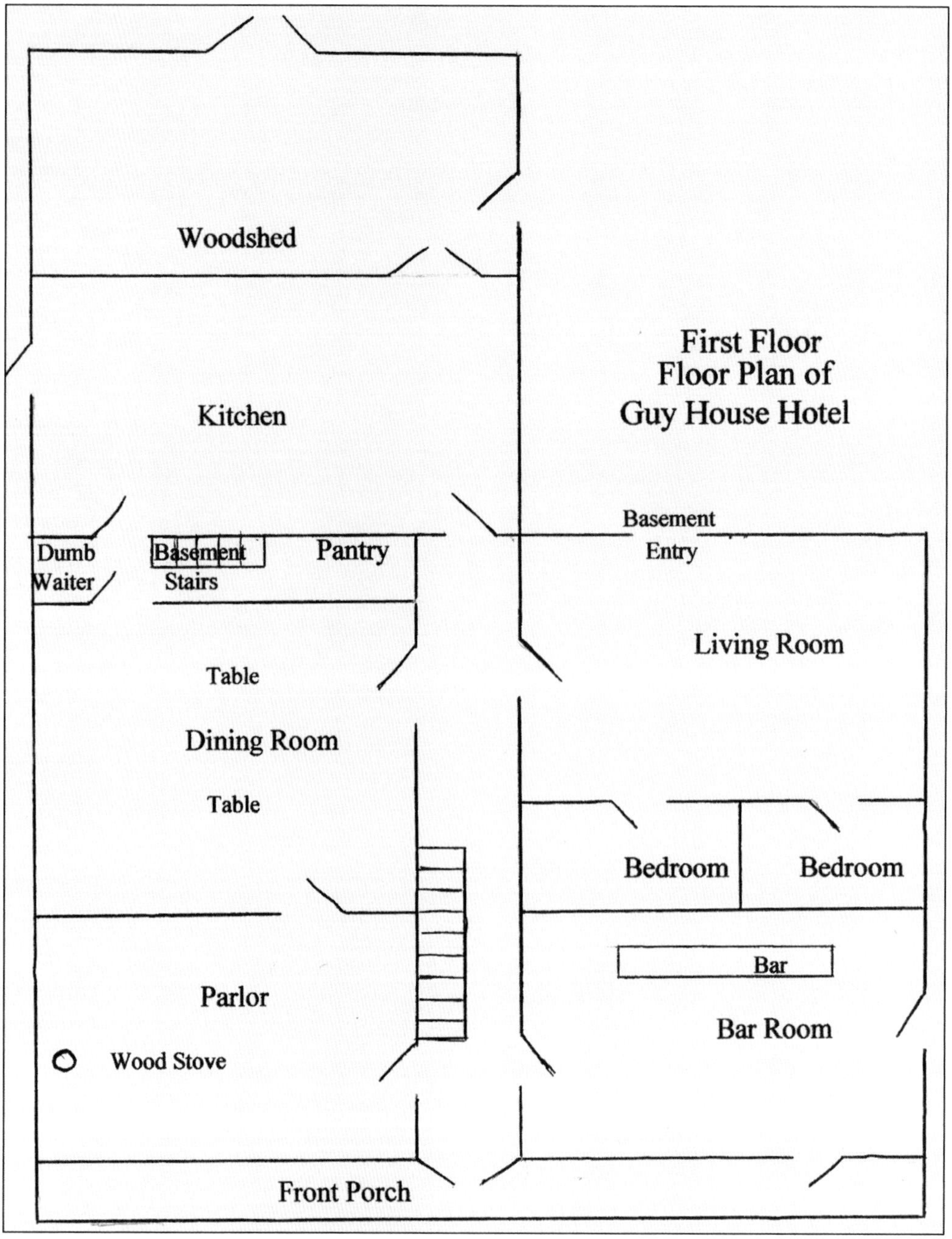

At age 70, Mary Guy Ashley, granddaughter of Jacob Guy, was the last member of the Guy family to operate the Guy House Hotel. Her husband, Dr. Don E. Ashley, an 1871 graduate of Western Reserve Medical College, practiced medicine in the county for many years. He died in 1917, and the funeral was conducted at the Guy House Hotel. The floor plan of the first floor of the hotel is shown here. The second floor had a long hallway opening to bedrooms for rent, a tiny "tramp's room" in the front where tramps could stay for free, and the large servants' quarters in the back. The third floor had a large dance floor with a painting of Jacob Guy and a recessed bandstand. (Courtesy of the Childs family.)

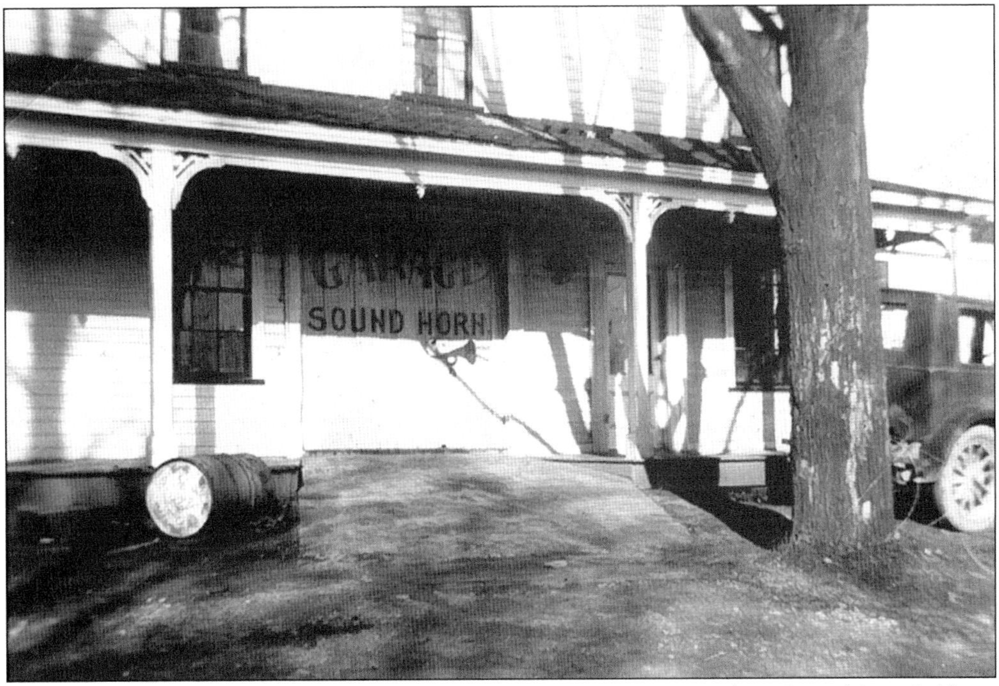

In 1928, Frank and Alice Childs, married two years and expecting their first of four children, purchased the buildings and six acres for $2,000. It was to have a dual role as their business and residence. It was minimally wired and had no indoor plumbing except a pitcher pump. Even so, first on the long list of priorities was to fix the leaking roof. Then Frank removed some inside partitions and added a set of folding garage doors to accommodate his car repair business, shown above. Below is one of many vehicles in the Childs' fleet. (Above, courtesy of the Childs family; below, courtesy of Lucile Stallard.)

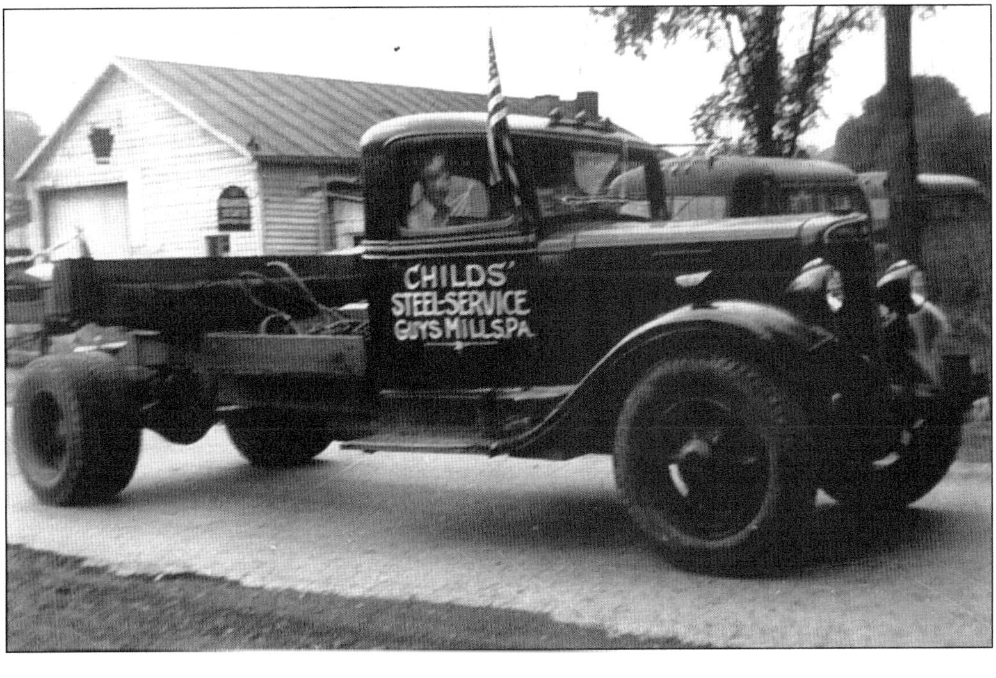

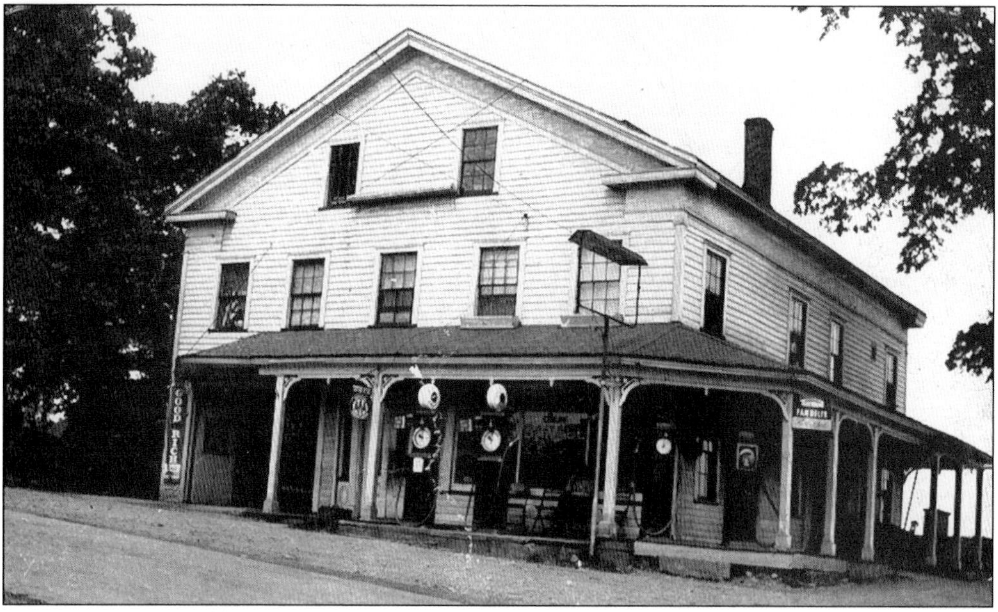

Gas pumps were added in 1929, as well as a gas delivery route, delivering gas in drums to area farmers. More interior partitions were removed, a state inspection area was added, and the machine and welding shop were expanded. Childs' Garage caught fire when Bird's Store/International Order of Odd Fellows (IOOF) hall burned across the road in 1933. Teen boys were dismissed from school to form bucket brigades. Water from three water pumps on the Childs property extinguished that fire. The IOOF hall did not fare as well. (Courtesy of Lucile Stallard.)

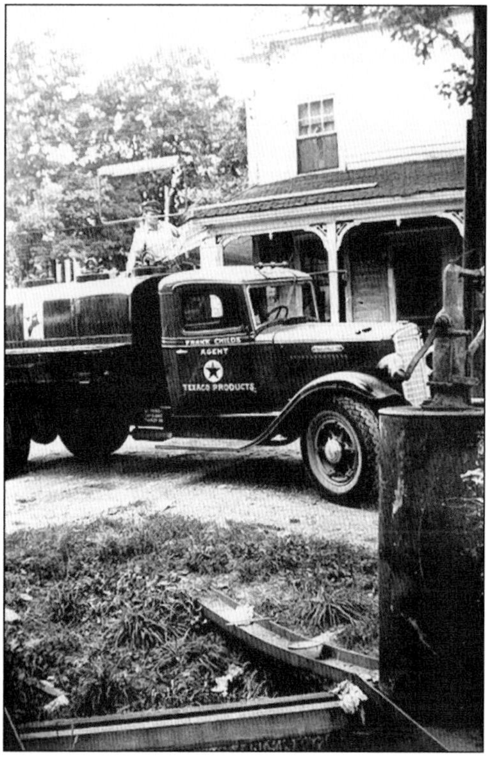

Frank Childs hauled gas from a Titusville refinery in this truck, and one day in 1936, the motor backfired and set the truck on fire. Immediately the truck was engulfed in flames, which shot high into the air. Adrenaline kicked in, and Frank saved three tires by removing them while the truck was on fire. The cab and one tire were ruined, but the 400 to 500 gallons in the tank did not explode. (Courtesy of the Childs family.)

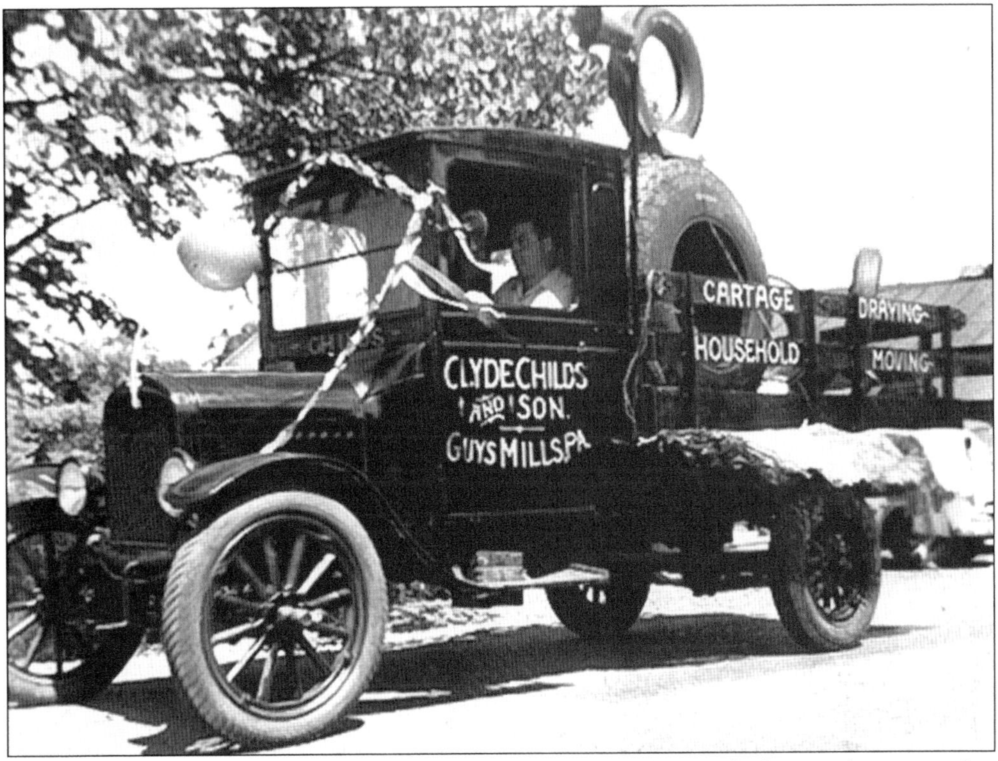

In the image above is one of many of Childs' Fourth of July parade floats, advertising that they offered household moving services. In 1943, Frank learned of the government releasing 16-ply surplus bomber tires. Though plagued with many physical ailments and setbacks, the wheels never stopped turning in Frank's engineering mind. These heavy-duty tires had been used only a few times on the B-29 bombers. He designed and manufactured the necessary rims and soon every farmer in the vicinity was using them on their farm equipment. Frank designed and built Childs' Logging Arches, also outfitted with bomber tires. His lettering and signage was done by Rudolph Hodge. (Above, courtesy of Brian and Judy Kirberger; below, courtesy of the Childs family.)

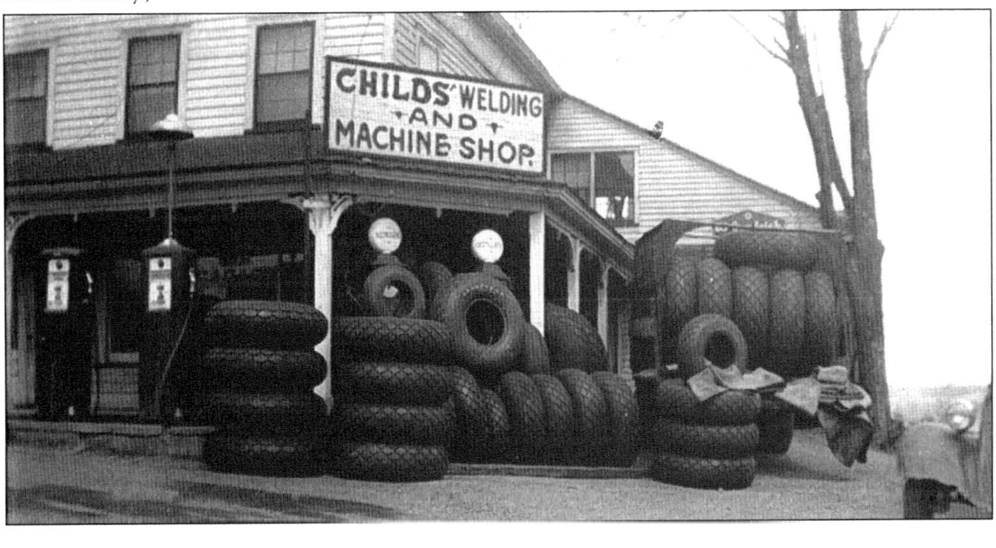

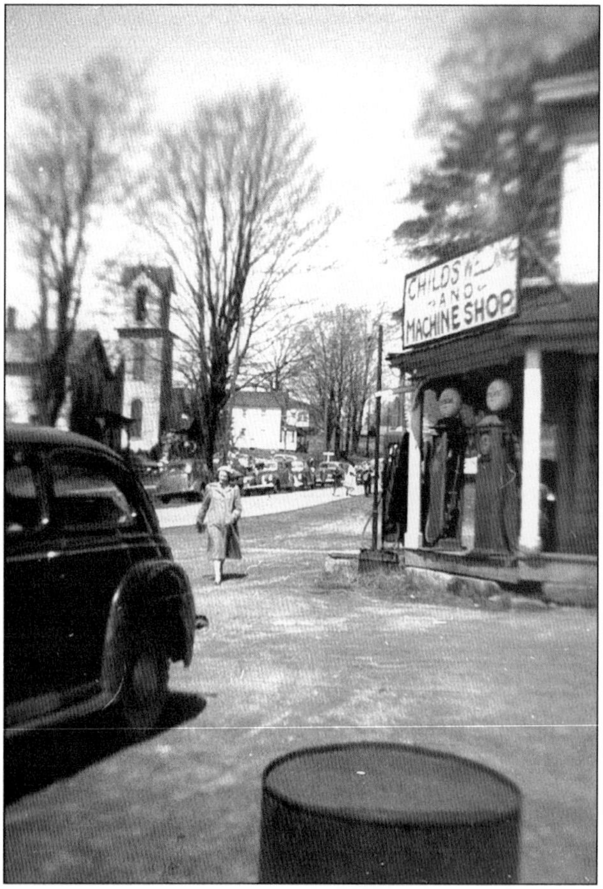

Seen at left, Marilyn Childs returns home from the Easter Methodist Church services in 1950. Their moving truck, purchased in 1953, is shown below. The Randolph East Mead School District purchased the property in 1964, and Mitchell Kosanovic purchased it from the school in 1965. In 1976, a developer purchased the property, the former Guy House Hotel was razed, and the new brick Guys Mills Post Office was built on the historic property. (Courtesy of Lucile Stallard.)

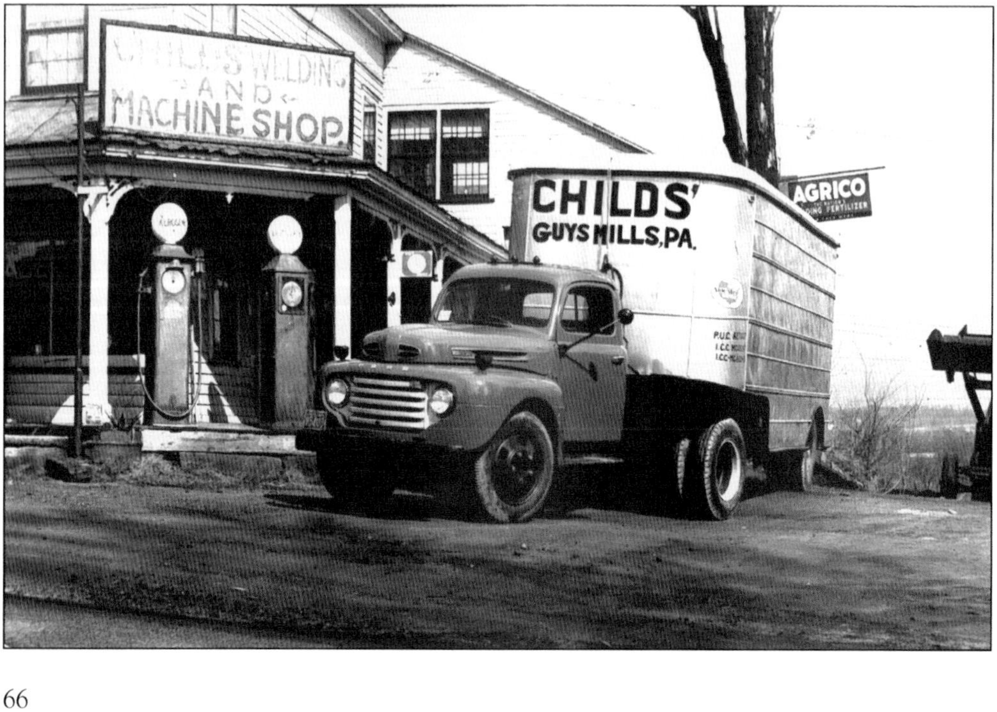

Six

They Communicated

Post Office History

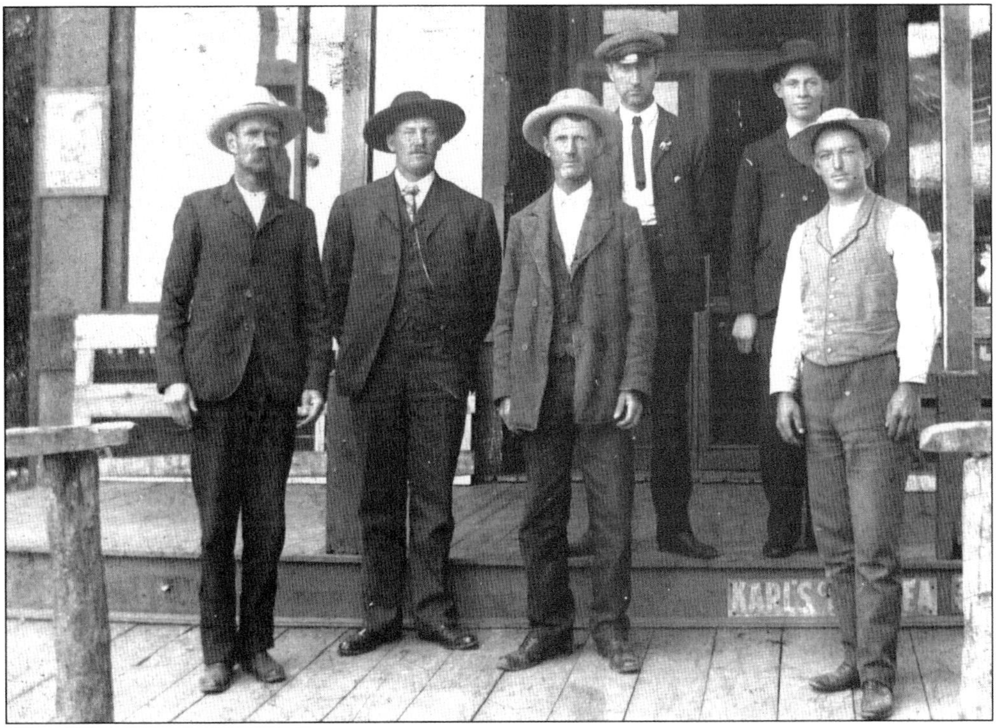

Abolitionist John Brown was the first postmaster in Randolph Township, serving from 1828 to 1835 in the northern township. The first Guys Mills Post Office was secured in 1830. By 1874, there were three in Randolph Township. Seen above, Guys Mills's first four rural mail carriers stand in front of Fred Bannister's store in 1903. From left to right are Ed Cooper, Emmett Burchard, William Blystone, postmaster Fred Bannister, postal clerk Karl Russell, and Guy Wygant. (Courtesy of Janet Marvin.)

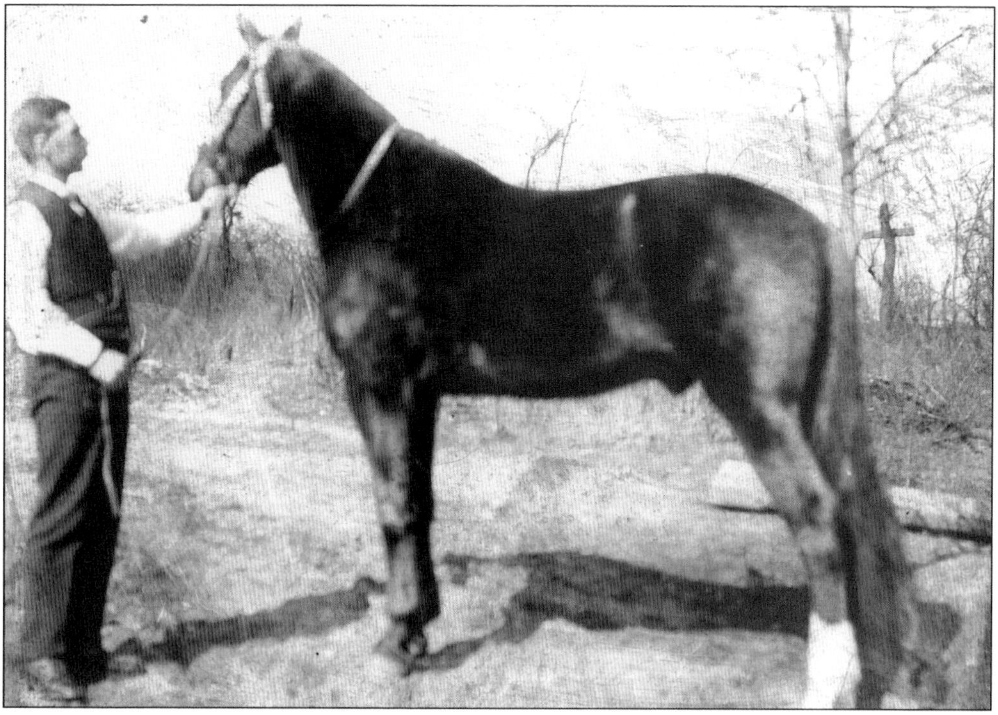

Clifford Isaac Graham, above, carried the mail by horse for eight years. He lived at Hickory Corners. Prior to rural free delivery, if mail remained unclaimed at the post office, the postmaster was required to advertise its presence in the local newspaper. Below is Ed Cooper, one of Guys Mills's original four mail carriers, with his mail delivery rig. Rural mail carriers were paid reimbursement per mile for using their own horses, sometimes referred to as "hayage." Clifford Hunter, Route 3 carrier, needed two horses on his daily 35-mile route. He would switch horses at a farm halfway through his route, alternating the horses at midday every day. With the advent of the automobile, a typical seven-hour mail route was cut to three hours. (Above, courtesy of Barbara Anderson; below, author's collection.)

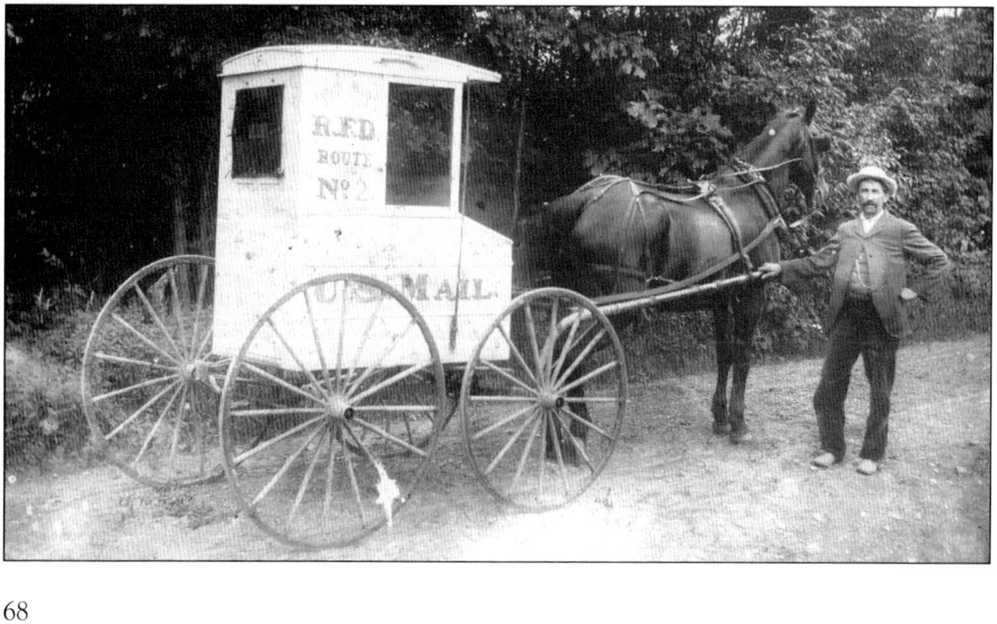

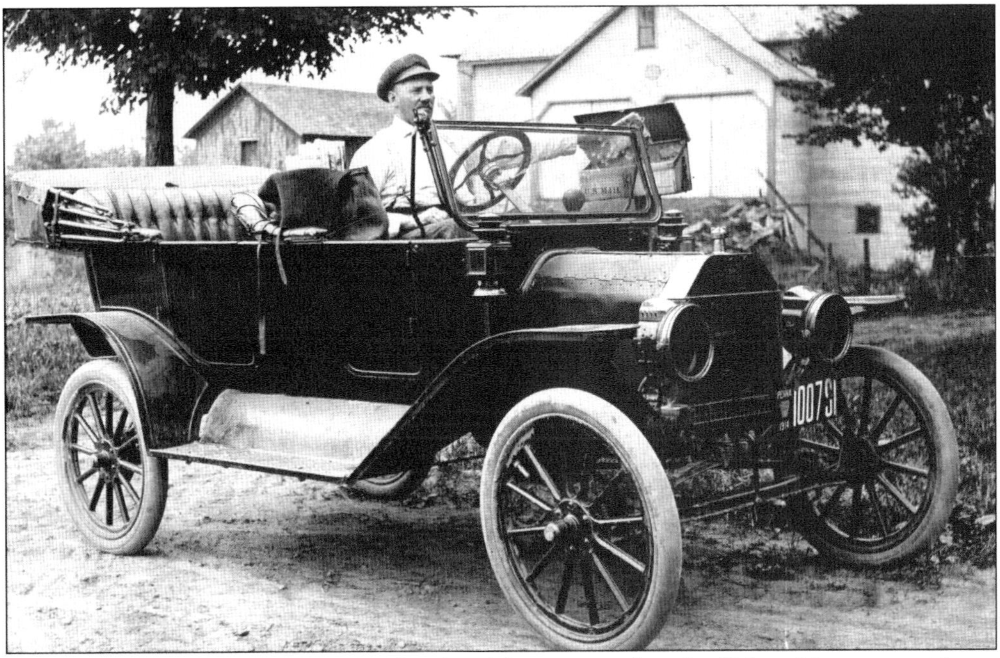

Guys Mills mail carrier Emmett Burchard is delivering mail to the Hilton Morrison residence (later the Paul Lang residence) in his 1913 or 1914 Model T touring car. Early Guys Mills mail carriers opted for cars in good weather and switched back to horses when the roads were bad in the winter. Below was one of the many locations of the Guys Mills Post Office. This building was on the intersection just south of the bridge. This building and others burned in 1945. After the fire, the post office was moved to the store building of David (Gerald) Bird Sr. (currently Norma's Store). (Above, courtesy of Janet Marvin; below, courtesy of Robert W. Waid.)

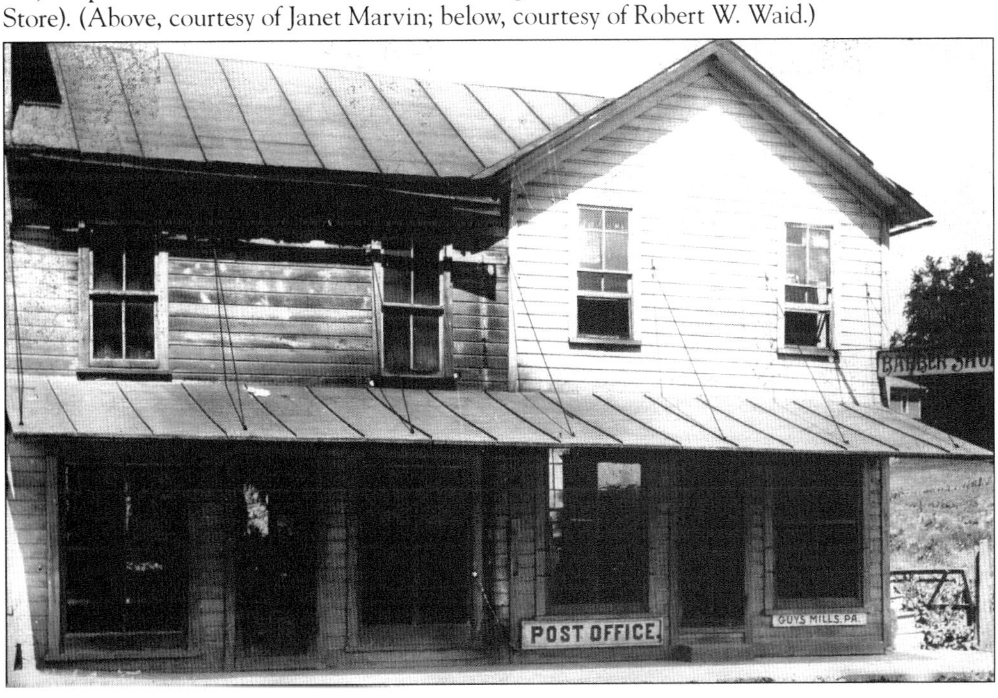

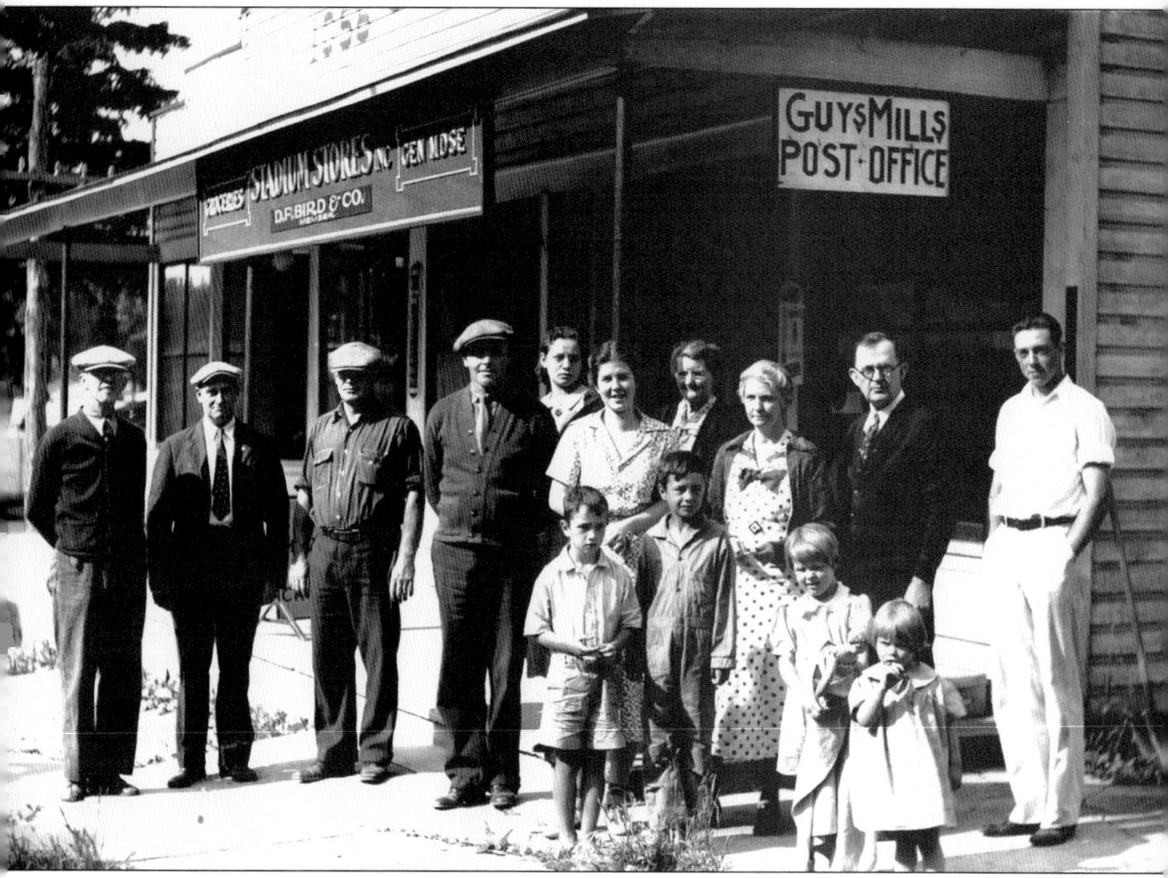

The post office was located in Bird's Store when this photograph was snapped in the 1930s. Seen here are, from left to right, Bert Brown, Route 2; Harold Hanks, Route 4; Clifford Hunter (who carried over two million pieces of mail in 31 years upon his retirement), Route 3; Guy Hall, Route 1; Dorothy Fantacci; Lila Bird, postal clerk; Jessie Bogardus; Kathryne Bird, postmaster; David (Gerald) Bird Sr., store proprietor; and David (Gerald) Bird Jr., store clerk. The neighborhood children are, from left to right, Wayne Corey, Marsden Corey, Lucile Childs, and Marilyn Childs. Rural mail carriers were sometimes the only people that isolated rural residents had regular contact with. Bert Brown is remembered for taking the time to fix a lady's wringer washer during his mail route. In wartime, carriers would go back out to hand deliver a letter from a son at war on their own time rather than making the family wait until the next day. (Courtesy of Sharon Hayes.)

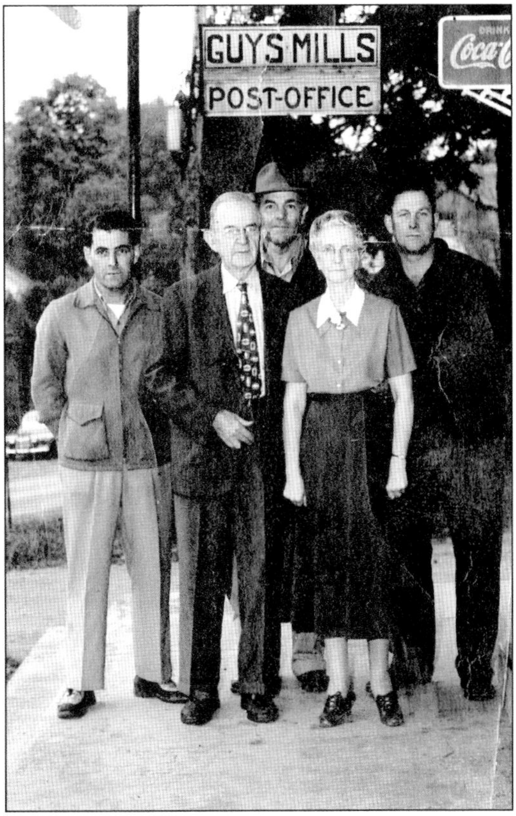

In 1952, David (Gerald) Bird Sr. is shown at right with his wife, postmaster Kathryne Bird. Rural mail carriers pictured, from left to right, are Phil Kinnear, Guy Hall, and Howard Webster. Seen below, the Guys Mills Post Office was located in the rear of Boyd's Store. Boyd's Store proprietor, Russell Boyd (left), hams it up with Jack Lingo (center), and Emmett Morehead. Today one can still see the mail slot to the right of the front doors at Norma's. This photograph was taken about 1956, just before the post office was moved from the store. It was relocated to the former Laibe's Store (the current location of Burchard's Photography Studio). (Right, courtesy of Sharon Hayes; below, courtesy of Russell and Virginia Boyd.)

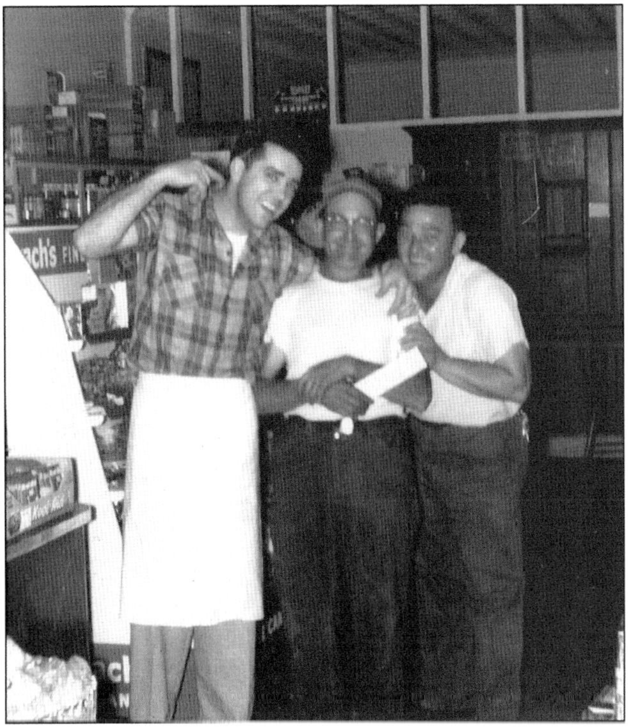

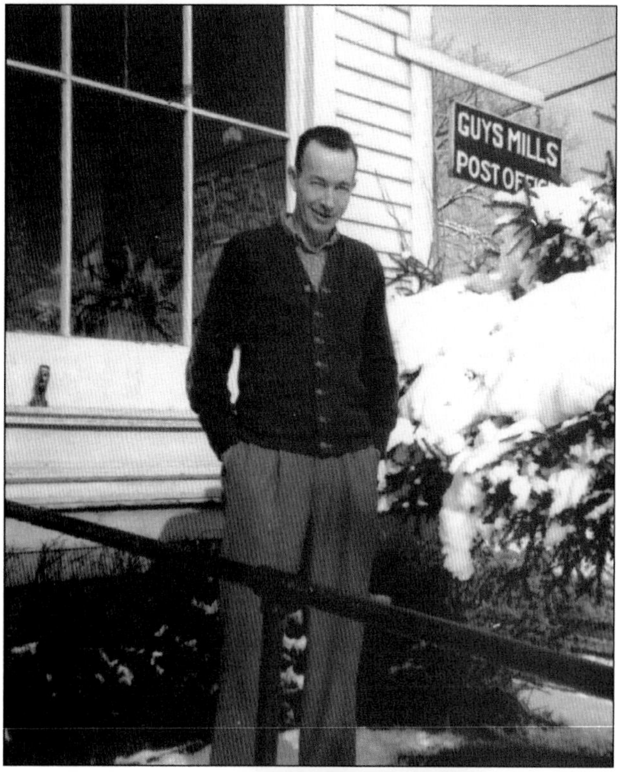

Located in the former Laibe's Store, postmaster Howard Byham (left) and postal clerk Marybelle Bird (below) faithfully served the community for many years. The post office was located there over 20 years. Since 1977, the Guys Mills Post Office has been located in the brick building on the former lot of the historic Guy House Hotel and Childs' Garage. (Courtesy of Leatha Humes.)

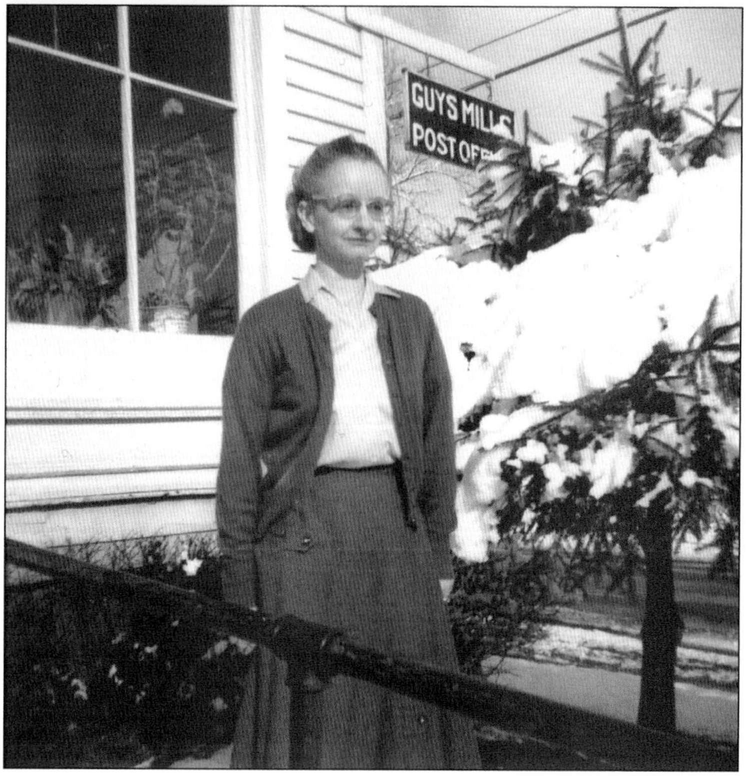

Seven

They Developed the Area

Businesses and Trade

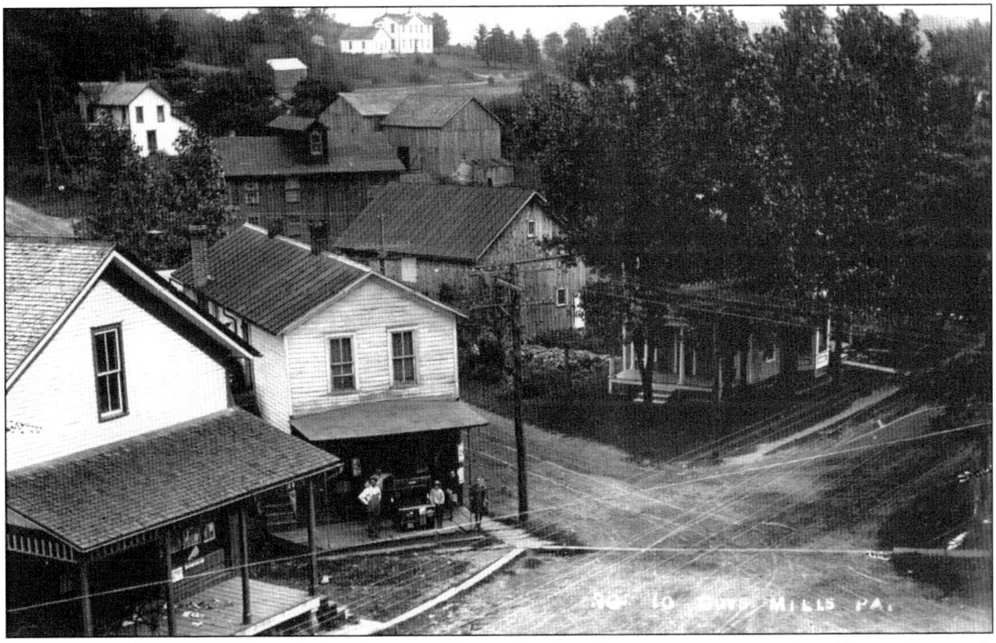

Erected in 1816 or 1817, Jacob Guy's sawmill was the first frame structure in the village that took its name. The mill wheel caught the millpond overflow to power the mill, the huge three-story frame building visible with a roof cupola in this rare 1910 postcard. Guy's son Franklin operated it for about 10 years after his father's death. It was later operated as a feed and gristmill powered by gasoline engines and was permanently abandoned around 1920. (Author's collection.)

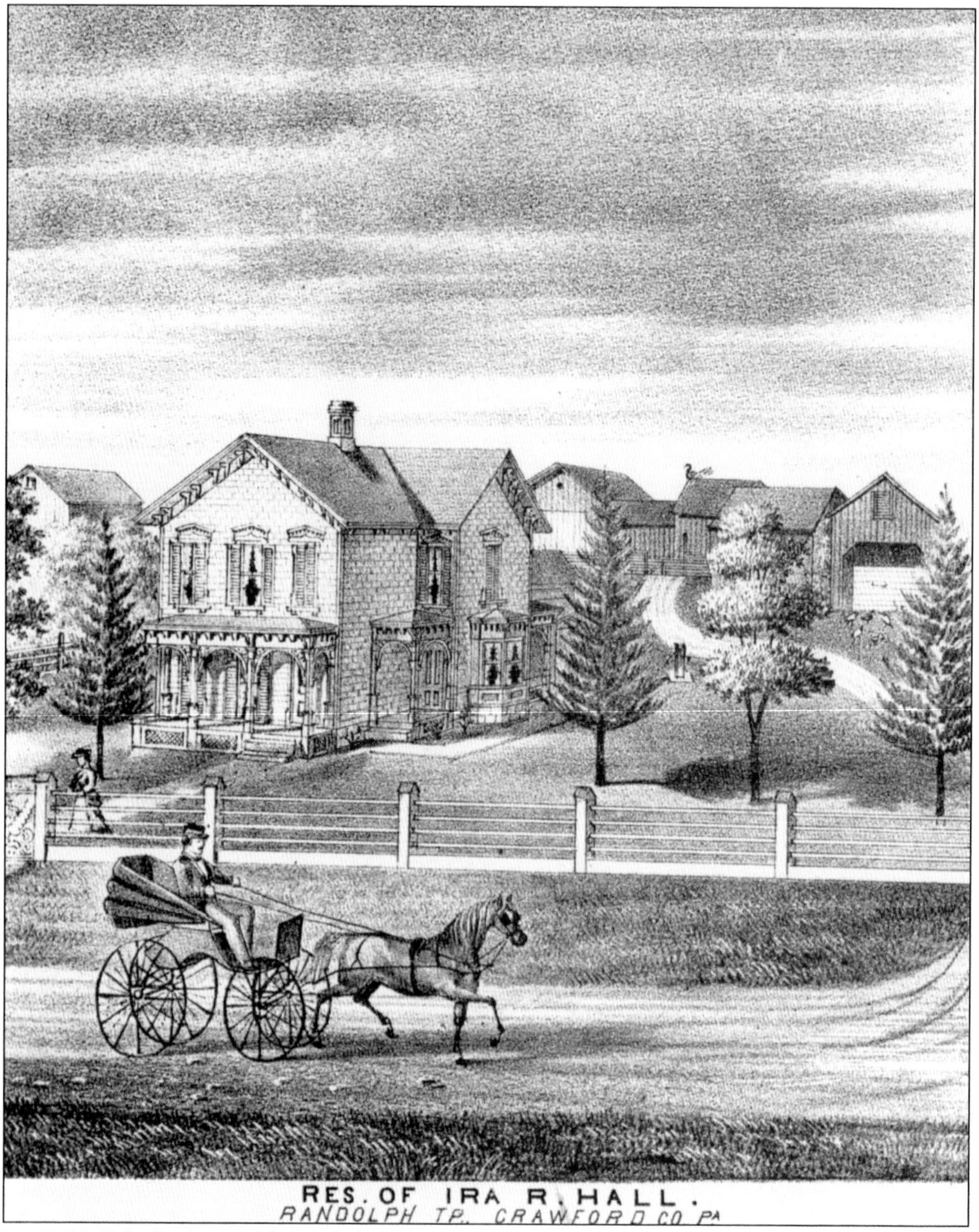

RES. OF IRA R. HALL.
RANDOLPH TP. CRAWFORD CO. PA

Ira R. Hall built this stately brick home in 1871, and it still stands today at Hickory Corners. He was the son of Leonard Hall, first settler of Hickory Corners, who immigrated here in 1817, walking the entire way from Vermont. Hall was an enterprising man, always working toward the advancement of religious and educational pursuits. He taught writing, held many township offices, and was Randolph postmaster (the post office was located in this home) and a Grange member. His obituary heralds him as an "exemplary man, kind, honest and true to his friends." He died at age 79 from injuries suffered from being thrown from a run-away buggy, and he was "of powerful frame and strong physic and enjoyed excellent health up to the time of the accident." (Courtesy of CCHS.)

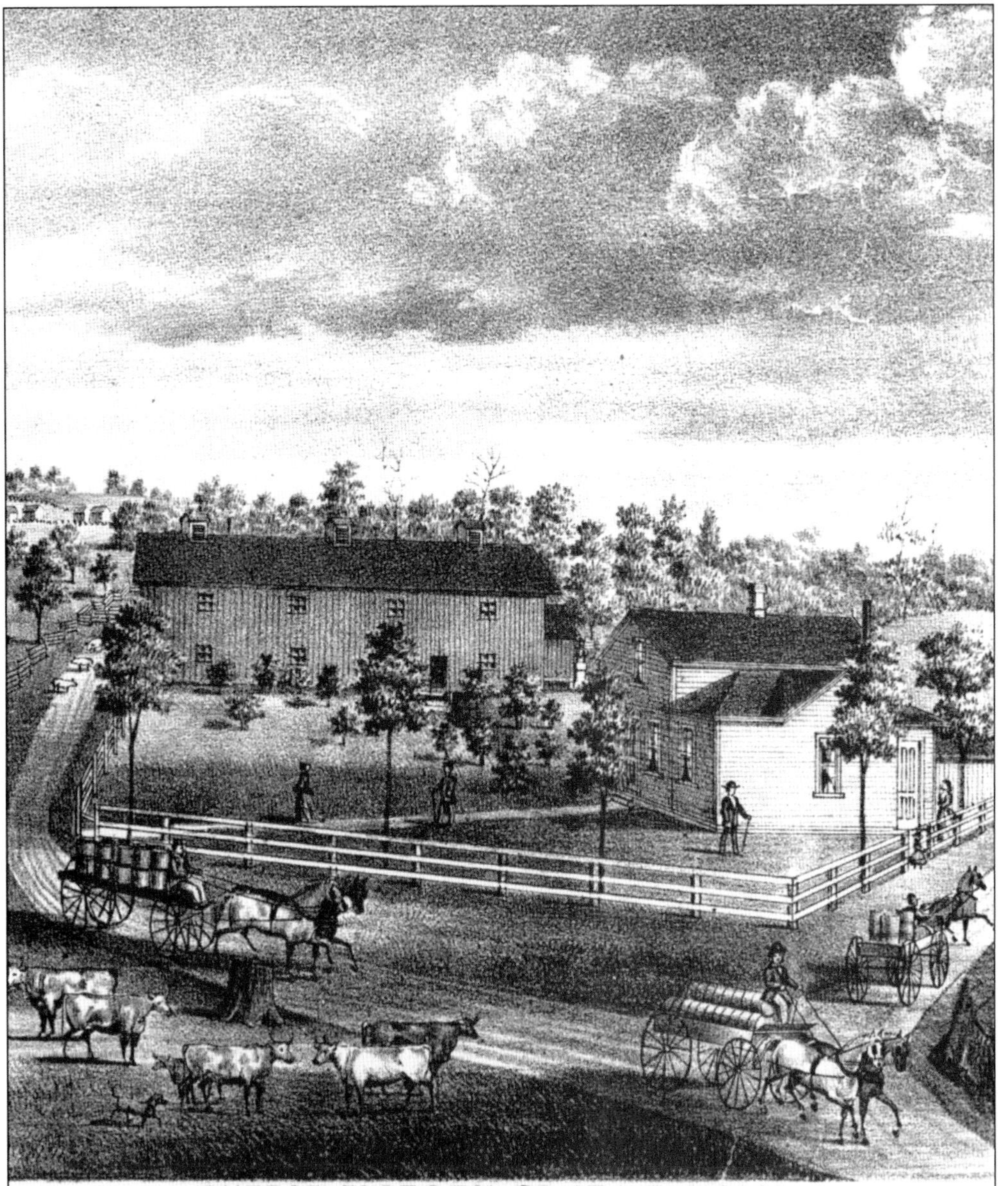

Hall built the Hickory Corners Cheese Factory in 1871 and soon built four more cheese factories in the area. Cheese factories were seasonal establishments, operating when cows had ample pasture and milk was plentiful. This was an important service to dairy farmers before the day of hauling milk to processing plants. Once the milk was dumped into the vats, the farmer pulled around back and filled his empty milk cans with whey to feed to his pigs. Hall was also extensively involved in stock raising, dairying, and farming. At the time of this picture, Hickory Corners consisted of a post office, church, store, blacksmith, cheese factory, and about 10 dwellings. (Courtesy of CCHS.)

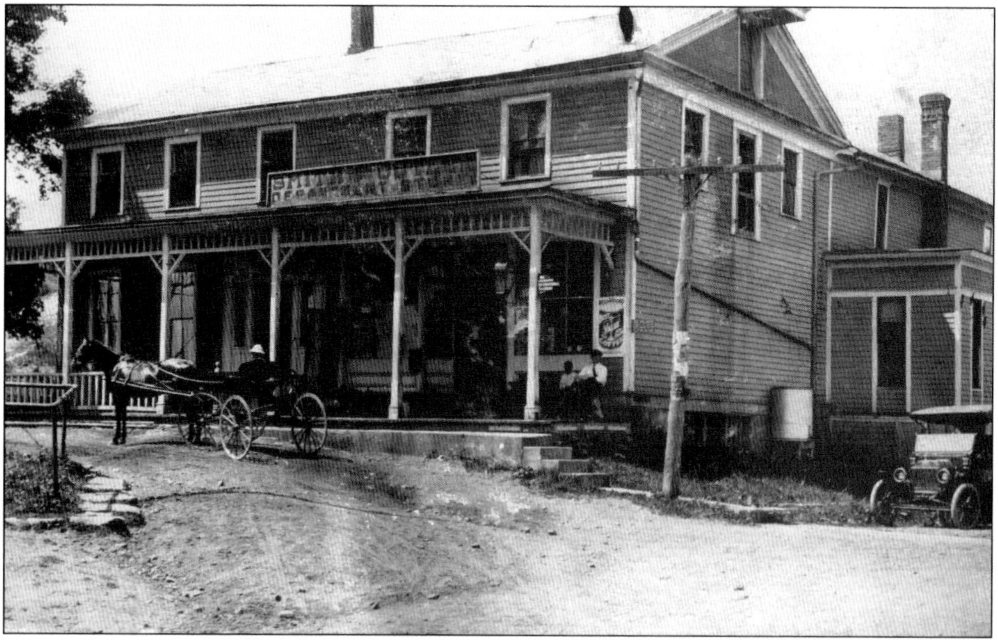

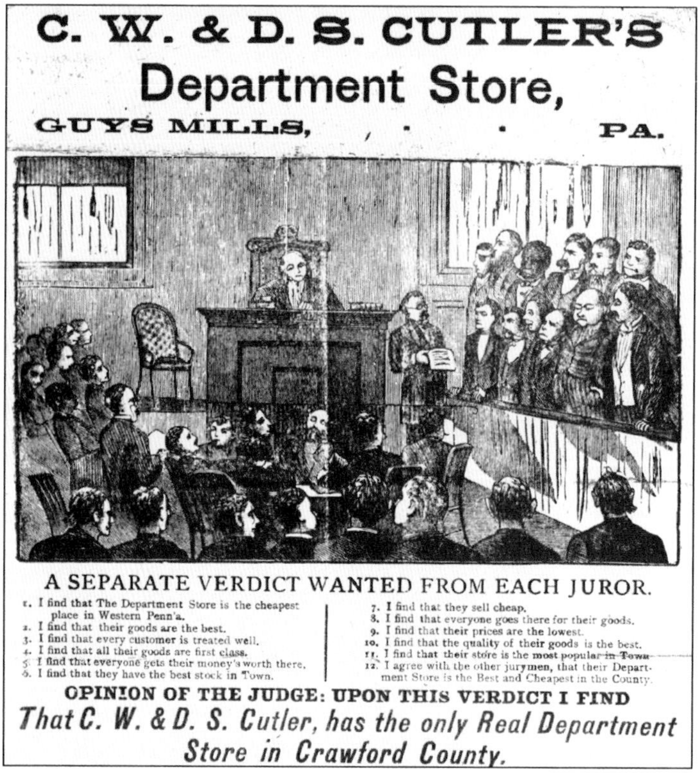

This site has always been a combination residential and commercial site. Jacob Guy established his general store at this location in 1833. Guy was followed by several owners, the most noted being the Cutler Brothers who added the second story for a meeting place for the lodge. Before the advent of the automobile made it easy to shop in Meadville, Cutlers carried such varied stock that they advertised their general store as "The only real department store in Crawford County." (Above, courtesy of Robert W. Waid; left, courtesy of the Childs family.)

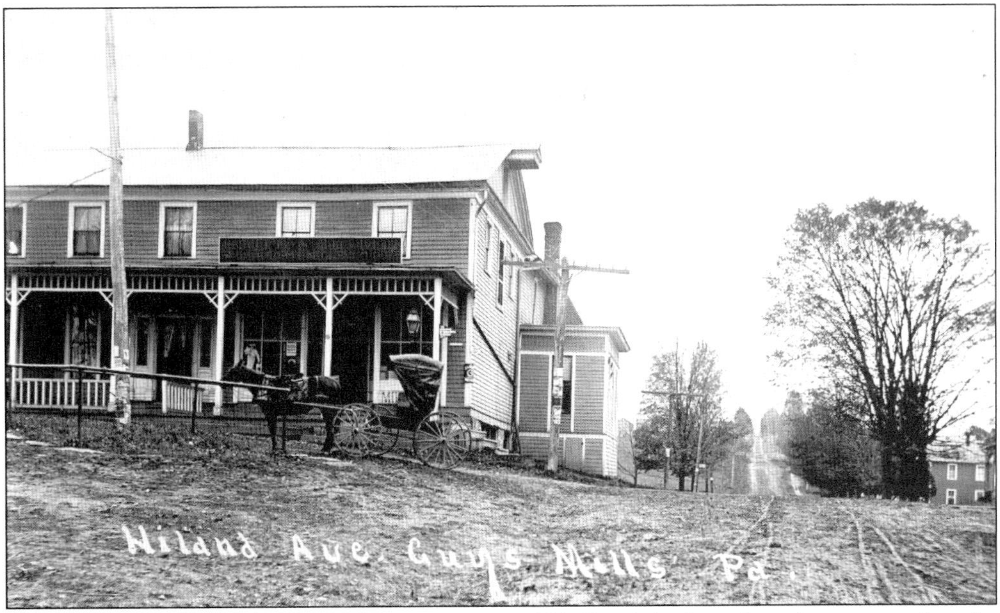

Pharmacist Den Smith became sole proprietor in 1900. Smith had a safe in the store, and in the absence of a bank in Guys Mills, he would cash checks, issue certificates of deposit, and provide other financial services. Karl Russell and Charles Kendall bought the building and stock in 1915. The next owners were George Laibe and John Beuchat. Laibe operated the store as sole owner then eventually leased the space out to other merchants. The last merchant to operate this building as a general store was David (Gerald) Bird Jr. from 1952 to 1955, shown below with his daughter. Through several more owners, it became Taggart's Upholstery Shop and the Guys Mills Post Office. It is the current home and photography studio of Dennis Burchard. (Above, author's collection; below, courtesy of Sharon Hayes.)

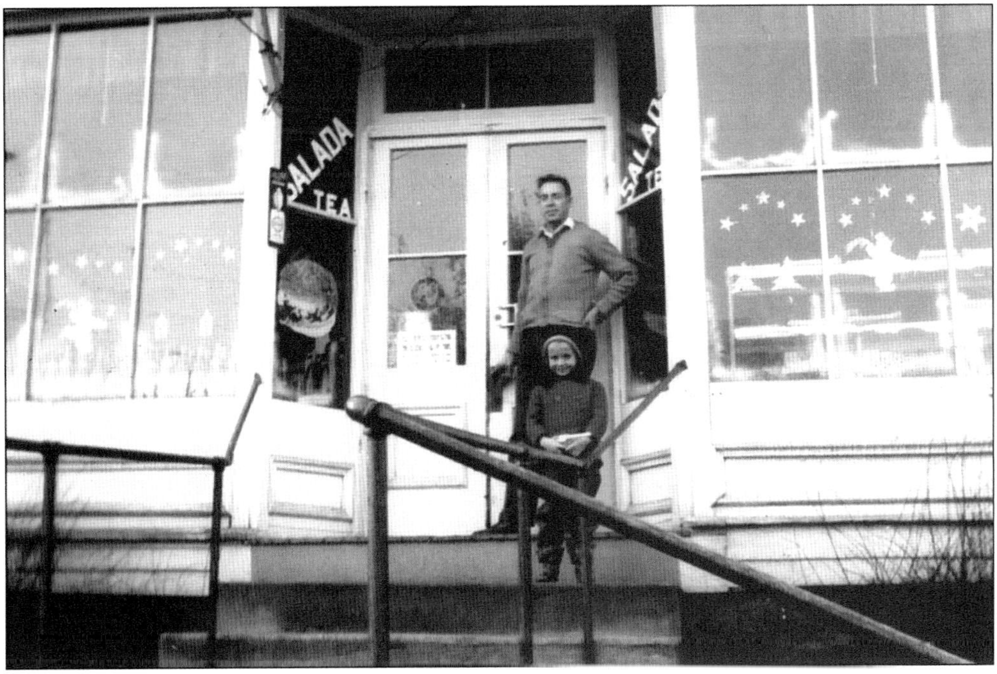

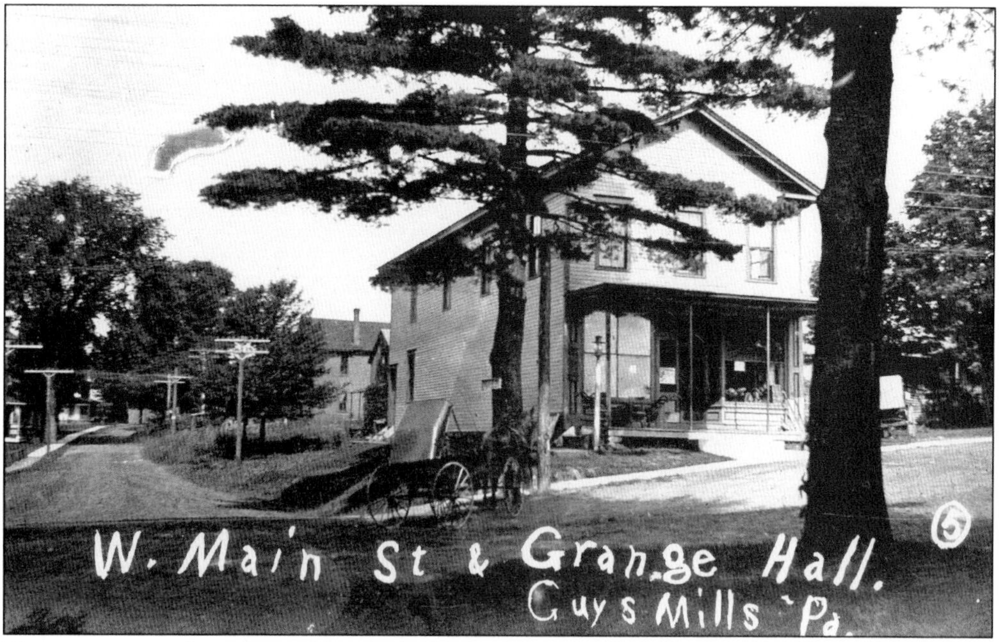

These two pages show the evolution of a familiar Guys Mills commercial building. The original 65-by-40-foot building, above, was built by Randolph Grange No. 190 about 1876. Grange meetings were held on the second floor, while the downstairs was rented by merchants John Radle and Knight Smith, who stocked it with an extensive supply of general merchandise. Later merchants renting this space were Chapin and Roueche, Roueche and Cooper, Delbert Gage, A. F. Gage and Son, and Corliss and Gillette. When the hall was sold to the IOOF No. 1056, they built large additions (below) to make space for a dining room and kitchen and continued to rent the bottom to merchants. The post office was located in the store and Randolph Grange rented the upper floor for meetings. (Above, author's collection; below, courtesy of Robert W. Waid.)

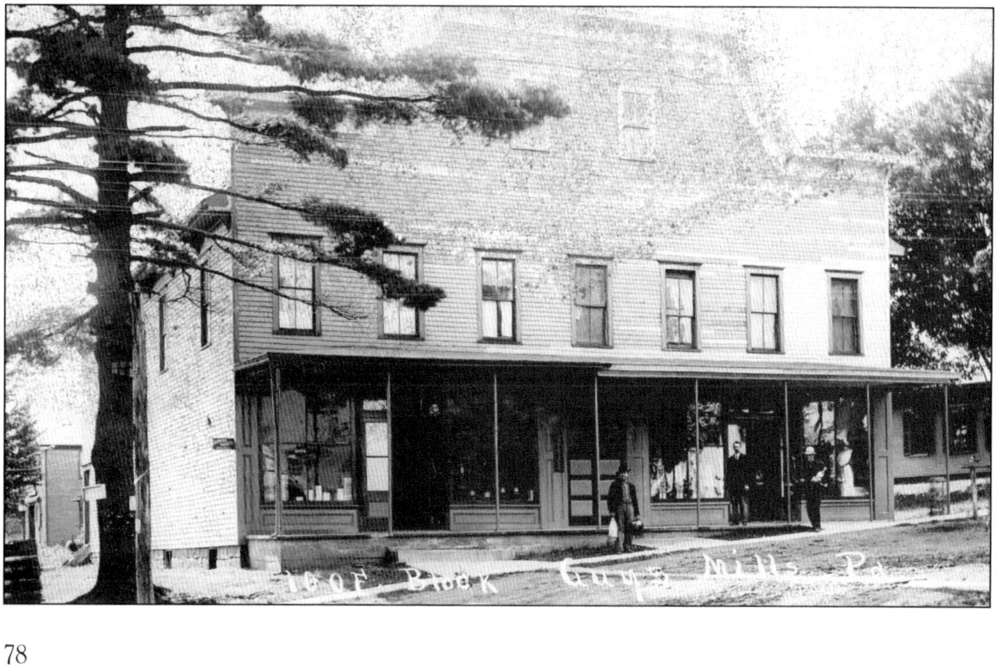

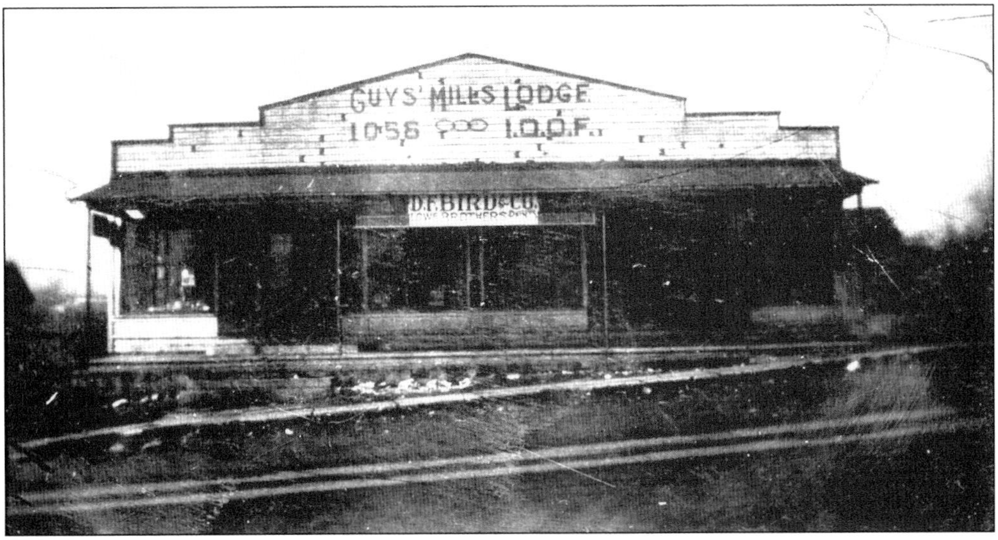

David (Gerald) Bird Sr. purchased the building in 1927. Bird's Store ledger shows interesting prices. One pound of coffee cost 43¢, a dozen eggs cost 10¢, and five pounds of sugar cost 35¢. The building was devastated by fire on March 10, 1933, while trying to thaw frozen water pipes. The post office was temporarily moved to Paul and Ancinohie Corey's house. A one-story building, shown above in 1944, was built in the spring. Merle Casler began renting the storefront in 1945. The photograph below shows Kathryne Bird with granddaughters Sharon and Carol. Beauty shops, doctors, and offices have rented the right side of the building. The Boyd family took over the store in 1950 and operated Boyd's Store until 1991 when Norma McFadden bought the building. It is now known as Norma's. (Above, courtesy of Lucile Stallard; below, courtesy of Sharon Hayes.)

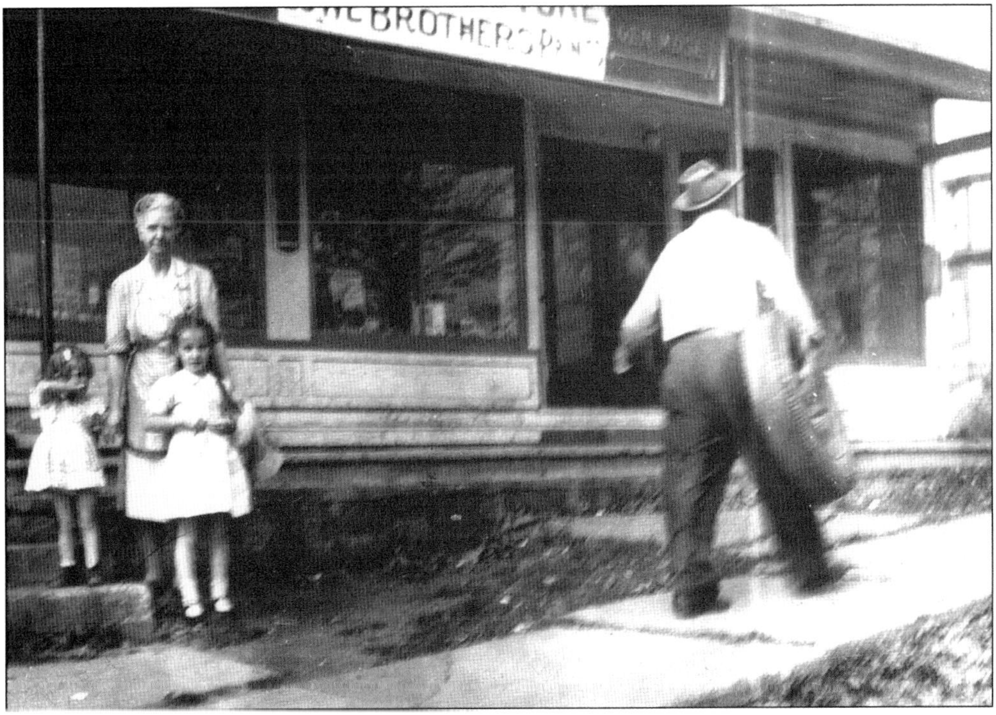

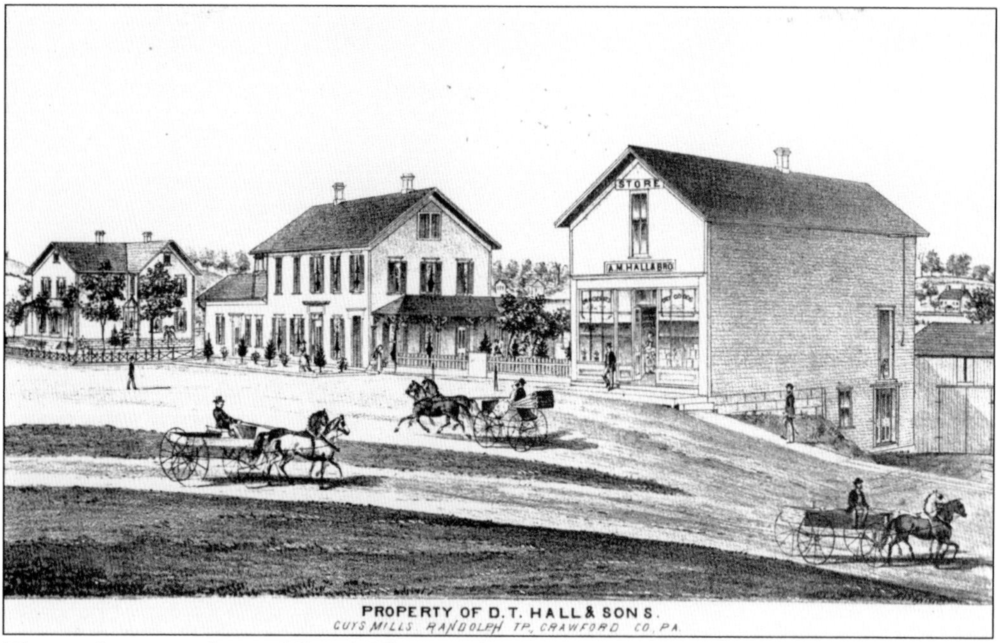

The northwest quadrant of Guys Mills was a busy commercial center consisting of four closely grouped buildings connected by board sidewalks and walkways. Seen above in 1876, D. T. Hall and Sons General Store and the Hall residence (later burned) were located here. The same store building (shown below on the right in 1914), when owned by Dr. Charles Burgwin, was converted into the Egg-win Poultry Plant, then Burgwin Apartments, then a folding chair factory. Also on this intersection was a carriage shop, tin shop, barbershop, post office, meat market, restaurant, township supervisors meeting room, and election hall. Cutler's Store was on the left. (Above, courtesy of CCHS; below, author's collection.)

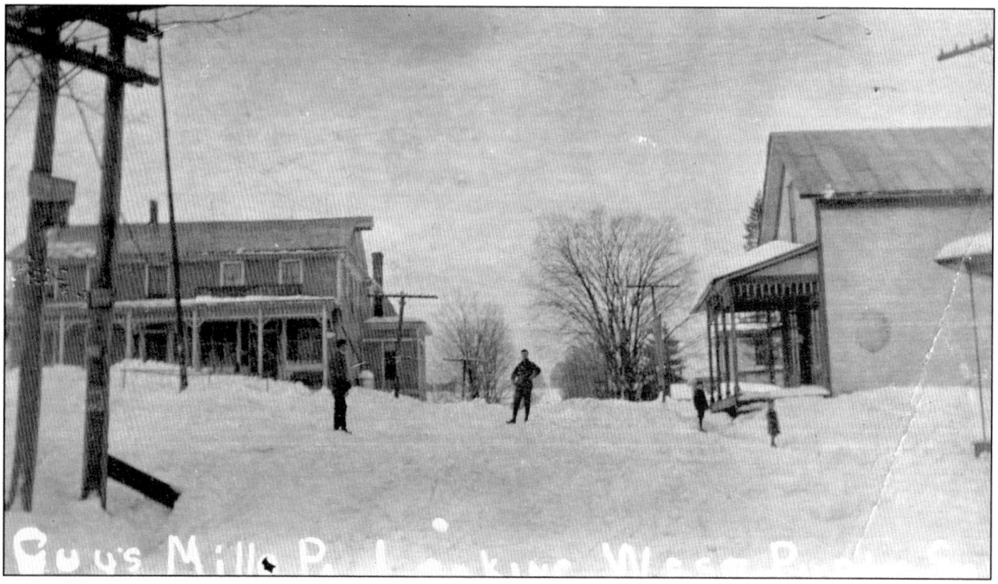

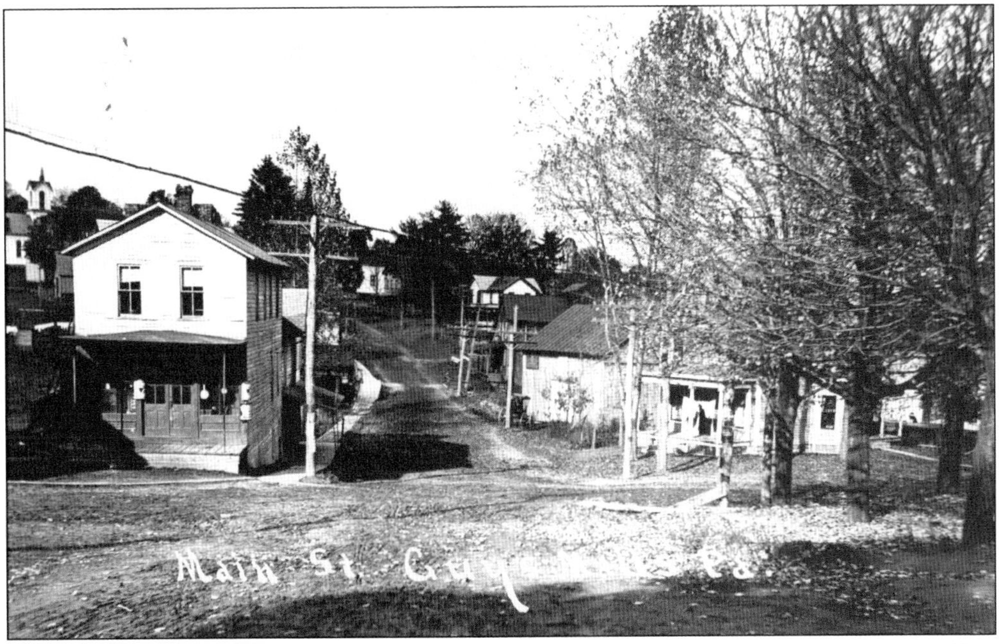

In the image above, the building on the left was Hesketh's Store and contained the post office. Art Hodge's Barber Shop was upstairs, offering 10¢ haircuts. Hodge had pictures cut from men's clothing catalogs pasted on his walls. From them customers could choose the New York–, Philadelphia-, Chicago-, or Boston-style haircuts. But no matter which they chose, everyone looked the same when they left. Notice the front porch of the mill, third building from the corner on the right in this 1910 postcard. The photograph below shows another view of this corner. A telephone alarm of one long ring followed by nine short ones alerted Guys Mills to the devastating fire in May 1945 that destroyed four buildings on this intersection and helped inspire the formation of the Randolph Volunteer Fire Department, which now stands on this site. (Above, author's collection; below, courtesy of Leatha Humes.)

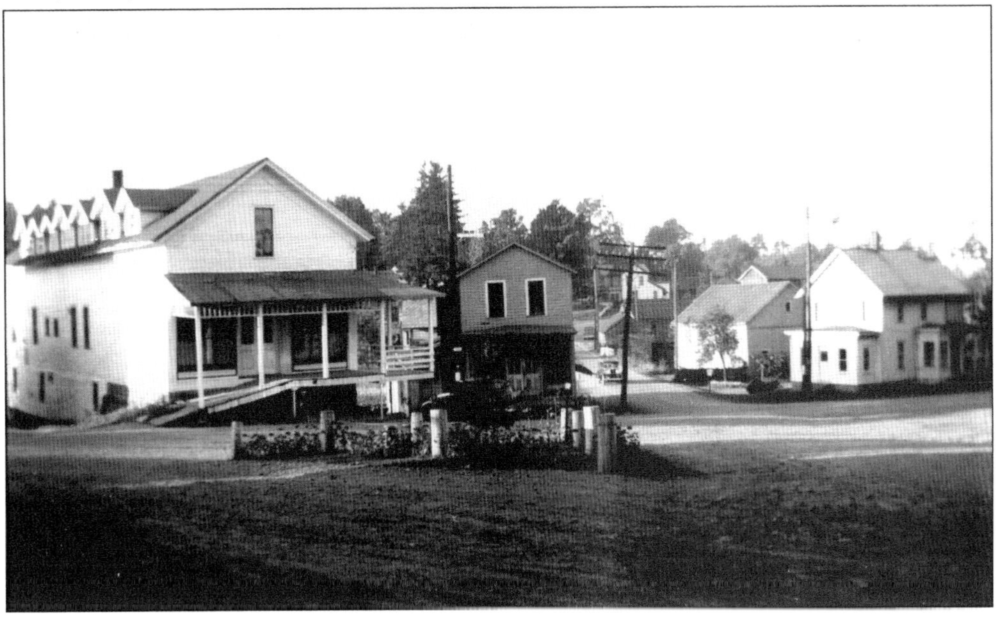

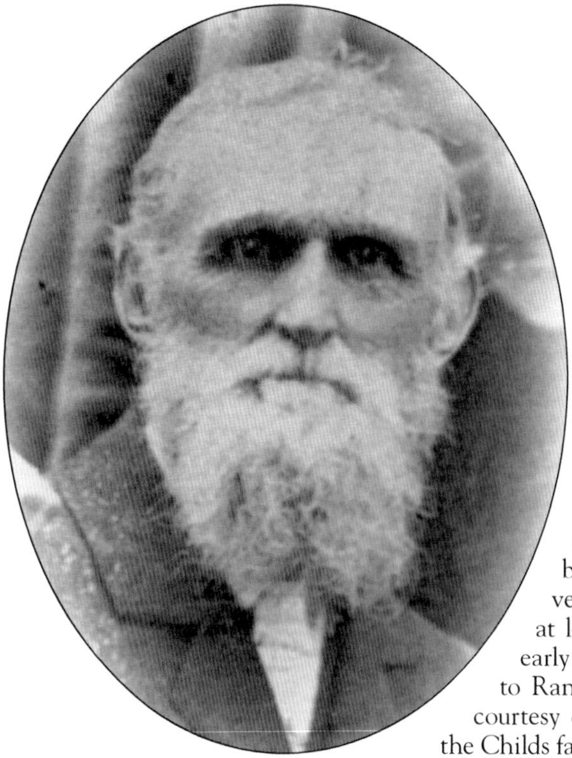

The Waid Funeral Home was established in Guys Mills in 1900. After attending Edinboro Normal School, a one-month embalming school in Pittsburgh, and becoming a licensed funeral director, Willard Cutler Waid purchased the funeral home (the current Kirberger home) from Philip Monroe and the furniture business from Charles Corliss. Waid ran the furniture shop in conjunction with the undertaking business. Willard was the son of Civil War veteran Seth Waid III (1835–1905), seen at left, and the grandson of Seth Waid Jr., early Randolph settler. Seth Jr. migrated to Randolph in 1916 at the age of 16. (Left, courtesy of Robert W. Waid; below, courtesy of the Childs family.)

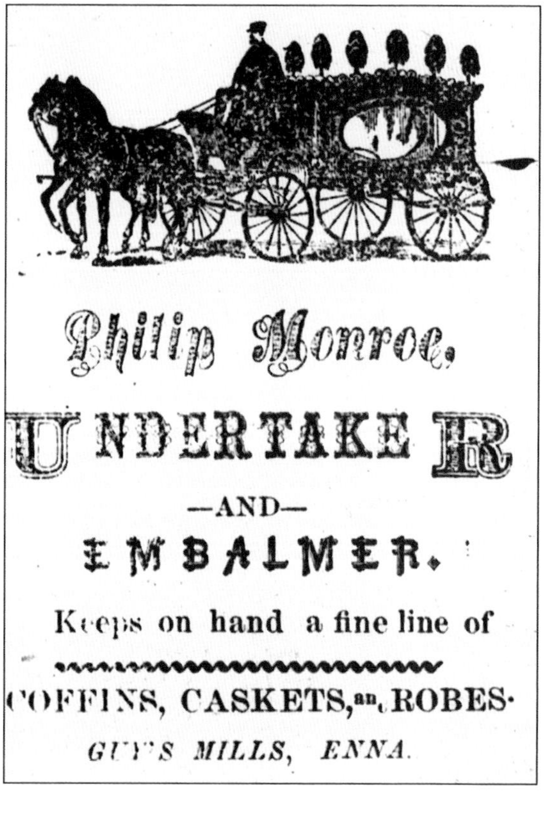

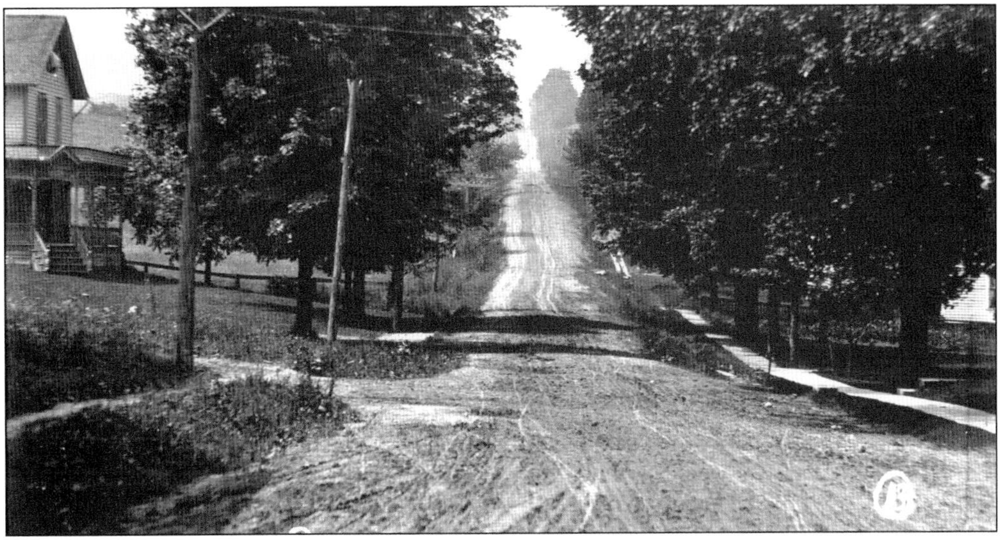

Funerals were usually held in the residence of the deceased or a church. If the residence was not large enough, the services were held at Waid's Funeral Home, shown above at far left. At the deceased residence, Willard prepared the body on their kitchen table, attending to embalming, cleansing, cosmetic needs, and dressing the body. Family members would often assist. The deceased would then be placed in their bed or Waid's Funeral Home's collapsible bed for viewing. Waid's Funeral Home also loaned chairs and lamps to help the family prepare to receive guests. Returning home to his furniture shop, Willard custom built the coffin. On the day of the funeral, the body was placed in the new coffin for the funeral then taken graveside by horse-drawn hearse or bobsled for winter funerals. Well-groomed matched teams were rented from farmers such as Harry L. Wentworth. In 1929, the establishment moved to Meadville. Son Leland Waid joined the business in 1936. It is now operated by Robert W. Waid and his sons Robert S. Waid, supervisor of the Meadville location, and Todd A. Waid, supervisor of the Conneaut Lake branch. Four generations are seen below, from left to right: Robert W. Waid holding son Robert S. Waid, Leland Waid, and Willard Waid. (Above, author's collection; below, courtesy of Robert W. Waid.)

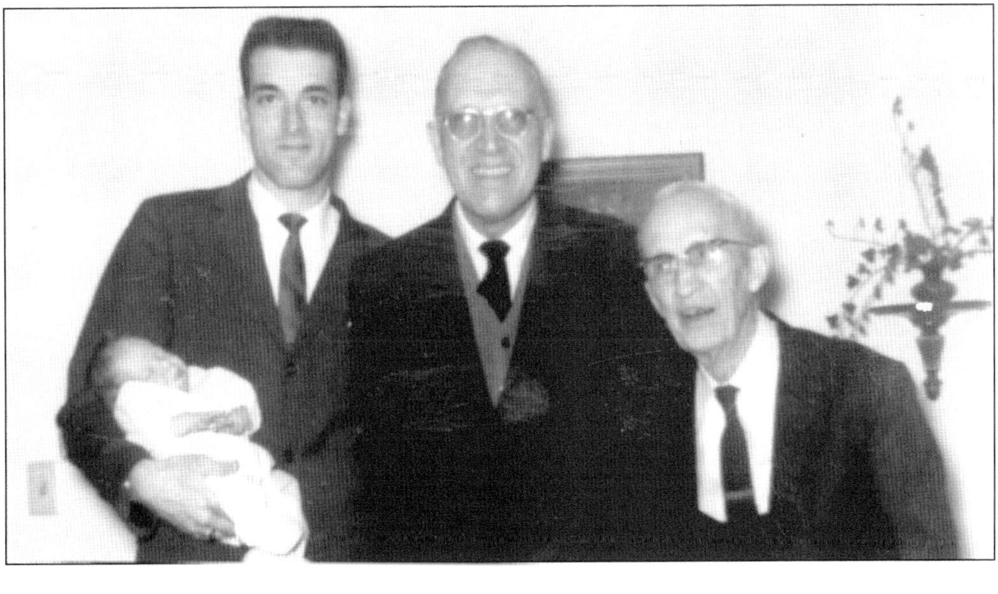

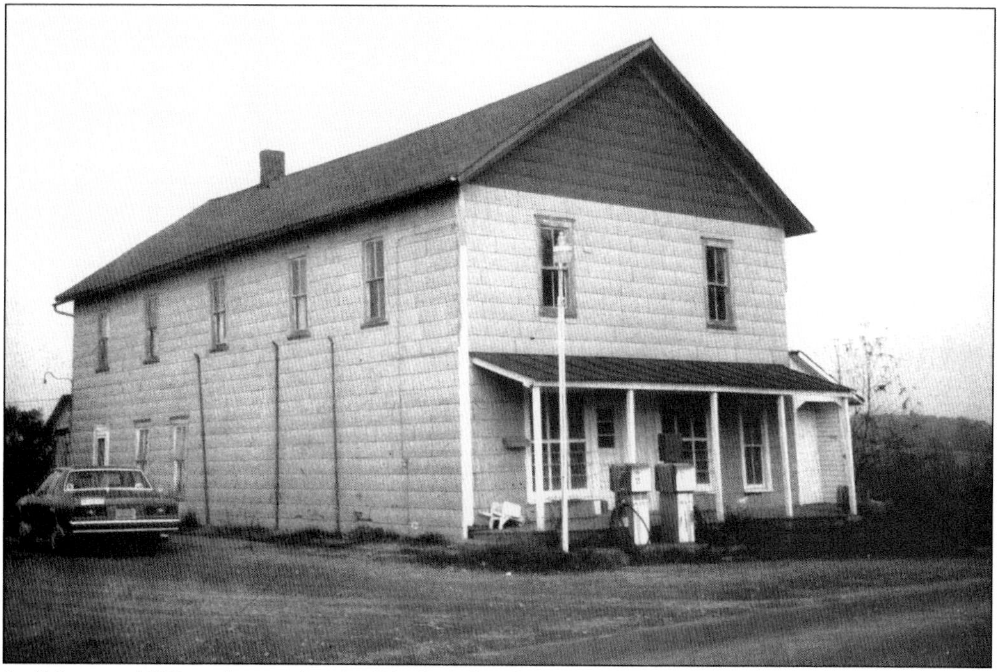

In February 1887, a charter for the Black Ash Chapter of the National Farmers Alliance and Industrial Union was issued to Albert O. Luce, Burton Bogardus, William H. Miller, Lewis Luce, and Edward Hatch. This huge building was erected with timbers donated by Congressman Joseph Sibley of Franklin. For years, the upstairs social hall hosted Alliance meetings, Black Ash Sportsman's Club meetings, Methodist Ladies Aid, wedding receptions, public dinners, dances, stage performances, and basketball games. The downstairs was leased to various general storekeepers including Reed, Welsh, Armstrong, Waid, Brown, Platt, Bickel, and Young. Tom Mattis had a gun shop there. The building included living quarters in the back. The building is now gone, the National Farmers Alliance and Industrial Union has disbanded, and the site is the home of Tom Young. (Above, courtesy of Tom Mattis; below, courtesy of Iris Armburger.)

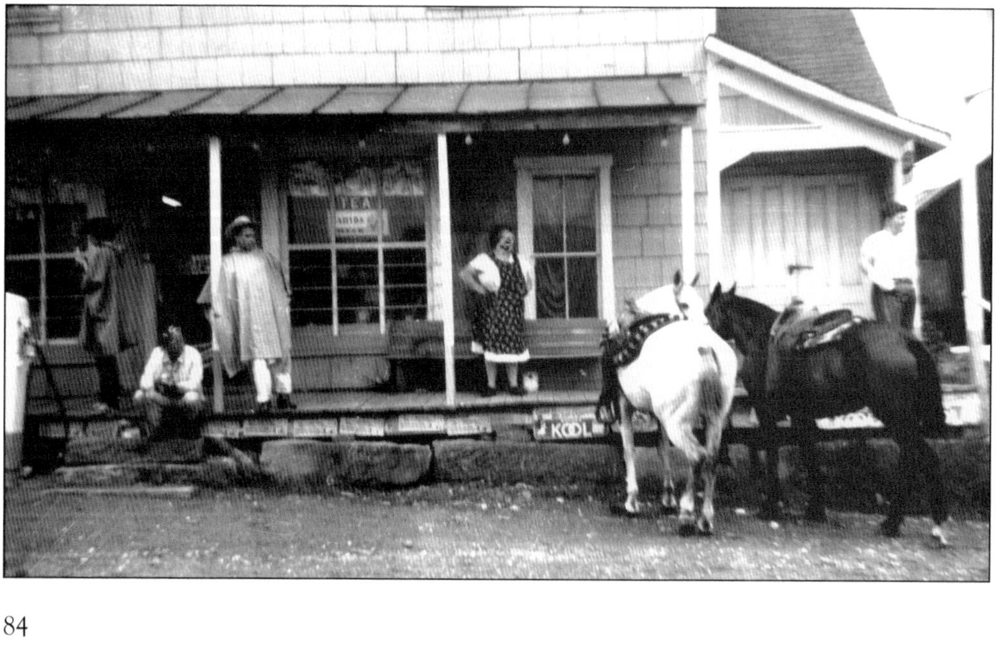

The sound of hammer and anvil rung out across Black Ash for many years. In his blacksmith shop east of Black Ash, Charlie Armstrong shows the smallest pony shoe he made and the largest, made for big teams. When he started blacksmithing around 1913, he charged 60¢ to replace a new shoe and could manufacture 60 to 70 shoes a day. (Courtesy of the Titusville Herald and Brian and Judy Kirberger.)

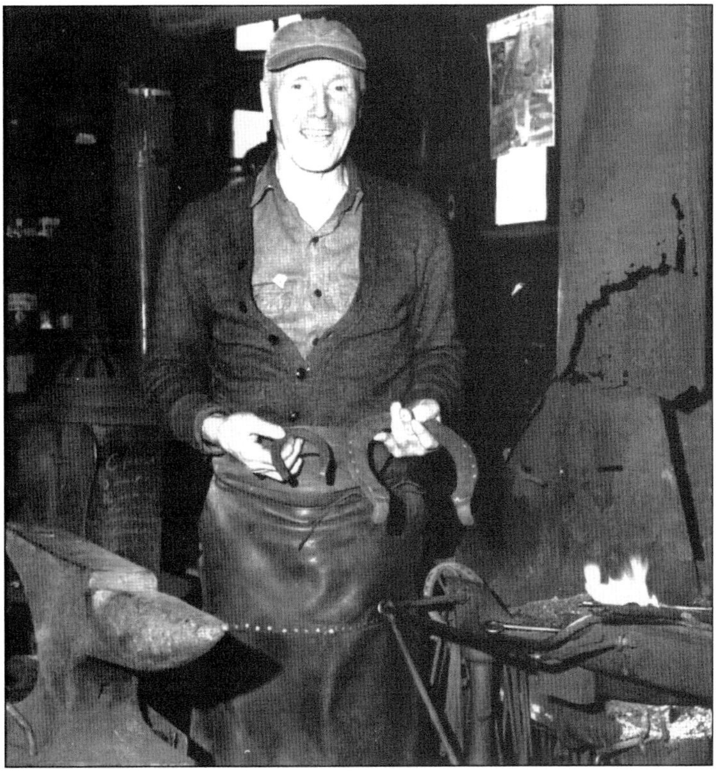

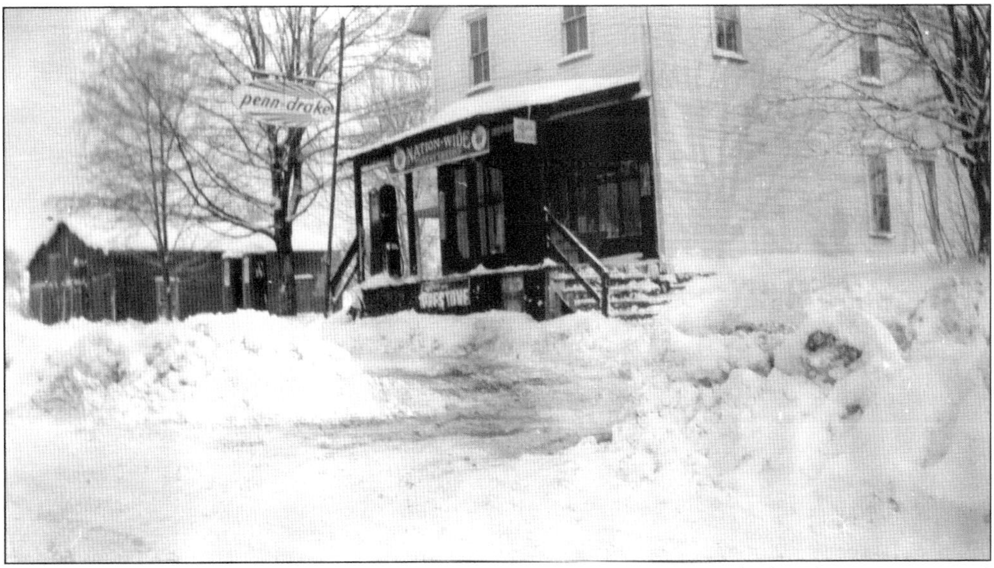

Herb Rambo ran a furniture store and a grocery store on Route 27 in Black Ash. Pettigrews and Uhlmans also operated the store at different times. They sold a wide range of stock, including gas and general merchandise. (Courtesy of Erna Bancroft.)

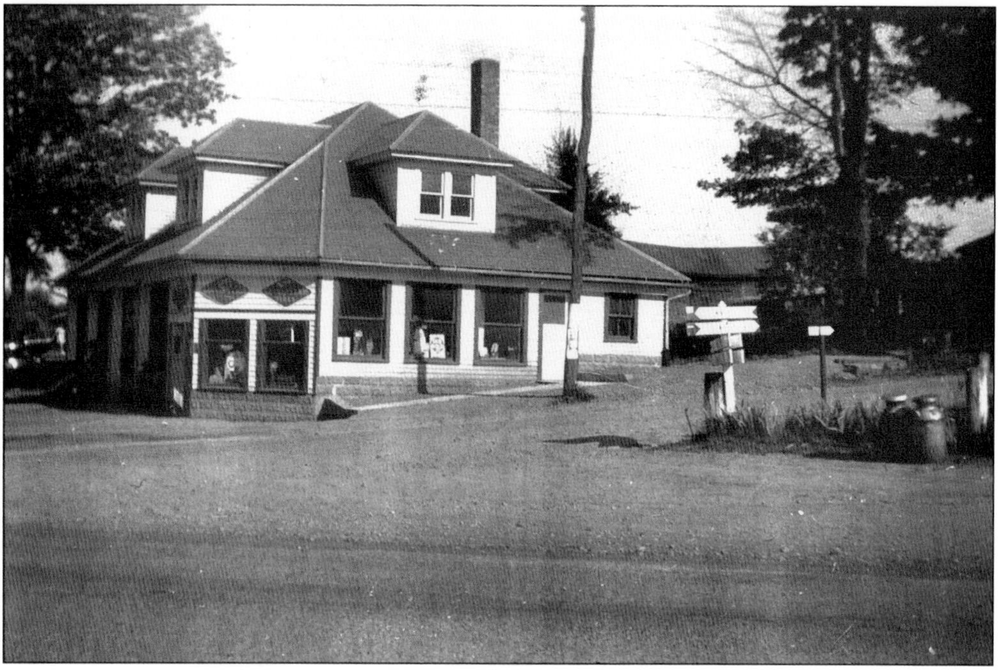

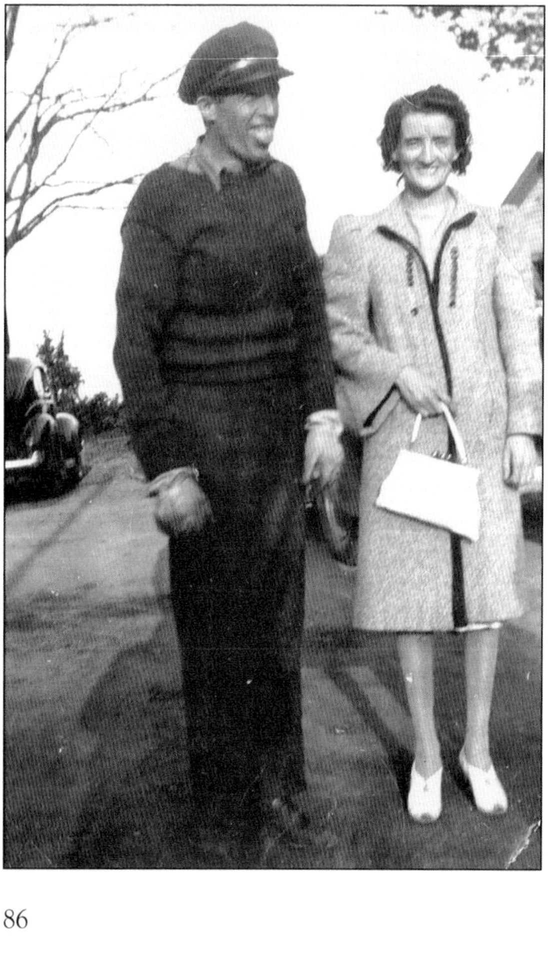

Bannister's General Store was torn down around World War I, and later Jim Welsh's garage and home stood here, just north of Wilford and Carolyn Miller's home in Guys Mills. Jim, a former employee of Frank Childs, repaired cars in his four-bay garage, delivered gasoline to area farmers, and sold Coreco Products. Jim and his wife, Nellie, and their children lived in the attached home. (Above, courtesy of Darlene Jablon; left, courtesy of Dorothy Anthony.)

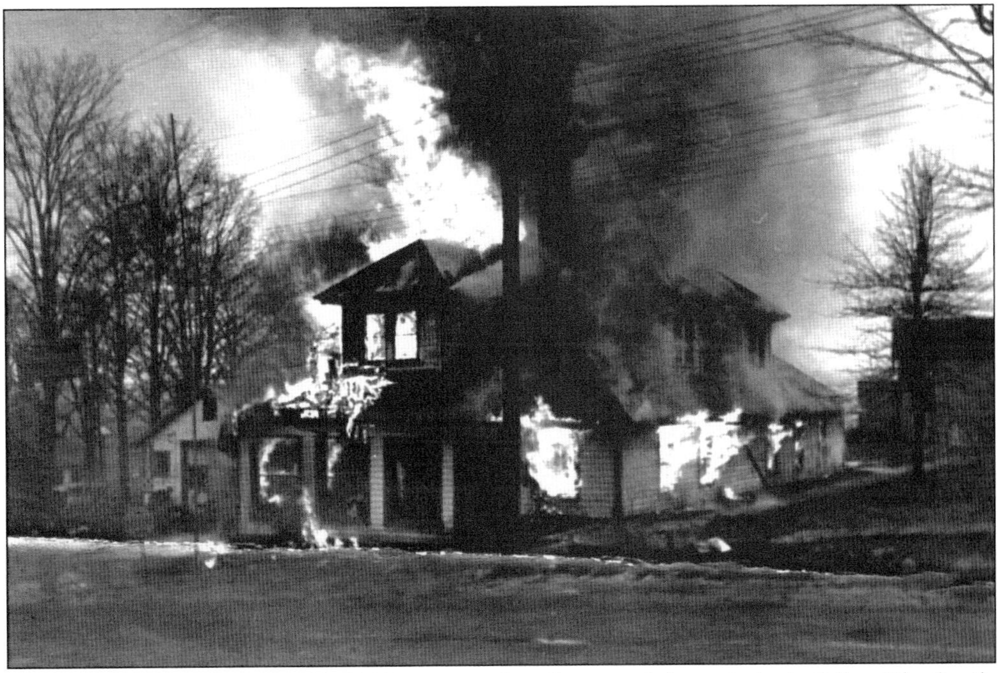

On the afternoon of January 20, 1944, a tremendous fire ripped through the building. The family was safe, but without a local fire department, the building was a total loss. Area citizens fighting the fire entered Joe Kaputa's home next door, ripped blankets off their beds, soaked them in their kitchen sink, and wrapped them around Welsh's gas pumps to prevent an explosion. Notice Kaputa's Garage on the left of the photograph above. The former Welsh's Garage site became a parking area for Kaputa's Garage, and Joe Kaputa took over the gas pumps. (Courtesy of the Childs family.)

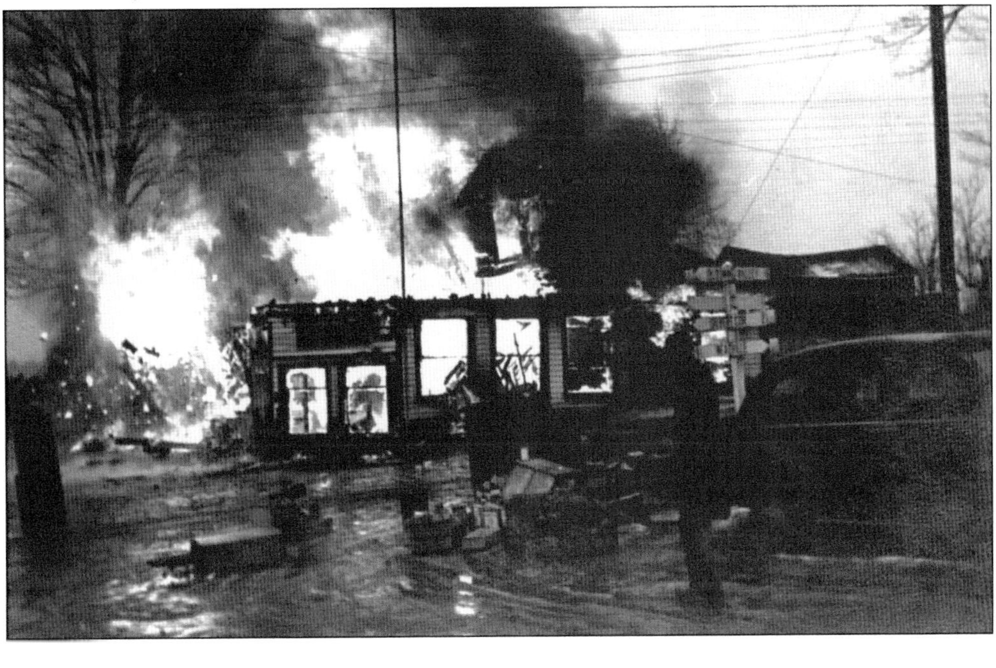

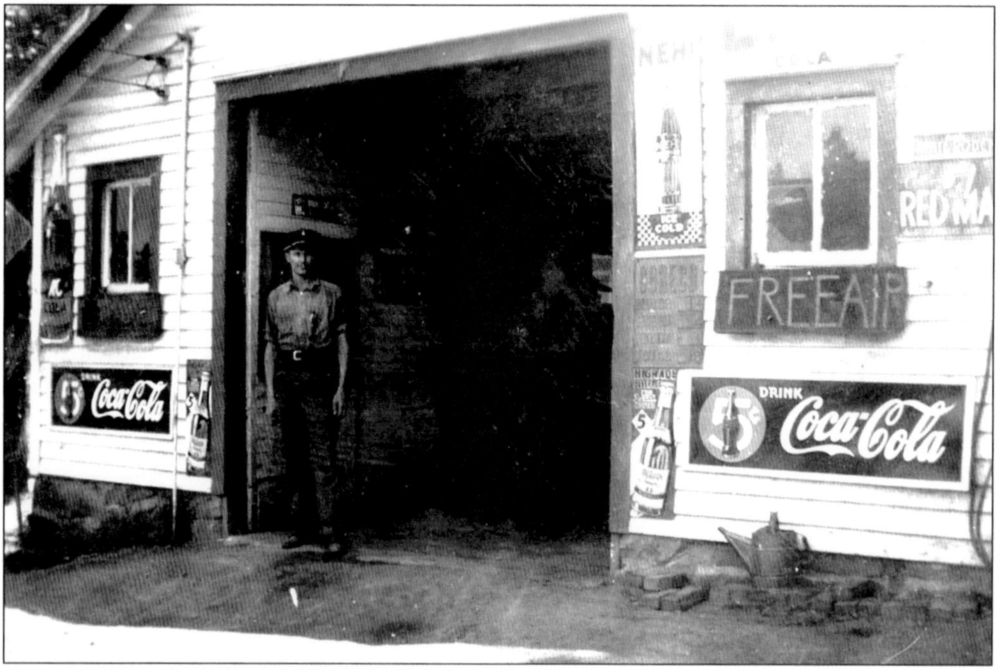

After Welsh's Garage burned, Joe and Bertha Kaputa started their business. These photographs show Joe in his garage and his large array of automobile supplies and general merchandise in the 1950s and 1960s. Ma's Root Beer, R.C. Cola, candy bars, a bag of peanuts or cashews, cigars, combs, and razor blades all cost 5¢ each. Fuel oil was 15¢, kerosene was 12¢, gas was 18¢, and high-test gas was 22¢ per gallon. (Above, courtesy of Darlene Jablon; below, courtesy of Dorothy Anthony.)

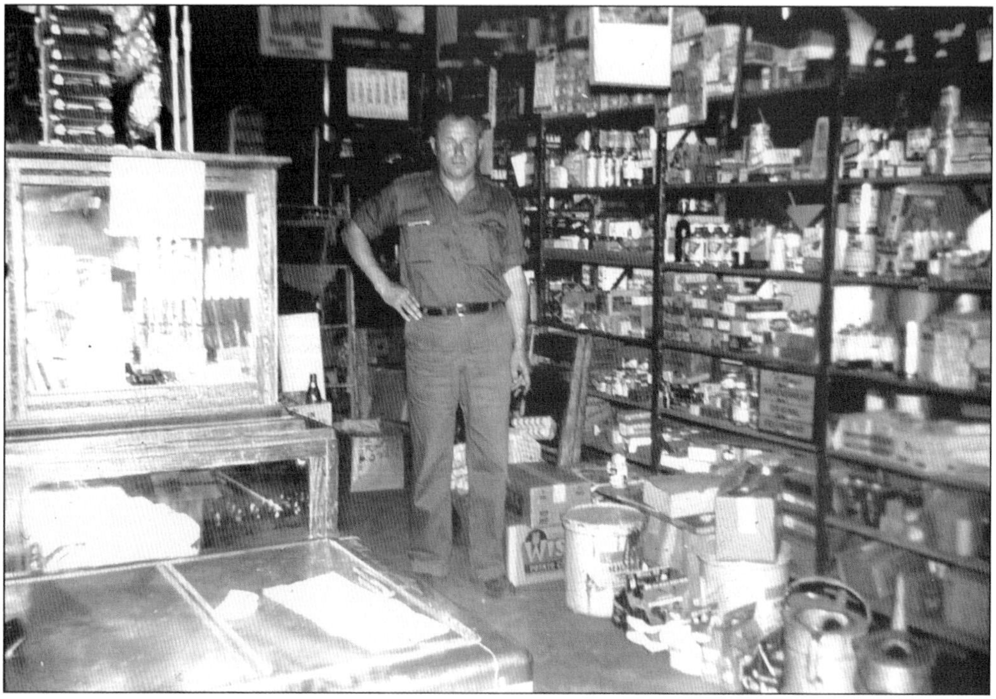

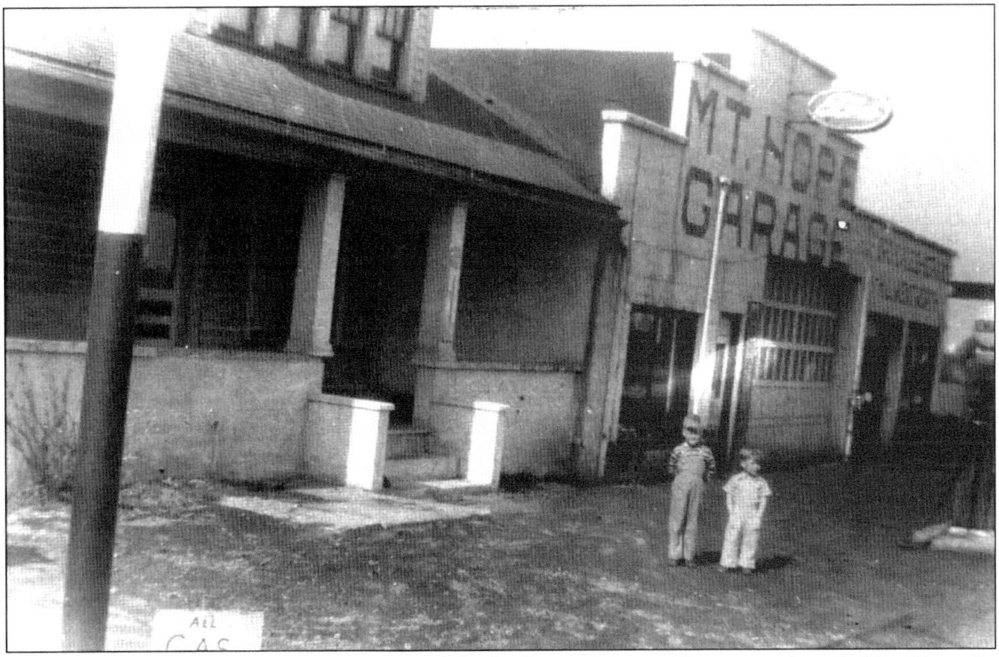

Wentworth Auto Sales, a full service Ford dealership at Mount Hope, was founded by Harry L. Wentworth in 1930. It was later run by sons Gaylord and H. Paul Wentworth and was purchased by John Bowser in 1983. In this photograph, Harold (left) and Allen Seber, sons of John L. Seber, pose in front of their house that was attached to the garage. John was employed for 26 years at Wentworth Auto Sales as automobile mechanic and service manager. Below, the front of the 1946–1947 Randolph High School basketball schedule sponsored by Wentworth Auto Sales revealed an early phone number, "4-R-6." Wentworth Auto Sales sponsoring the school sports calendar is a tradition that continues today. (Above, courtesy of David and Marilyn Boyd; below, courtesy of Wenna Bean.)

PHONE GUYS MILLS 4-R-6

WENTWORTH AUTO SALES

(MT. HOPE GARAGE)

Sales Ford **Service**

R. D. 2 **Guys Mills, Pennsylvania**

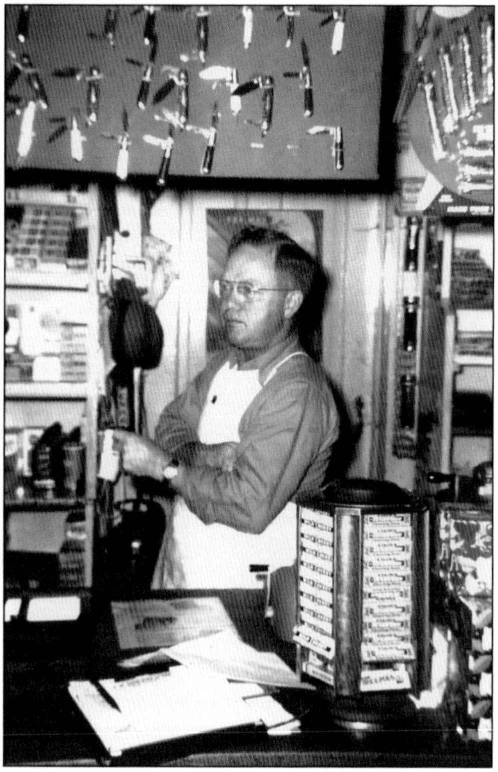

In the image at left, Walter Foulk waits on his customers at Mount Hope General Store. He owned and managed this store for 11 years. Below is a typical advertisement for the Mount Hope General Store, showing its vast array of merchandise. In the early 1900s, Harley Cutshall owned the Mount Hope General Store. Cutshall served as Crawford County Sheriff from 1922 to 1925. He then served as Crawford County commissioner from 1928 until his death in 1930 and was succeeded by Hugh Cutshall to complete the term. (Left, courtesy of John Foulk; below, courtesy of Betty Nelson.)

FOULK'S MT. HOPE STORE

WE TRY TO CARRY EVERYTHING A GENERAL STORE SHOULD HAVE. IF WE DON'T HAVE IT, WE WILL GET IT FOR YOU. SHOP & SAVE HERE

BIG REMNANT SALE!

Stephens Unbleached Linen Crash Toweling only 39 cts a yd.

GLOVE DEPT.

Canvas	Gloves	Jersey	Gloves
Monkey-face	"	Women's	"
Leather-face	"	Boy's	"
All Leather	"	Red Jer. Hunt	"
Rubber	"	Plastic Treatd	"

Hunting Season Is Here.
SHELLS, AMMUNITION, DRYBAK HUNTING CLOTHES and just the Footwear you need. See us now.

We carry good stock of WINDOW GLASS in standard sizes. Fix windows now. Watch that Radiator! Peak Permanent Anti-Freeze at $3.50 a Gal. Alcohol base at $1.25 a Gal,-both Pennsoil Products. Bring in your Eggs! 50 cts for pullet & 60 cts for large eggs. Open evenings.

DRUG DEPARTMENT We carry at our Mt. Hope Department Store a fine line of drugs of which we will tell you later.

»»»»» MT. HOPE GENERAL STORE «««««

WALTER F. FOULK. PROP.

MEAT IS A MUST FOR A MAN WHO DOES HARD MANUAL LABOR -and there has been a SHARP RISE in meat prices lately. However, in order to protect our customers, we will continue to sell QUALITY MEATS at the LOWEST POSSIBLE PRICE. REMEMBER, "YOUR WELFARE IS OUR BUSINESS."

WE HAVE A COMPLETE STOCK OF STEAKS--ROASTS--FRESH PORK--BACON--WEINERS--HAMBURG--BOLOGNA--LUNCHEON MEATS--FROZEN FISH, all at ROCK BOTTOM PRICES.

SHOX-STOK ELECTRIC FENCER $14.50
Elec. Fence Insulators--$3 per 100 Elec Fence smooth wire, half-mile coils.-$7.95 2 point Barb Wire-$5.45 the Roll 4 pt, $7.45
PENNSYLVANIA POWER MOWER $109
REO-21 Inch $104 REO 22 inch TRIMALAWN $189

LOCAL HISTORY. In the year 1822, Jonas Byham left his family in Worcester County, Massachusetts and journeyed on foot and alone 600 miles through the wilderness to Crawford County, where his brother John had settled a short time before. In the fall of 1822, he returned, again on foot, in 12 days, or 50 miles a day, to Massachusetts, truly no small physical feat.

FOR SALE: FARMALL F-20 TRACTOR in good running order. Robert Heath, R D 2, Guys Mills.

PRINTING

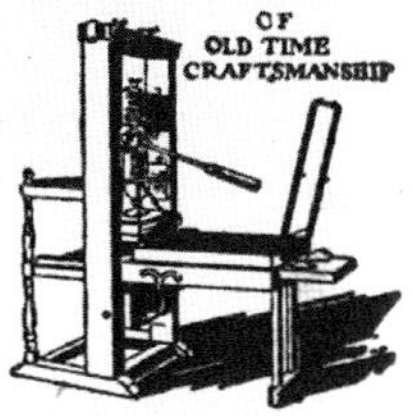

RAYMOND E. SMITH
MANAGER
PHONE 14--R--2

WARREN W. FOULK
MECHANICAL SUPT.
PHONE 2--R--2

THE SMITH PRESS

GUYS MILLS PENNSYLVANIA

PRINTING

CARDS, TICKETS, CIRCULARS, FOLDERS, POSTERS, MENUS, PROGRAMS, LETTER--HEADS, BILL--HEADS, FORM--LETTERS, PAMPHLETS OR WHAT HAVE YOU FROM A CARD TO A 12 X 14 INCH BILL--POSTER. WE HAVE ALL NEW EQUIPMENT,

Old Ben Frankln did not have much of a printing press, (pictured above) but he printed a Nation from it. We can't print a nation, but we can print your business into a GOOD STATE. We will print anything for anybody except matter contrary to pnblic morality, subversive propaganda and counterfeit money. We won't print that even for the Government. We have no crushing overhead, no big wage scales to make costs excessive WHY GO WHERE YOU MUST PAY MORE WHEN YOU CAN GET IT DONE AT HOME FOR LESS?

FOR PRINTING, TRY THE SMITH PRESS.

Foulk mailed out seasonal advertisements every few weeks to announce sales and new merchandise at the Mount Hope General Store. (Courtesy of Betty Nelson.)

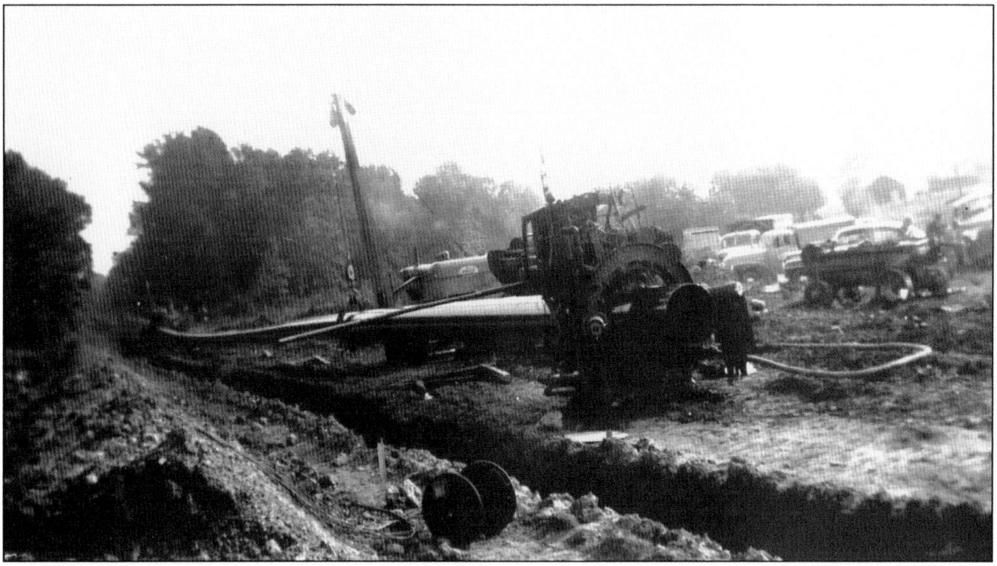

The high-pressure Tennessee gas line snakes from south to north through Randolph Township on its way to the highly populated cities on the northeastern seaboard. The Randolph Township portion was constructed and laid in 1950. (Courtesy of Shirley Gregory.)

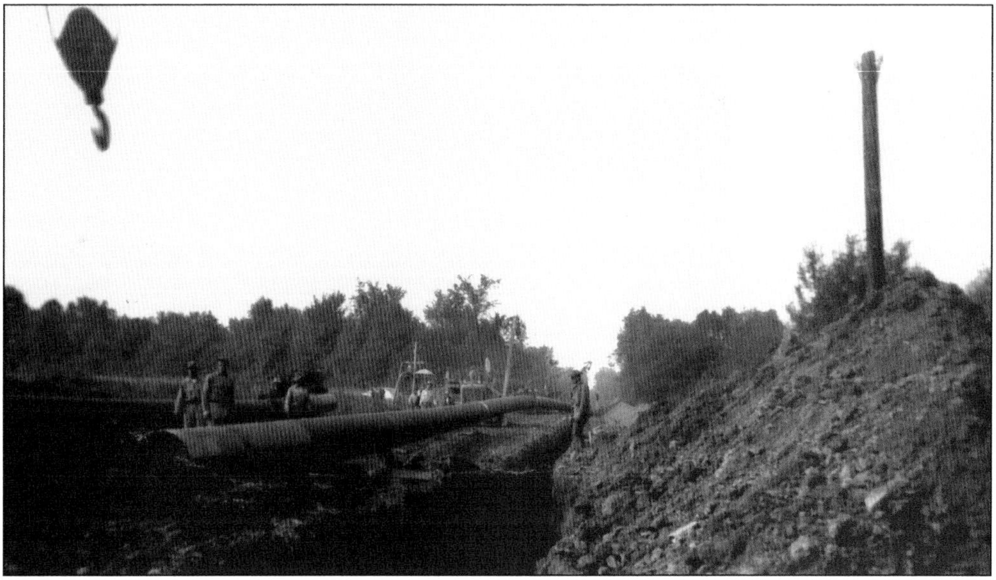

Eight

They Protected
Randolph Volunteer Fire Department

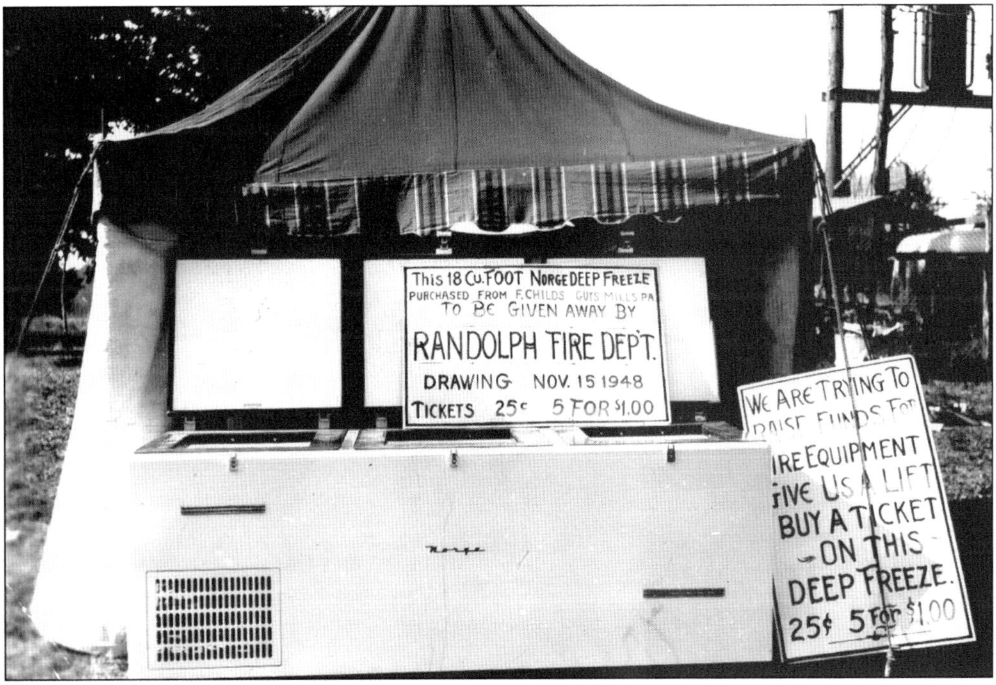

In the 1930s and 1940s, several devastating fires destroyed public buildings and homes in Guys Mills. The townspeople felt hopeless. This prompted public township meetings to discuss the establishment of the Randolph Volunteer Fire Department. One thing that stood in their way was money. This new Norge deep freezer was bought from Frank Childs in 1948 to help raise money to buy the first fire truck. (Courtesy of the Childs family.)

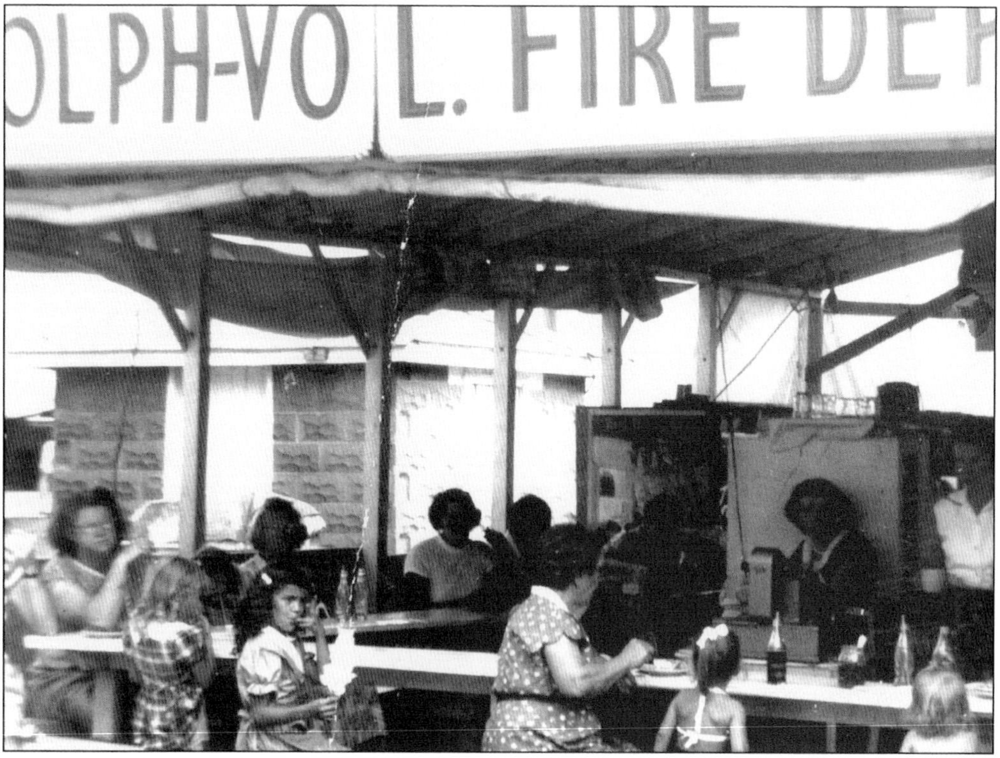

Seen above, the annual food stand at the Crawford County Fair raised money for fire equipment and eventually a new fire hall; workers still are laughing about a missing dishrag that was later found in a pot of gravy. The annual fair food concession continues today, but without dishrag gravy. Seen below preparing food for another 1948 fund-raiser in a makeshift kitchen in Walter Kent's basement are, from left to right, Ellen Williams, Marian Waid and son, Jeanette Nageotte, Frances Virtue, Flossie Kent, Joie Cooper, Helen Wright and son, Inez Heme, and Leona Casler. The first fire truck was purchased the following year. Merle Casler was fire chief at the time. (Above, courtesy of Brian and Judy Kirberger; below, courtesy of Virginia Sanner and Sharon Hayes.)

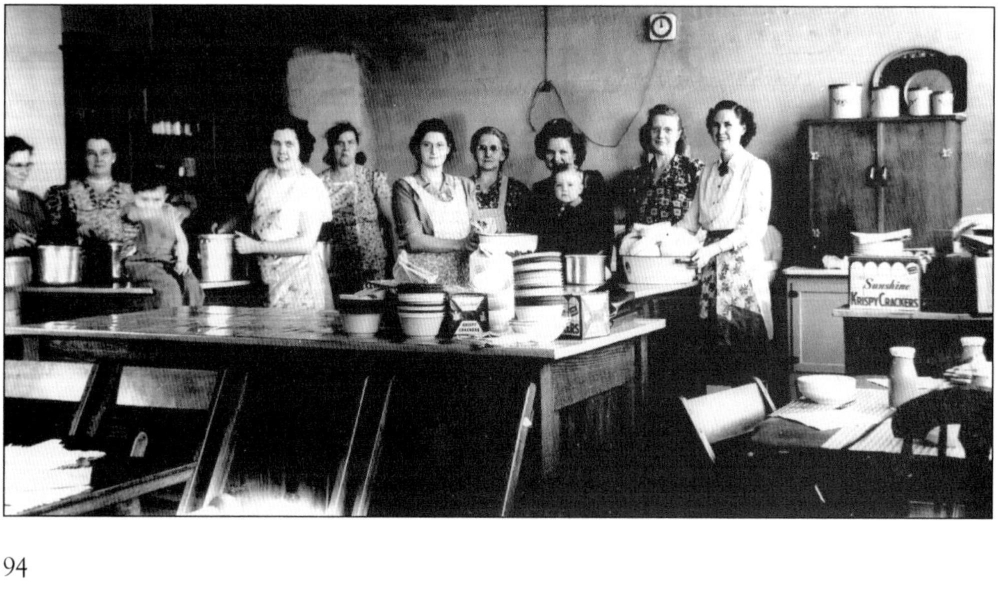

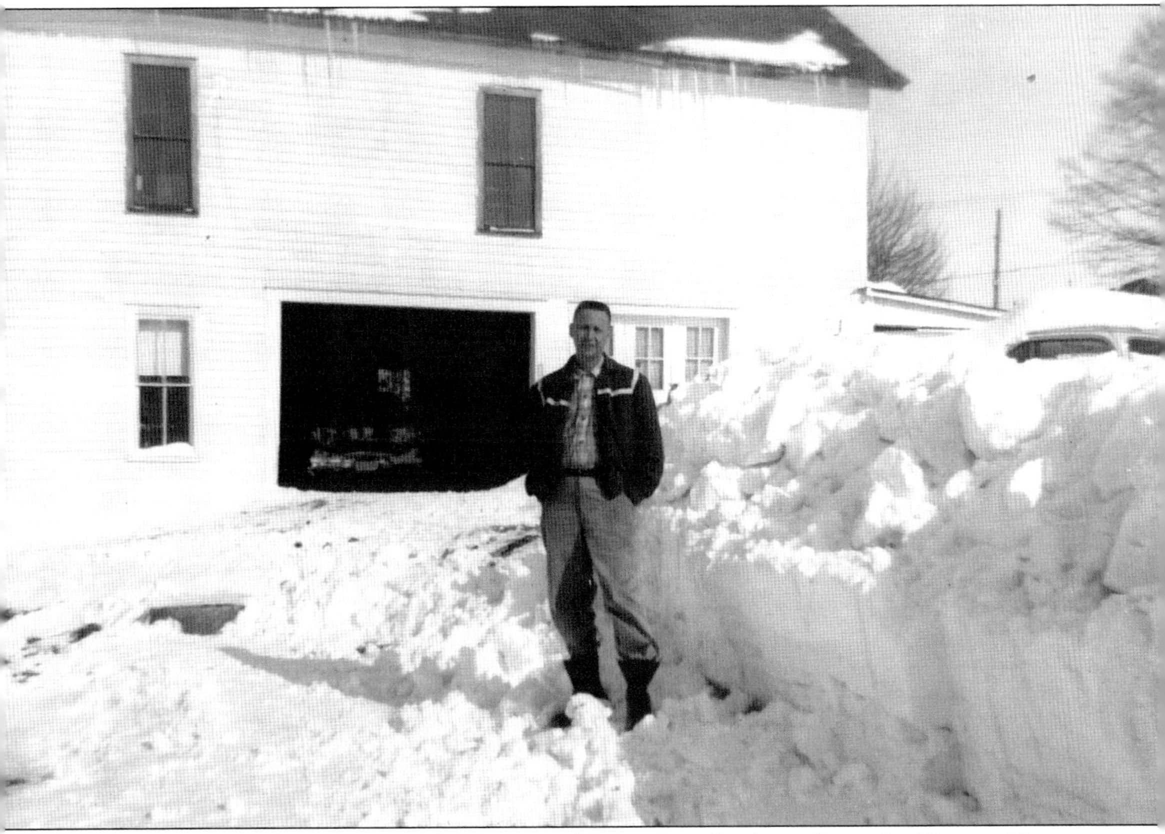

The first fire truck was purchased in 1949 and housed in this large frame building at Victor Armstrong's residence until the fire hall was built in 1956. Fourth of July floats were built there, and food for the firemen's Crawford County Fair booth was prepared there before the fire hall was built. This building had formerly been undertaker Willard Waid's furniture store where he built coffins. This list of past fire chiefs was supplied by Steve Potts: Merle Casler (1949–1952), Walter Kent (1953–1964), Dale Boyd (1965), Fred Neff (1966), Russell Boyd (1967), George Rockefellow (1968), Charles Reynolds (1969–1972), Walt Kelly (1973–1975), Russ Kimmell (1976–1977), Norm Bogardus (1978–1979), Bill Wooley (1980), Gary Hollabaugh (1981–1986), Joe Rudy (1987–1989), Dave Mailliard (1990–1996), Todd Crago (1997), Dave Mailliard (1998–1999), Vern VanTassel (2000–2003), Dave Mailliard (2004), Ed Smith (2005), Tad Acker (2006), Shaun Welsh (2007), and Steve Potts (2008). (Courtesy of Brian and Judy Kirberger.)

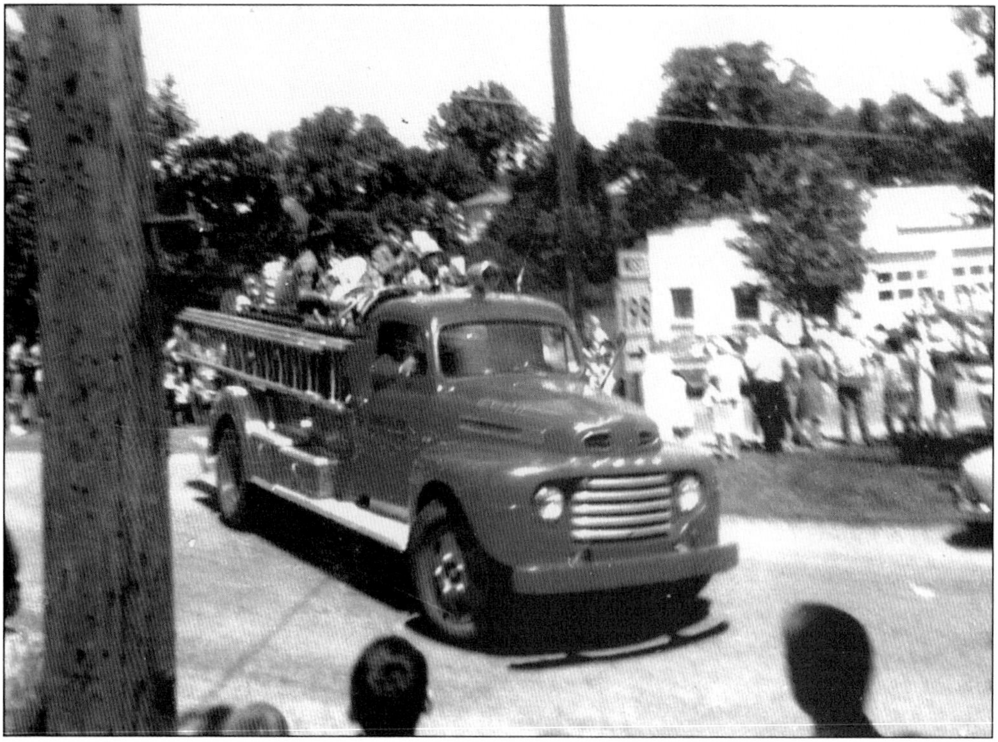

Everyone loves a parade, and the firemen love them, too. The Randolph Volunteer Fire Department sponsored Fourth of July parades and fireworks in Guys Mills for many years. Spectators caught these two Randolph trucks on film in the 1960s. The photograph above shows the Randolph Volunteer Fire Department in the background. This building was finished in time for the big 1956 Fourth of July celebration. The 1956 celebration included a turkey dinner ($1.25 for adults), auction, card party, dance, talent show, and fireworks. Ironically the Randolph Volunteer Fire Department is built on the site of the devastating fire of 1945. The photograph below shows the side of Boyd's Store. (Above, courtesy of Darlene Jablon; below, courtesy of Janet Marvin.)

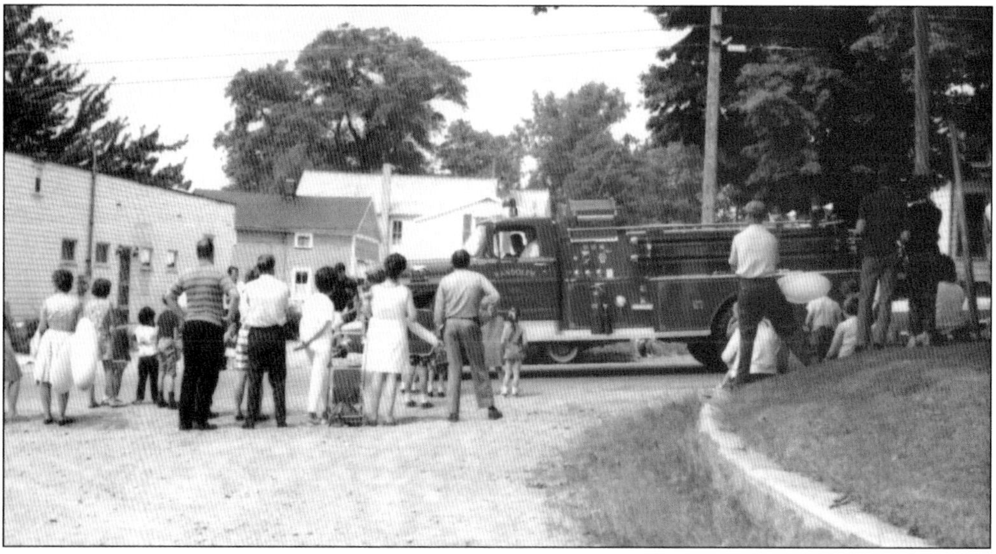

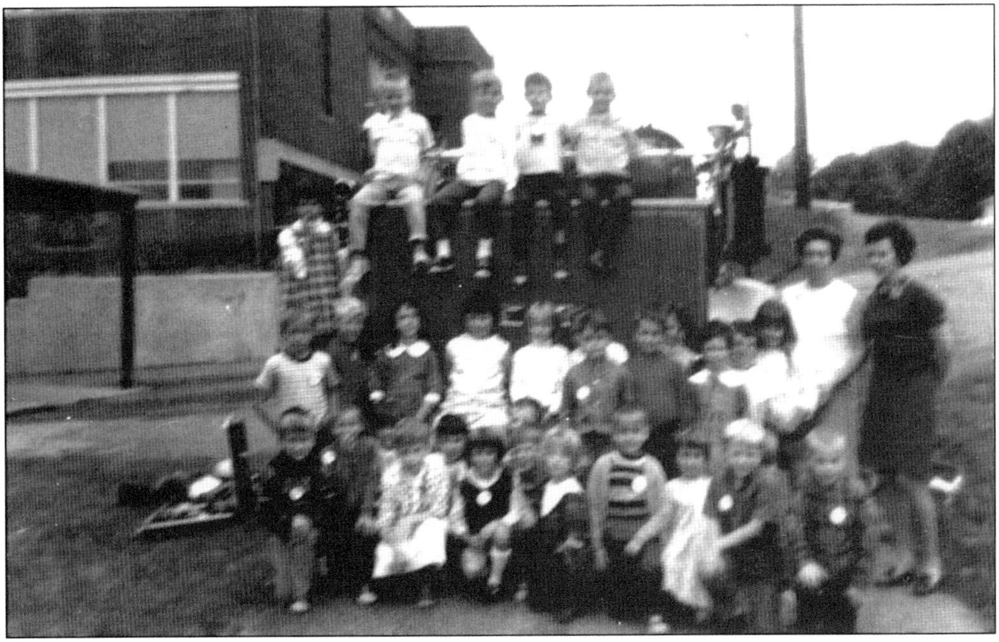

Educational programs at Randolph East Mead Elementary School taught youngsters the importance of fire safety and fire prevention. School secretary Norma McFadden and Audine Mangus let the children explore the fire truck. (Courtesy of Myrtle Bogardus.)

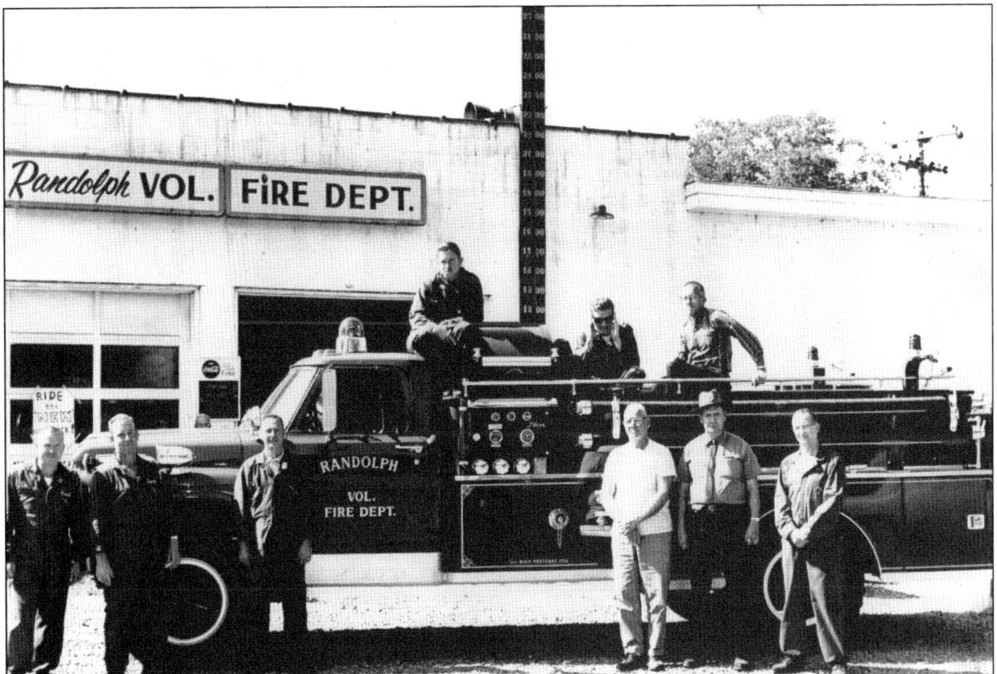

Proudly showing off a new truck in front of the station are, from left to right, (first row) Harold Beerbower, George Rockefellow, Victor Armstrong, Harry Burchard, constable Paul Miller, and Wilford Miller; (second row) David Marvin, Charles Reynolds, and Winton Flaugh. (Courtesy of Brian and Judy Kirberger; photograph by Edward Gray for the Meadville Tribune.)

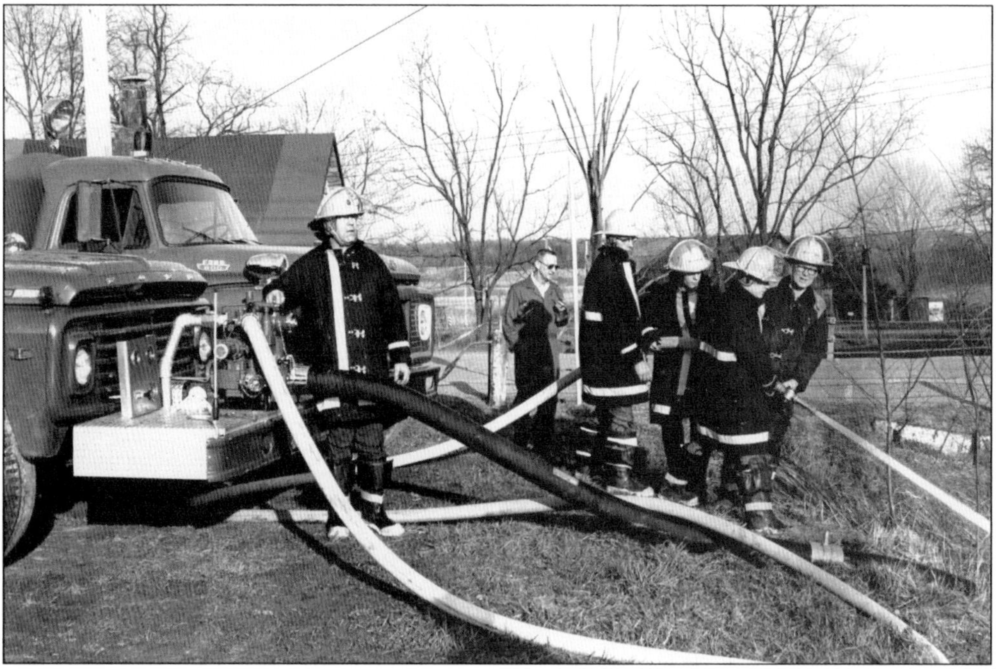

Testing hose pressure at the creek are, from left to right, Dorcy Bowersox, Victor Armstrong, Ed Mangus Sr., two unidentified, and Ron Sanner. Sanner tells of a house fire one winter that was so cold the all the firemen's water hoses froze solid. (Courtesy of the Meadville Tribune and Brian and Judy Kirberger.)

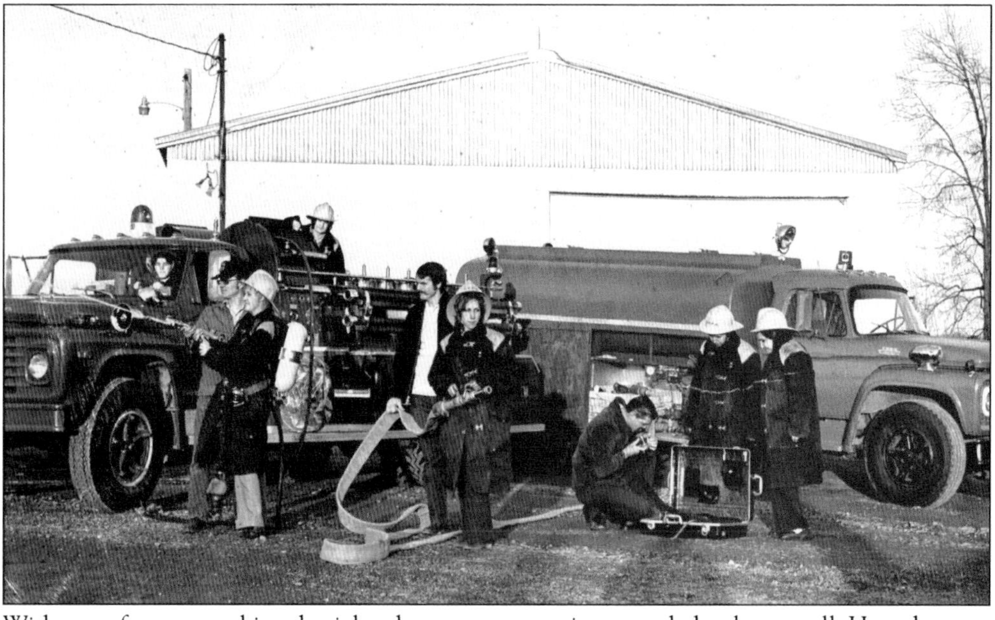

With most firemen working day jobs, the women sometimes needed to be on call. Here the men are briefing the ladies on correct procedures at the Randolph Township building. Mary Kelly is in the driver's seat, and Nancy Jones is in the back of the truck. On the ground, from left to right, are Russ Kimmel, Judy Kirberger, Walt Kelly, Bobbie Geer, Joe Jones, Audine Mangus, and Ilene Bowersox. (Courtesy of the Meadville Tribune and Brian and Judy Kirberger.)

Nine

They Played
Music, Sports, and Civic Organizations

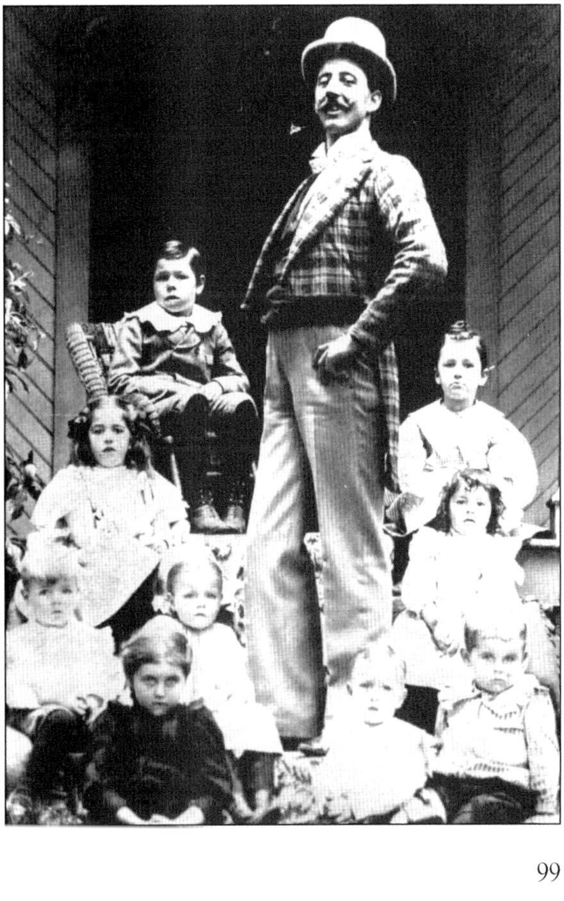

Hickory Corner's famed son Clifford Isaac Graham was a vaudeville-style singer and dancer. Invited to perform with W. C. Fields in New York City, he preferred to spread his entertainment locally and won many talent shows. Here in 1898, he is posed with the area children, clockwise from top, Amy Wilder, Audeen Graham (Kirk), Karl M. Graham, Clifford Baugher, Leo "Smith" Graham, Otto Graham and Gracia Graham (Pardee), Georgia Baugher, and John C. Graham. (Courtesy of Barbara Anderson.)

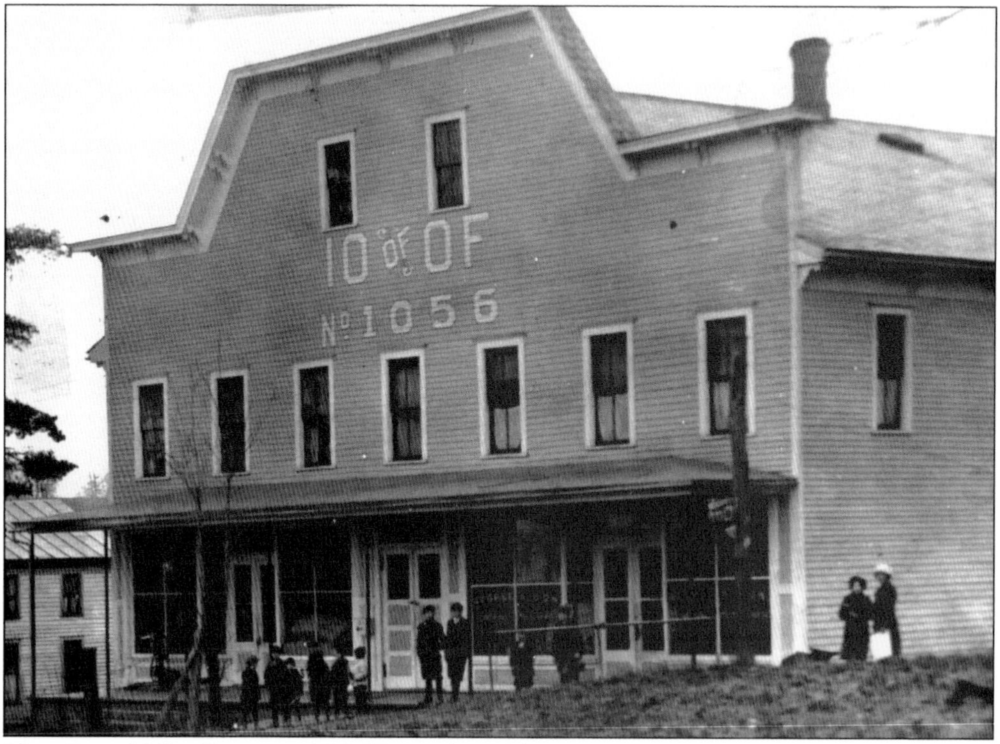

The Guys Mills Chapter of IOOF conducted their meetings upstairs in the IOOF hall until a fire in March 1933 destroyed their meeting place. A. F. Gage and Son were general storekeepers on the first floor at the time this postcard was photographed around 1916. This is the current location of Norma's. One of their many projects was promoting sports such as girls' basketball. The 1910–1911 IOOF champions pose here. School sports were uncommon at this time, so community teams were often formed. (Above, author's collection; below, courtesy of Sharon Hayes.)

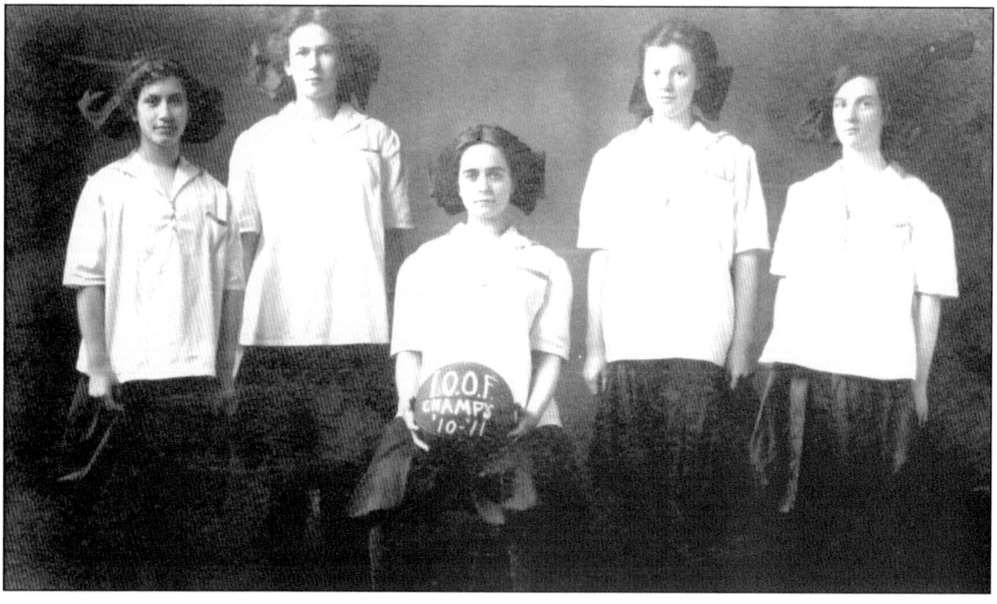

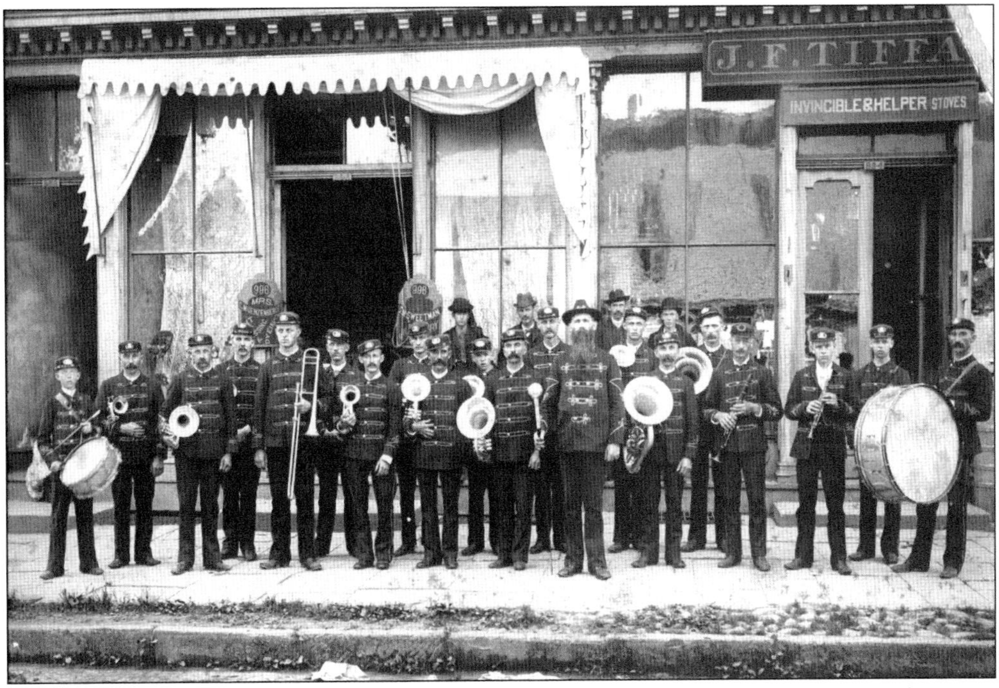

The Guys Mills Community Band attained regional celebrity. Organized in the early 1870s, it continued for 25 years. It was a drawing card for picnics, political and patriotic gatherings, and many community affairs. Pictured are, from left to right, (first row) Eddie Roueche, Leon Roueche, Dell Gage, Dr. Jim Wilson, John Wright, Frank Roueche, Ed Roueche Sr., Dudley Cutler, Henry Roueche, two unidentified, Don Ashley Jr., and Hank Lingo; (second row) Alec Gates, Pen Haight, two unidentified, Charlie Cary, Ben Waid, and Herm Hotchkiss. The gentlemen in back without uniforms are unidentified. (Courtesy of Sally Hotchkiss.)

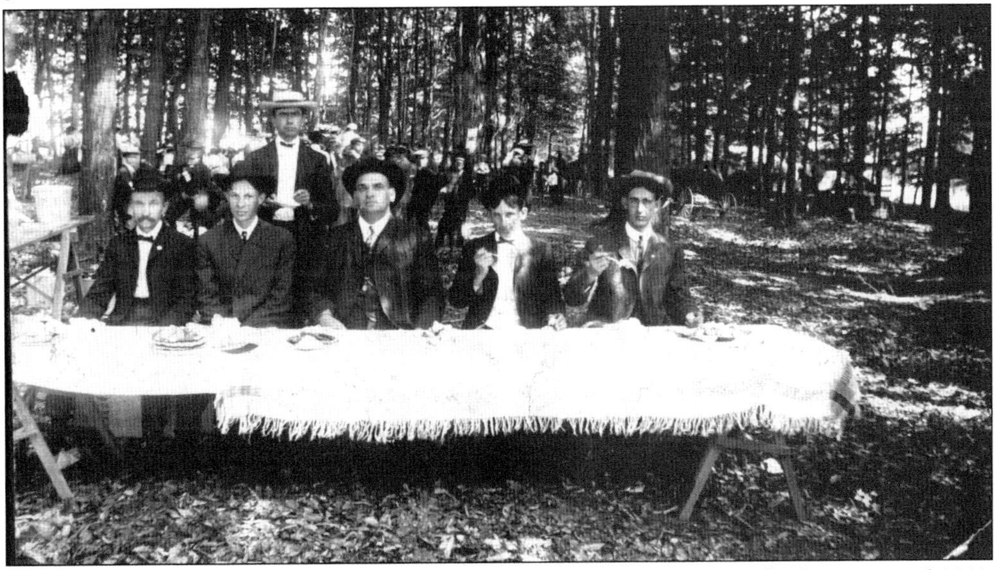

What appears to be a pie-eating contest has attracted some of Guys Mills' finest around 1901. Pictured are, from left to right, Charles Russell, Karl Russell, Clinton Gilbert (standing), Den Smith, Judd Lingo, and Charles Cutler Jr. (Courtesy of Wilford and Carolyn Miller.)

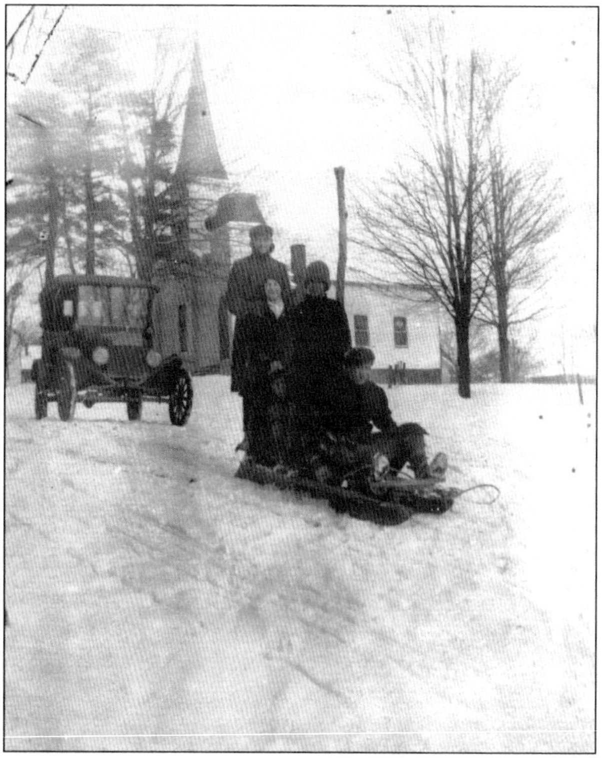

The Collins family is tobogganing down Main Street in Guys Mills in 1923 or 1924. Orval Collins is standing in the back, and his older brother Devere is sitting in the front. The Congregational church provides the background. (Courtesy of Barbara White.)

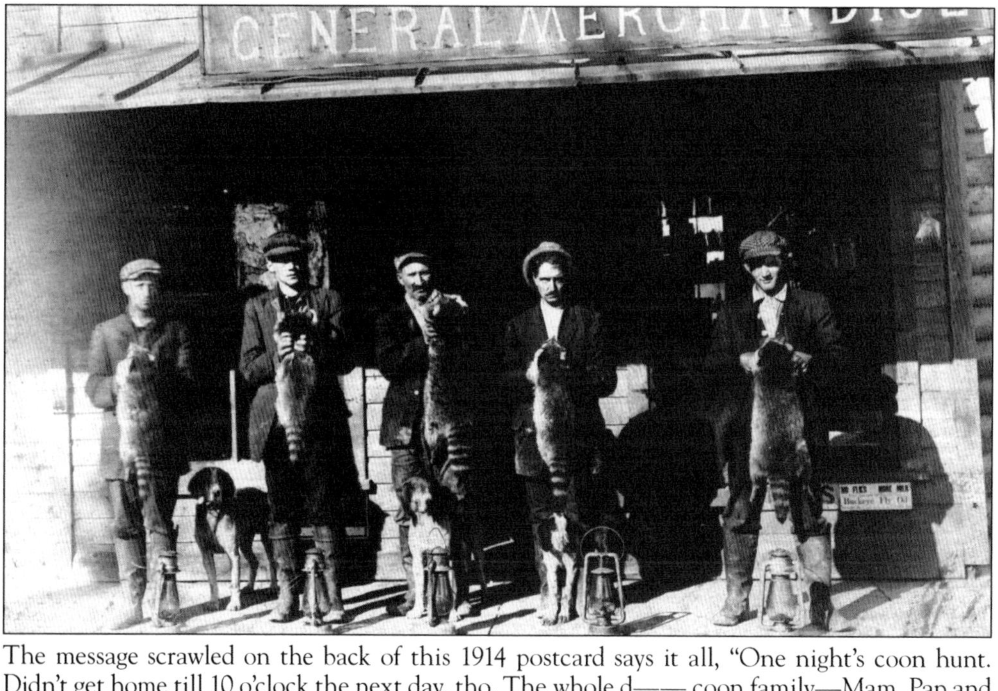

The message scrawled on the back of this 1914 postcard says it all, "One night's coon hunt. Didn't get home till 10 o'clock the next day, tho. The whole d—— coon family—Mam, Pap and all the kids." Pictured with their dogs and lanterns are, from left to right, Lee Cooper, Clyde Smith, Hank Lingo, Clayton Wygant, and Claude Hunt. (Courtesy of Russell and Virginia Boyd and the author.)

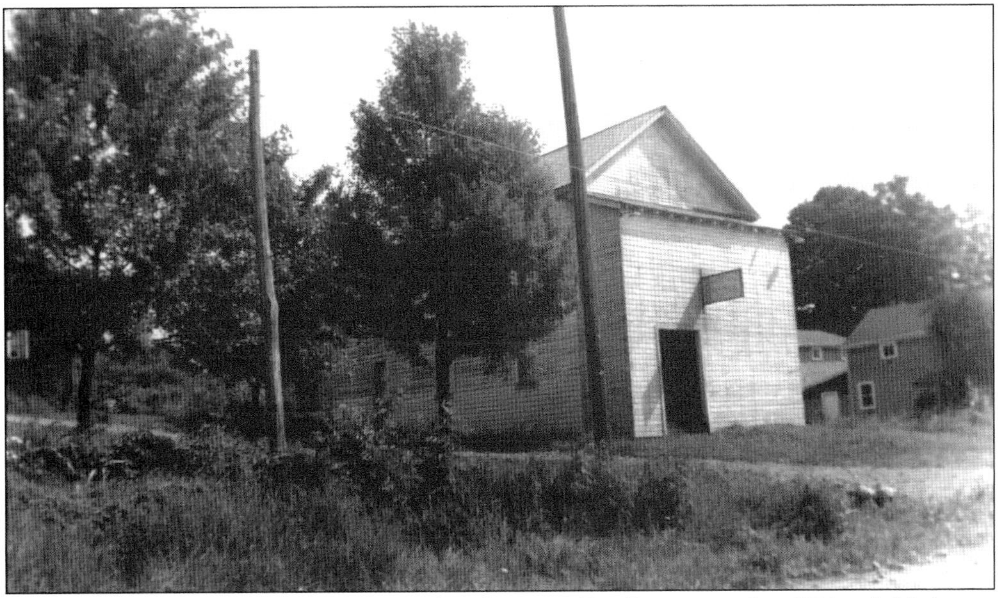

Randolph Grange No. 190, Patrons of Husbandry, was officially organized in 1874 with 50 charter members. Their first master was Philip M. Cutshall, who also was a two-term state representative from 1897 to 1900. They met several places before buying and remodeling Leon Roueche's Blacksmith's Shop (above), dedicating it in 1939. Randolph Grange meetings were held here until they disbanded in December 1993. This is the current location of Bogardus' Auto Repair on Plank Road. The Randolph Grange officers and members in the 1930s are shown below. Frenchtown Grange disbanded in 1941, Blooming Valley Grange disbanded in 1961, and Mount Hope Grange disbanded in 1968. Randolph welcomed these members to join their chapter. (Above, courtesy of Lucile Stallard; below, courtesy of Janet Marvin.)

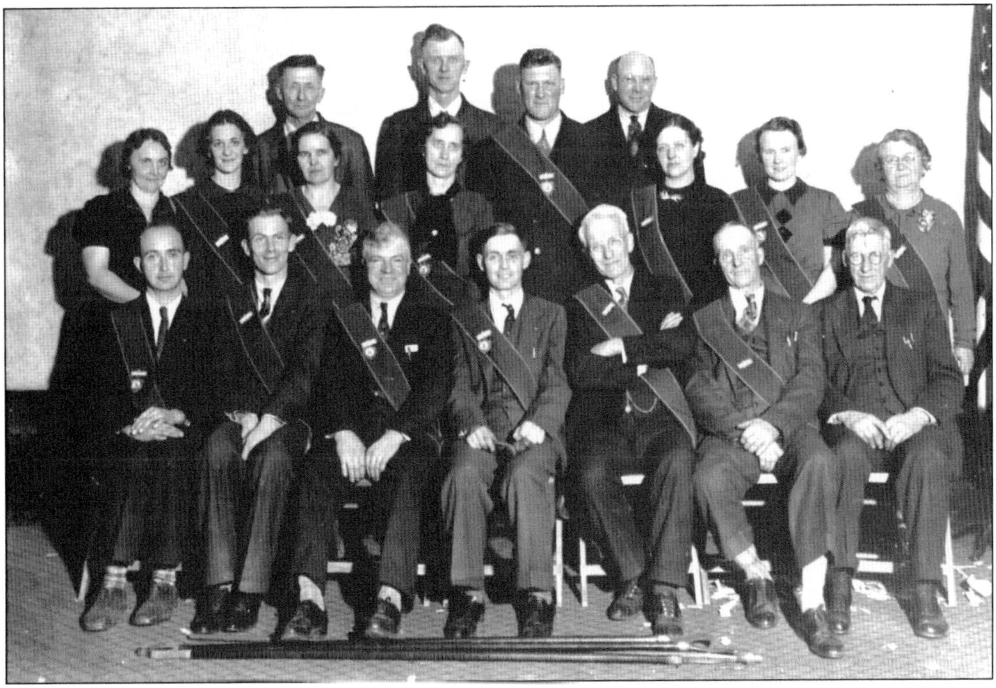

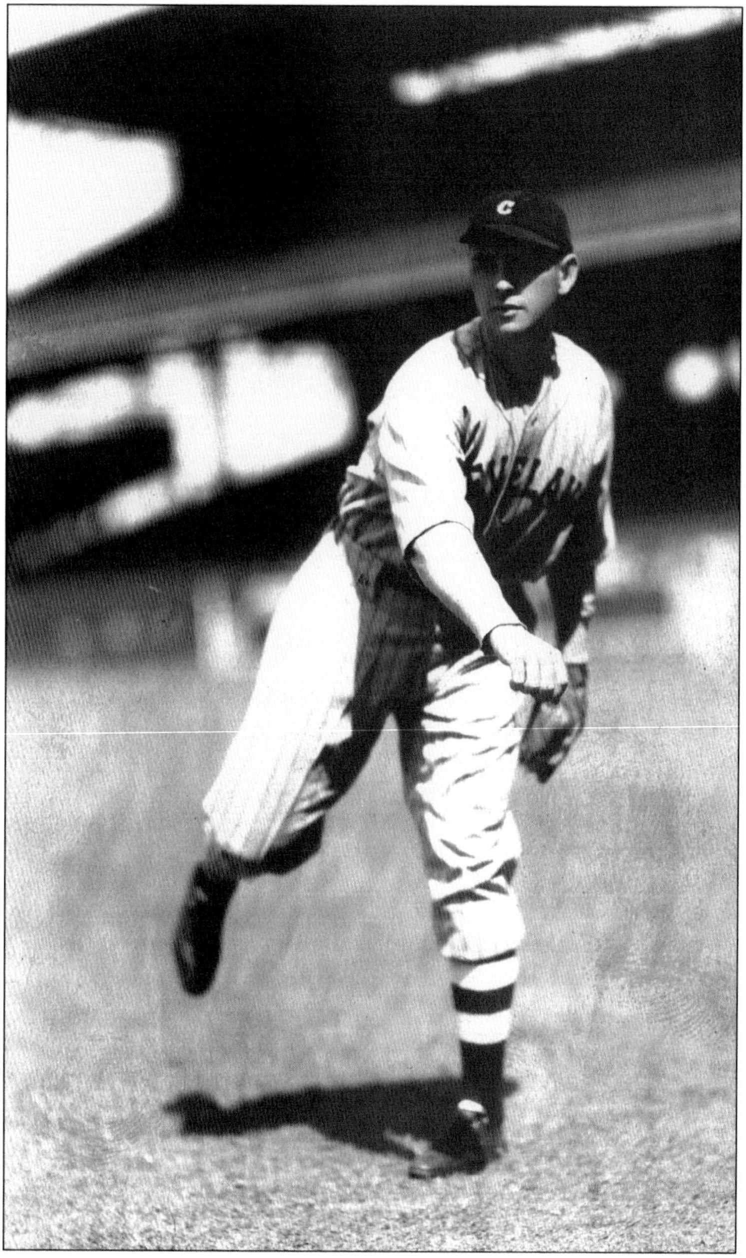

Clint Brown, born in Black Ash in 1903 and known as the Black Ash Flash, had a 15-year major league pitching career. It began in September 1928 with the Cleveland Indians, whom he continued to play with for eight years as a starting pitcher. He amassed a 56-61 record and a 4.42 ERA, pitching in 189 games, 128 as a starter. He also had eight career shutouts. Traded to the Chicago White Sox in 1936, they made Brown into one of the first relief aces in baseball history. From 1936 to 1950, Brown pitched in 197 games (195 in relief) saving 53 while posting a 29-28 record with a 3.99 ERA. He led the American League in saves in 1937 with 18, and in 1939, he set the pace with 11 relief wins. He also set a major league record in 1939 with 61 appearances. He closed out his career returning to Cleveland in 1941 making 48 appearances in his last two seasons. He passed away in 1955 at just 52 years of age. (Courtesy of Mark Roche.)

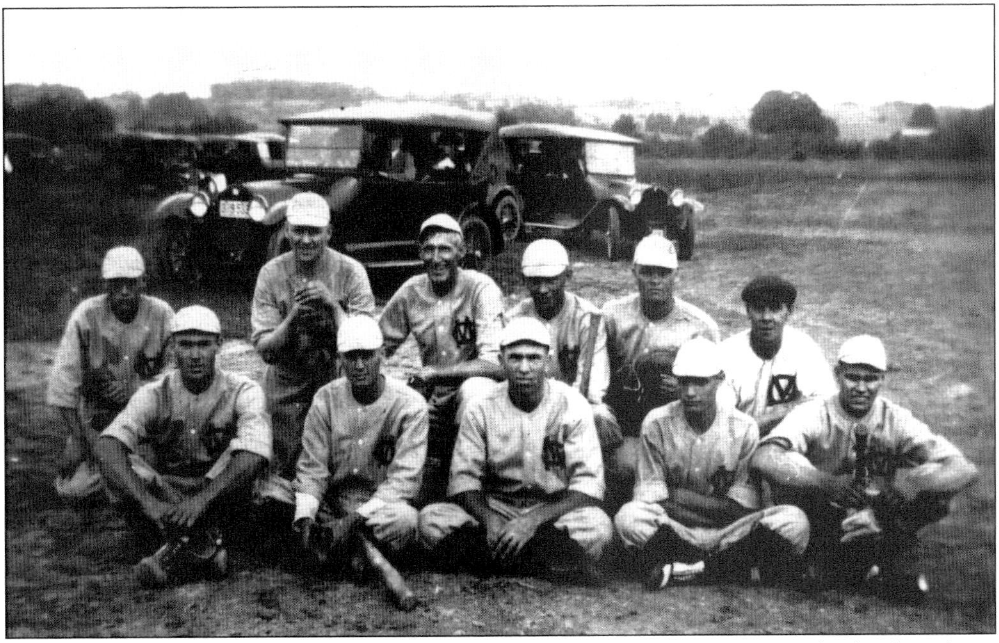

The old Guys Mills baseball field was across the road from Union Cemetery, back a long lane. Cars filed out of these baseball grounds in 1922 as the Guys Mills Baseball Team poses for a group photograph. Pictured are, from left to right, (first row) Charles Burchard, Chester Lingo, Howard Boyd, and two unidentified; (second row) unidentified, Walter Burchard, Brice Walker, unidentified, Lee Luce, and unidentified. (Courtesy of Janet Marvin.)

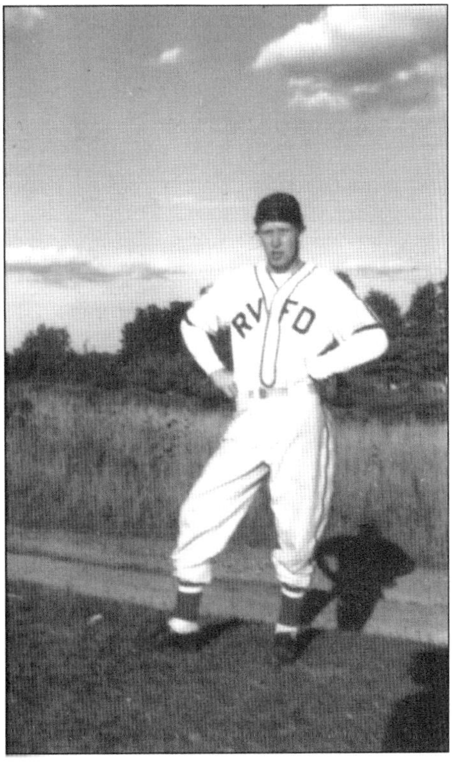

David Marvin, shown here in a Randolph Volunteer Fire Department baseball uniform in 1955, also organized the All-Points Softball League. They played under the lights at the Randolph East Mead School fields. Eight teams played there, beginning about 1962. There were two teams from Guys Mills, Marvin managed the team simply known as the Guys Mills Team. The other team was known as the Guys Mills Gophers. (Courtesy of Janet Marvin.)

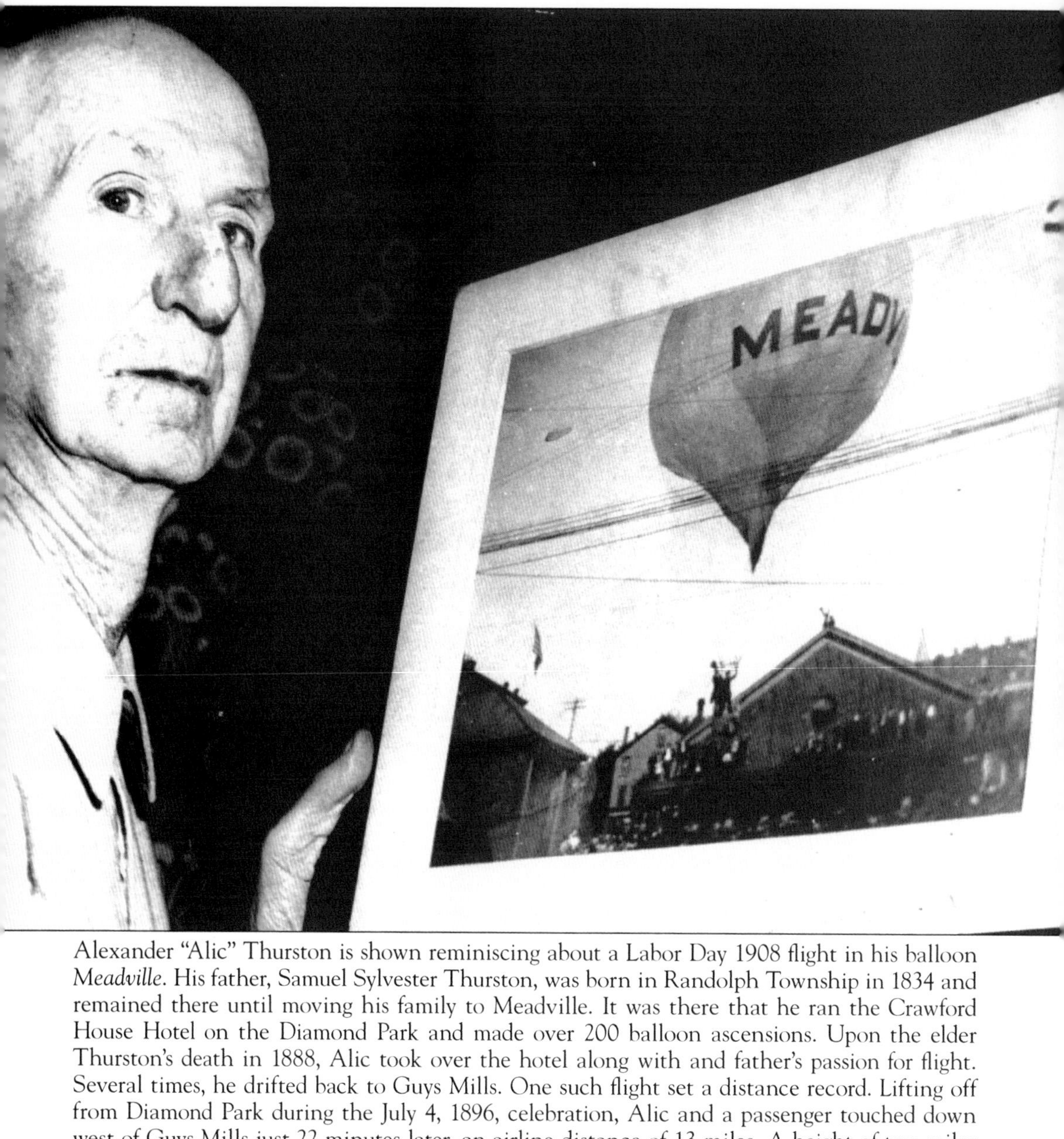

Alexander "Alic" Thurston is shown reminiscing about a Labor Day 1908 flight in his balloon *Meadville*. His father, Samuel Sylvester Thurston, was born in Randolph Township in 1834 and remained there until moving his family to Meadville. It was there that he ran the Crawford House Hotel on the Diamond Park and made over 200 balloon ascensions. Upon the elder Thurston's death in 1888, Alic took over the hotel along with and father's passion for flight. Several times, he drifted back to Guys Mills. One such flight set a distance record. Lifting off from Diamond Park during the July 4, 1896, celebration, Alic and a passenger touched down west of Guys Mills just 22 minutes later, an airline distance of 13 miles. A height of two miles and a speed of over 35 miles per hour were obtained. The Thurston name lives on through Meadville's Annual Thurston Hot Air Balloon Event. (Courtesy of CCHS.)

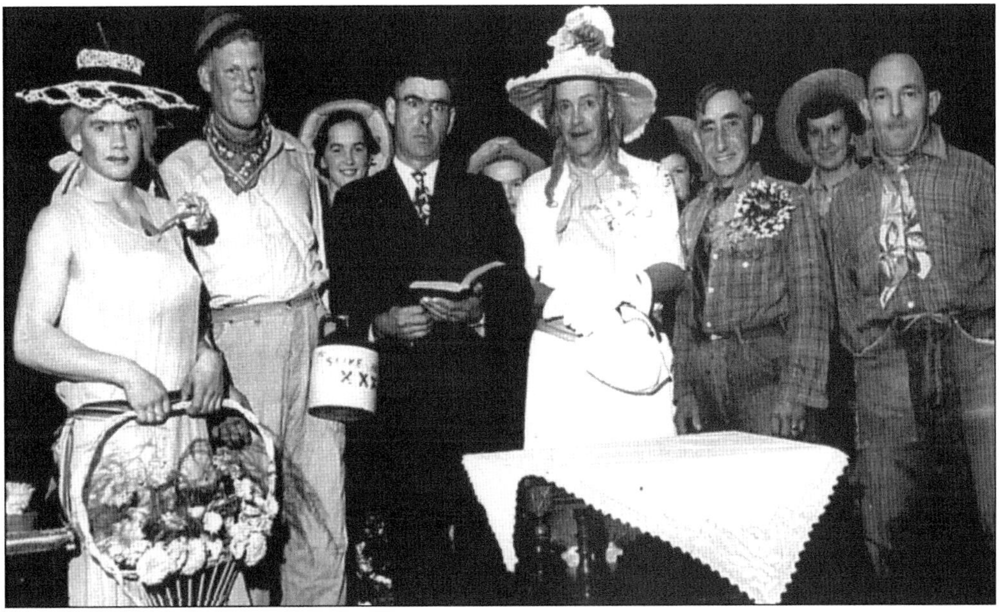

Local history is seasoned with a healthy sense of humor. Entertainment was self-made and lighthearted. Here actors posed after a mock shotgun wedding skit at the Randolph Grange Hall in 1950. Pictured are, from left to right, (first row) Donnie "Snuffy" Smith, bridesmaid; Walter Burchard, father of the bride with shotgun and moonshine; "Reverend" Raymond Skiff; Homer Clark, bride; Aurie Blakeslee, groom; and Jack Lingo, best man. (Courtesy of Carolyn Miller and Virginia Sanner.)

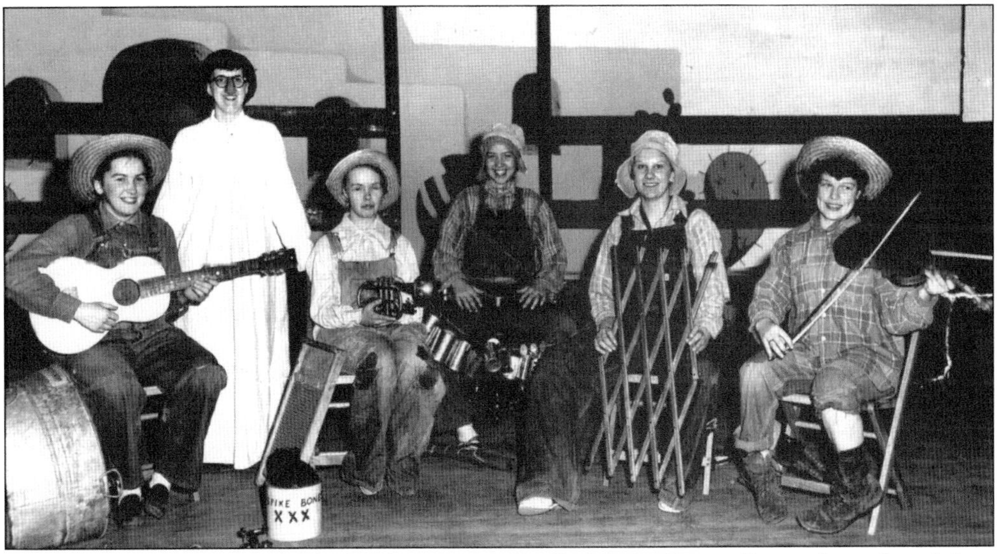

Wedding music was provided by local "musicians" called Spike Bones. Pictured are, from left to right, Reenie Buckle, Carole Kindervater, Virginia Bogardus, Barbara Smith, Wanda Burchard, and Winona Trevethan. These teens fashioned themselves after the popular musical comedian "Spike Jones and His Musical Depreciation Revue," making cheerfully deranged music and talented mayhem. Ballads receiving Spike Bones treatment were punctuated with gunshots, whistles, washboards, cowbells, and beating on pots and pans. (Courtesy of Virginia Sanner, photograph by Hildebran.)

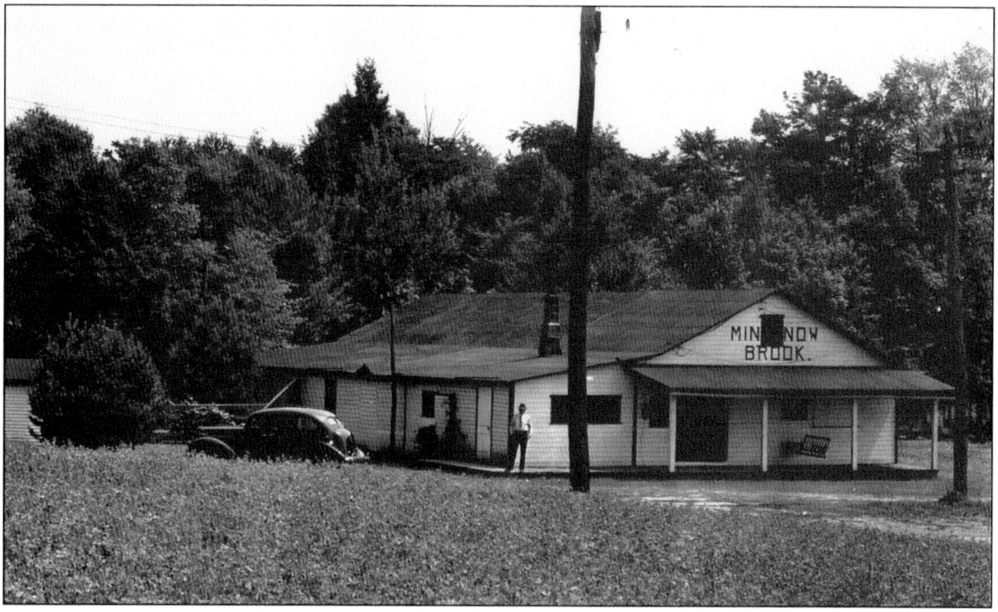

Minnowbrook Dance Hall on Townville Road was a very popular place on Saturday evenings. Russell and Helen Beuchat bought it from Jack and Frank Ardry around 1945. The Beuchat family lived in the attached apartment. Hot dogs, hamburgers, and soft drinks were served, but no alcohol, because Randolph Township was dry. The last dance was held in the mid-1950s. (Courtesy of Marilyn Steadman.)

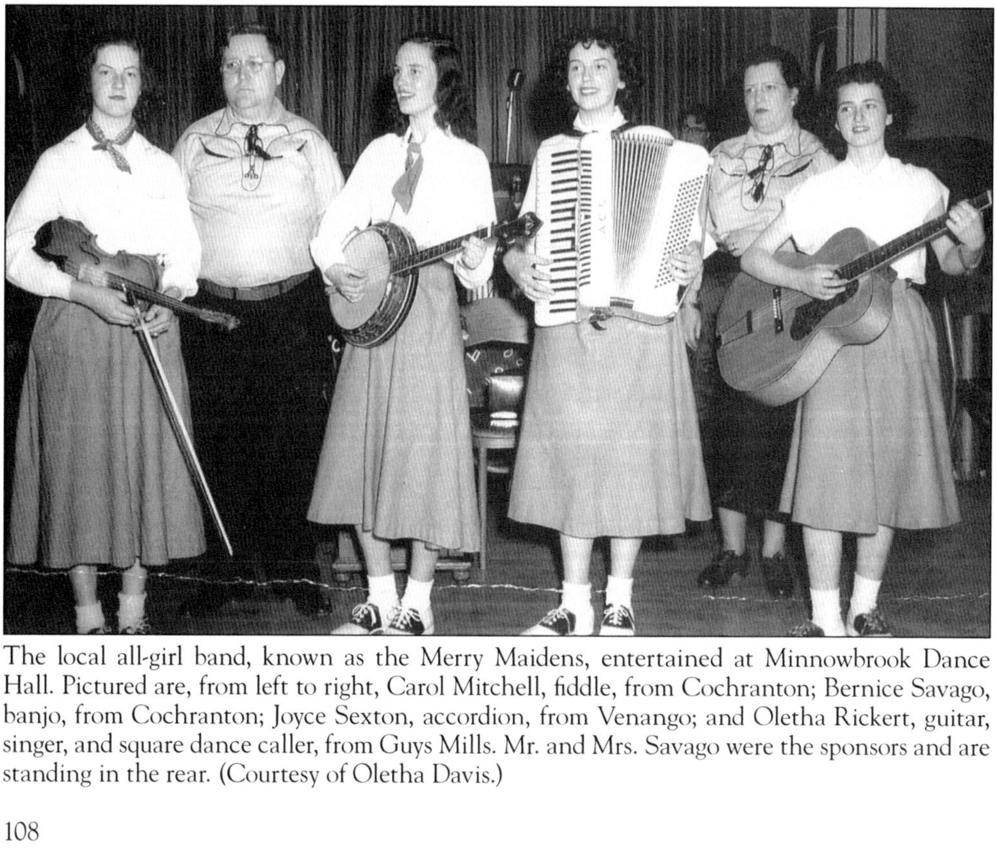

The local all-girl band, known as the Merry Maidens, entertained at Minnowbrook Dance Hall. Pictured are, from left to right, Carol Mitchell, fiddle, from Cochranton; Bernice Savago, banjo, from Cochranton; Joyce Sexton, accordion, from Venango; and Oletha Rickert, guitar, singer, and square dance caller, from Guys Mills. Mr. and Mrs. Savago were the sponsors and are standing in the rear. (Courtesy of Oletha Davis.)

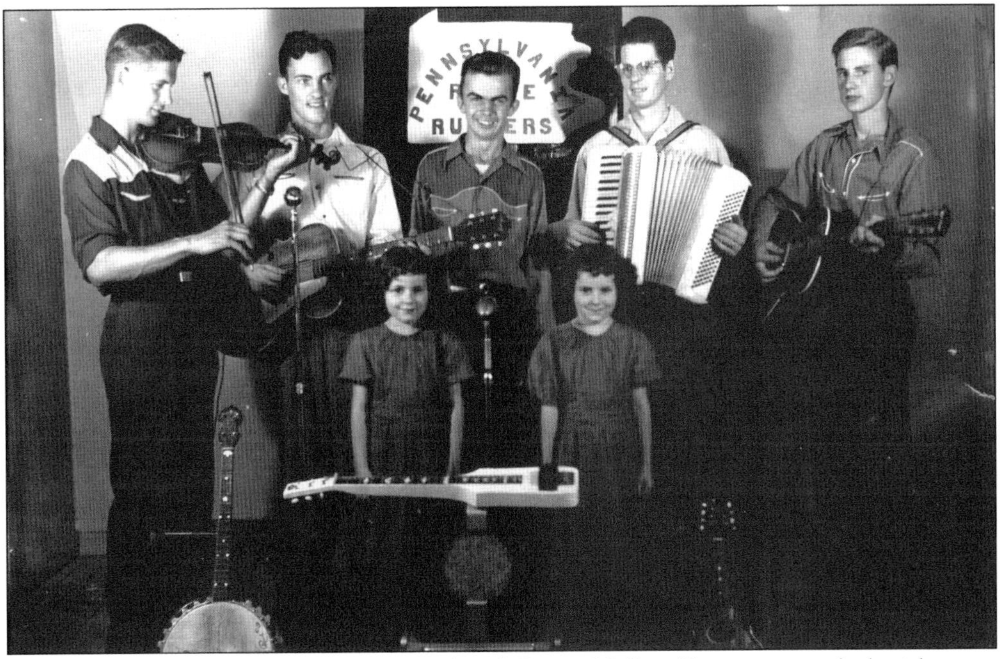

Live music was a huge draw to the Minnowbrook Dance Hall and having a cute little girl or two belting out ballads did not hurt. These bands played polkas, waltzes, square and round dances, and more. In the photograph above, the Pennsylvania Ridge Runners pose for a promotional photograph. Seen below are the ever-popular Ray's Ramblers around 1958, which consists of, from left to right, Ray Boyle, band leader; George "PeeWee" Wasko; John Miller; Bob Burlison; and Bob McGowan. Ray's daughter Donna Rae Boyle is in the front. Later, Bob McGowan and his brothers Dick and Tuck formed the Playland Playboys who played at Playland Campgrounds. (Above, courtesy of Marilyn Steadman; below, courtesy of Marilyn Steadman and Kim Templin.)

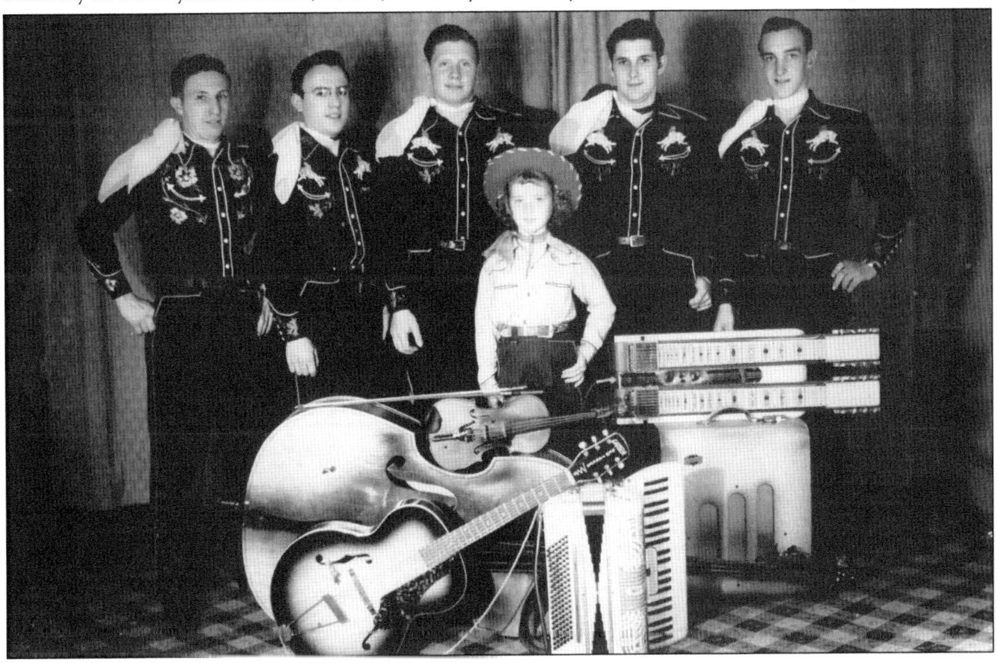

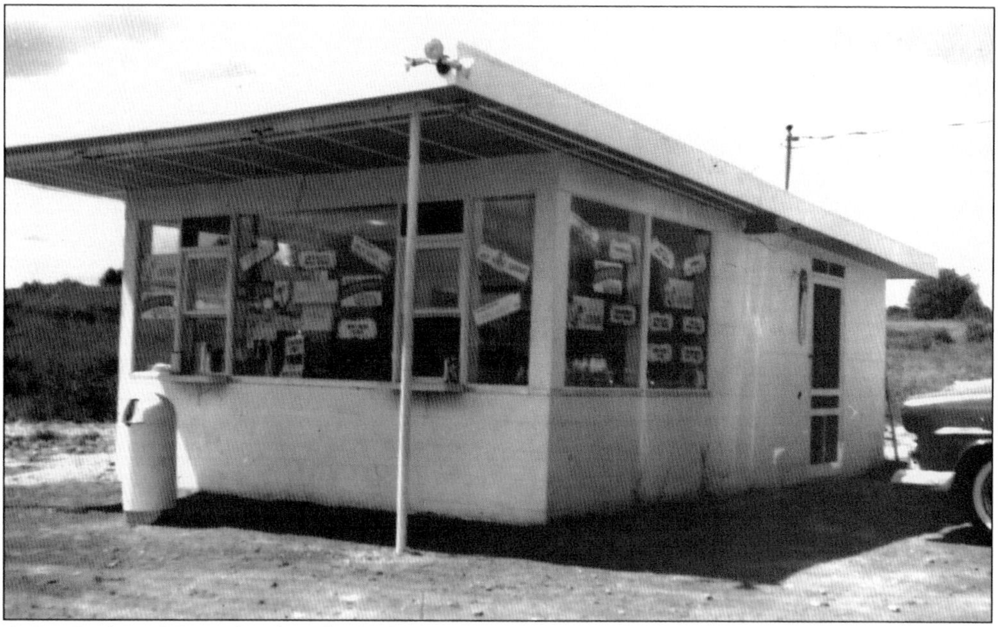

A. E. "Bud" and Dorothy Sliter built the Dari Dell in 1957 on the intersection of Routes 198 and 27, where they sold delicious frozen custard for many years. Through several owners, it evolved into Granny's Restaurant. In 1985, owners Dorothy and Aaron Yoder named it the Fooder Gong (Dutch for "feed alley") Restaurant and enlarged it. Currently owned by Dorothy, it is a variety store. (Courtesy of Dorothy Sliter.)

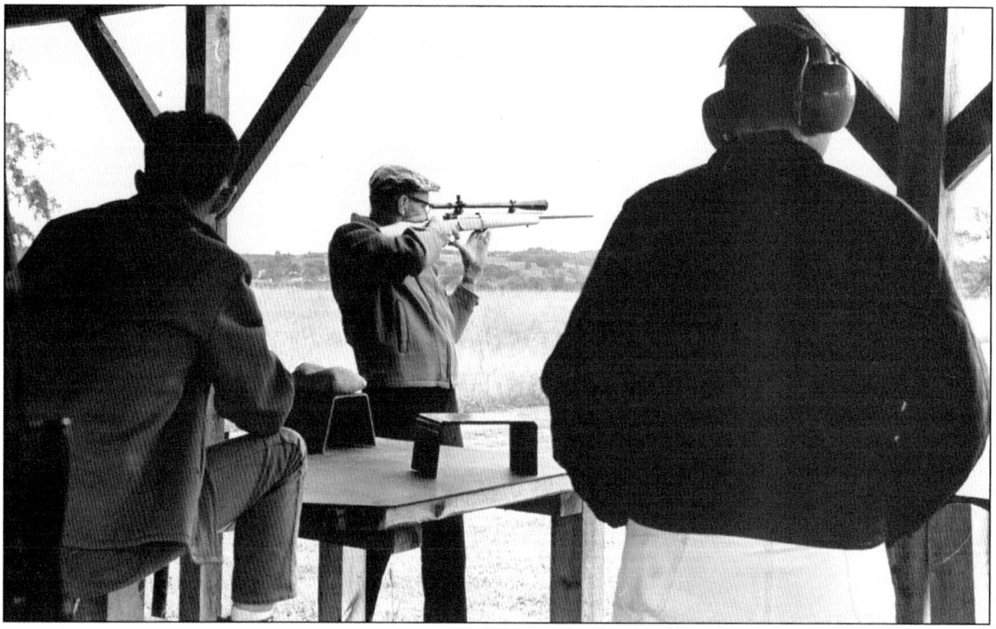

The Black Ash Sportsman's Club had a shooting range on Shaffer Road. In this image, from left to right, Harold Smith, John L. Seber, and Ray Graham practice at that range. Seber is shooting a gun that he built, a custom 219 Zipper with Mauser action and curly maple stock. This range was closed when stray bullets fell on Edgewater Golf Course. The club now meets on their 118-acre grounds on Clark Road near Black Ash. (Courtesy of John L. Seber.)

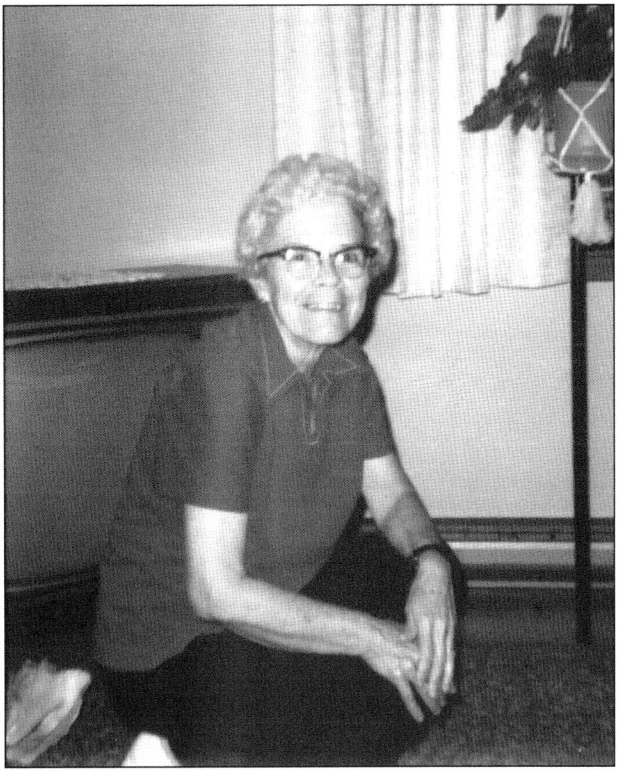

Edgewater Golf Course was a favorite nine-hole public course for area golfers. It was founded by Leo (below) and Helen Mailliard (right) and their son and daughter-in-law Don and Donna Mailliard. It opened in July 1967 on Route 198 "Johnnycake Street." Leagues and Sunday golf tournaments were enjoyed by the golfers. (Courtesy of Donna Mailliard.)

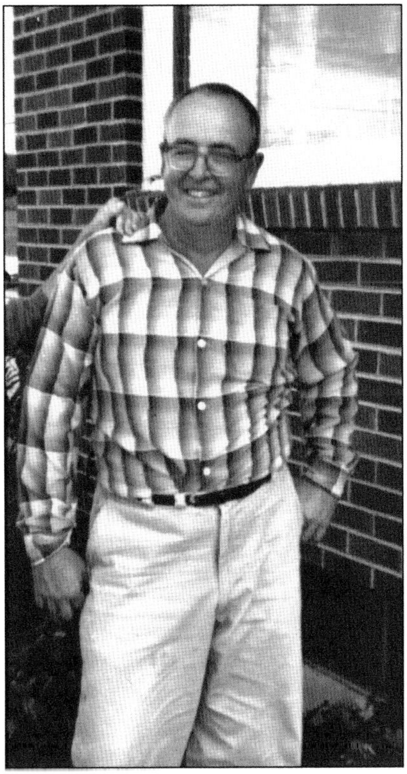

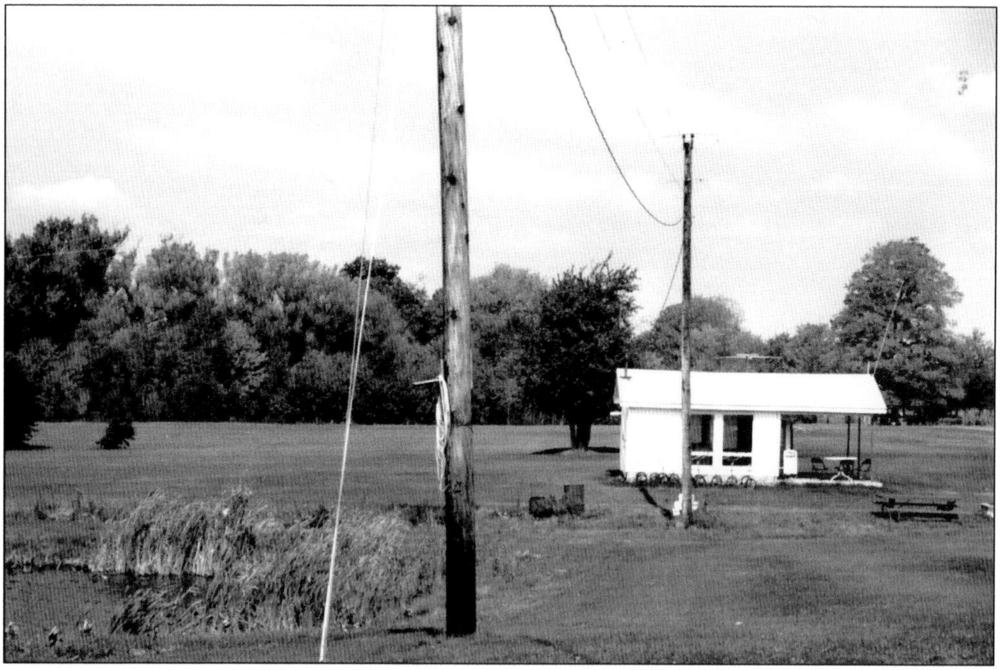

Edgewater Golf Course measured a challenging 2,168 yards around ponds with a beautiful finish in the woods. The course was par 34 for 9 holes and par 69 for 18 holes. Don and Donna's children, Mark, Jill, and Kathleen (seen below), worked every season, meaning all three generations were actively engaged in the business. Kathleen and Mark manicured the course, and Jill was in charge of the clubhouse. Many area students and senior citizens were also employed at the golf course. Edgewater continued in operation for 23 years, closing in October 1989. (Courtesy of Donna Mailliard.)

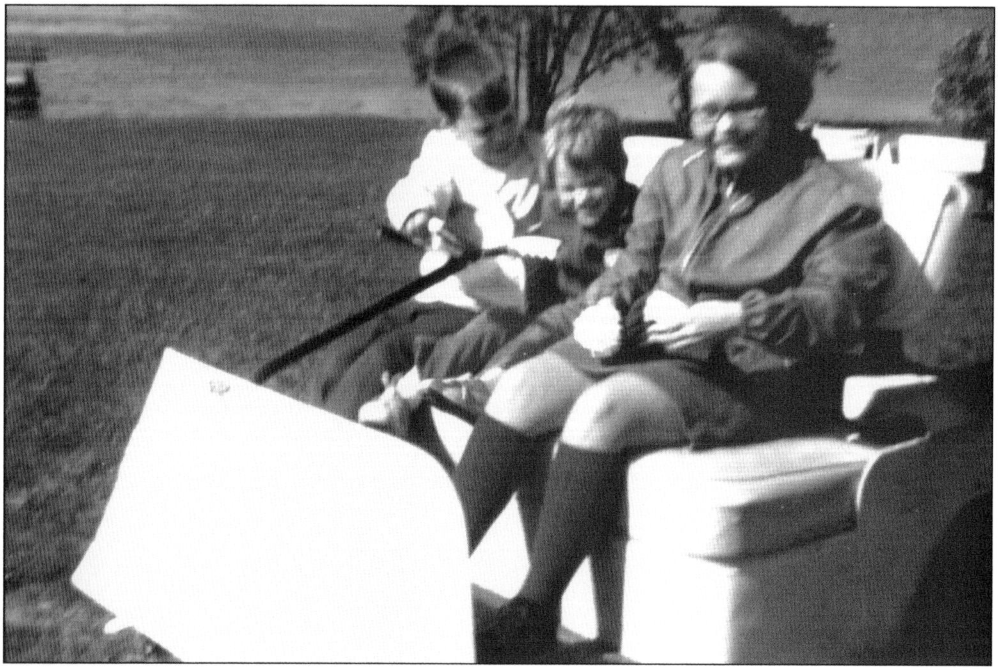

Ten

THEY CELEBRATED
INDEPENDENCE DAY

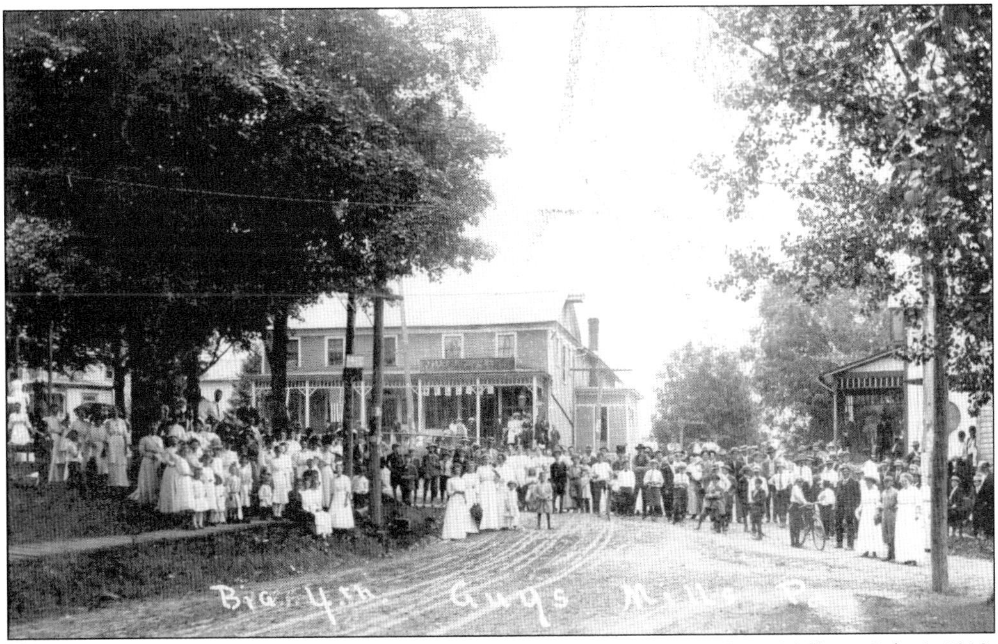

Over 200 area residents crowd together on the main intersection in Guys Mills on July 4, 1912, to be captured by the photographer's shutter, proving that celebrating Independence Day is a long-standing tradition. In the background, Smith and Cutler's Department Store beckoned "Welcome" with signs and an American flag hanging from the gingerbread porch trim. (Courtesy of Robert W. Waid.)

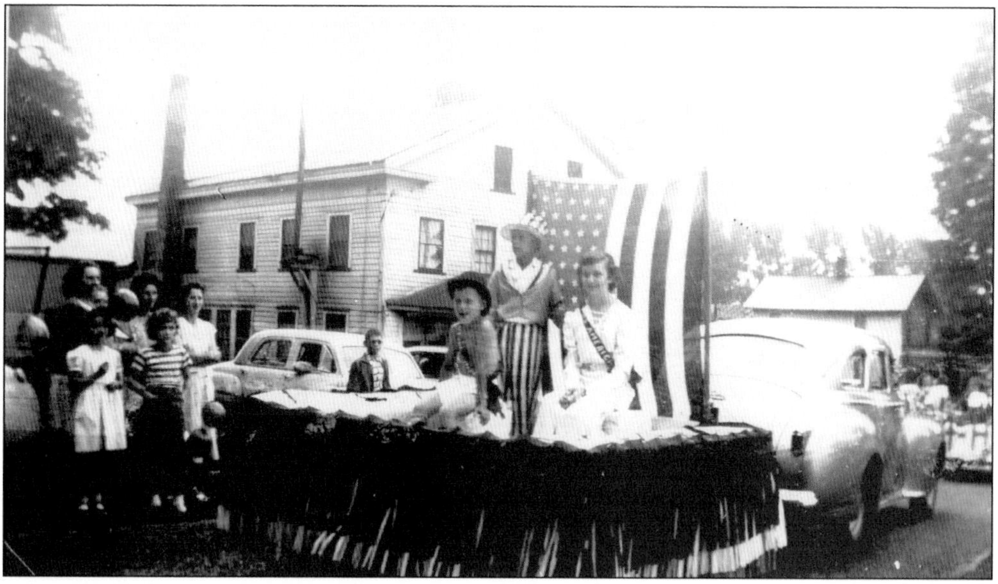

After World War II, the mid-1940s parades usually took a patriotic theme. Above, children portraying Baby New Year (in diaper and top hat), Uncle Sam, and Miss America rolled down Main Street in Guys Mills backed by the American flag. Childs' Garage is in the background. Below, soldiers proudly lead the Randolph East Mead Missilemen Marching Band. This photograph was shot just prior to the building of the Randolph Volunteer Fire Department in 1956. Notice the empty lot. (Above, courtesy of Brian and Judy Kirberger; below, courtesy of Sharon Hayes.)

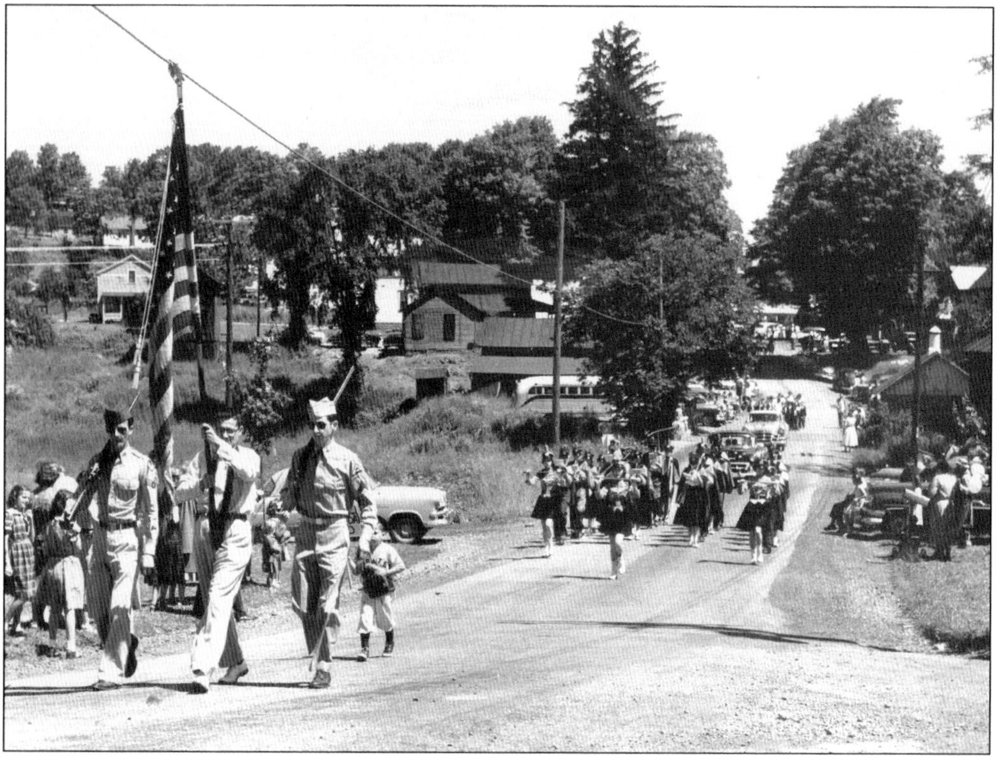

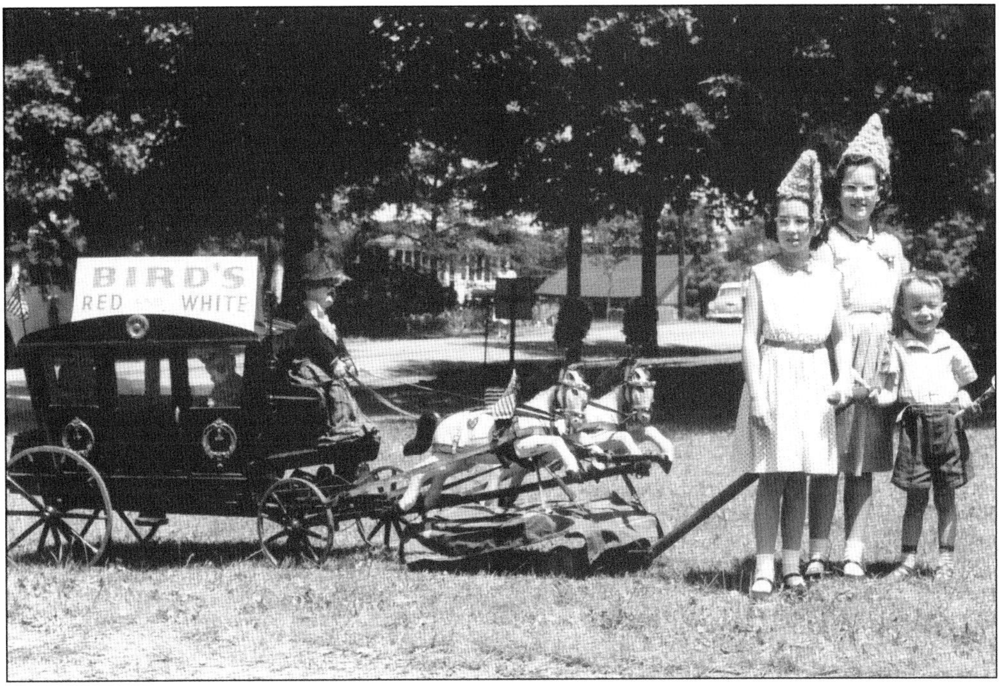

Sharon, Carol, and Lyle Bird are ready to represent Bird's Store in a Fourth of July parade in the early 1950s with this miniature carriage. (Courtesy of Sharon Hayes.)

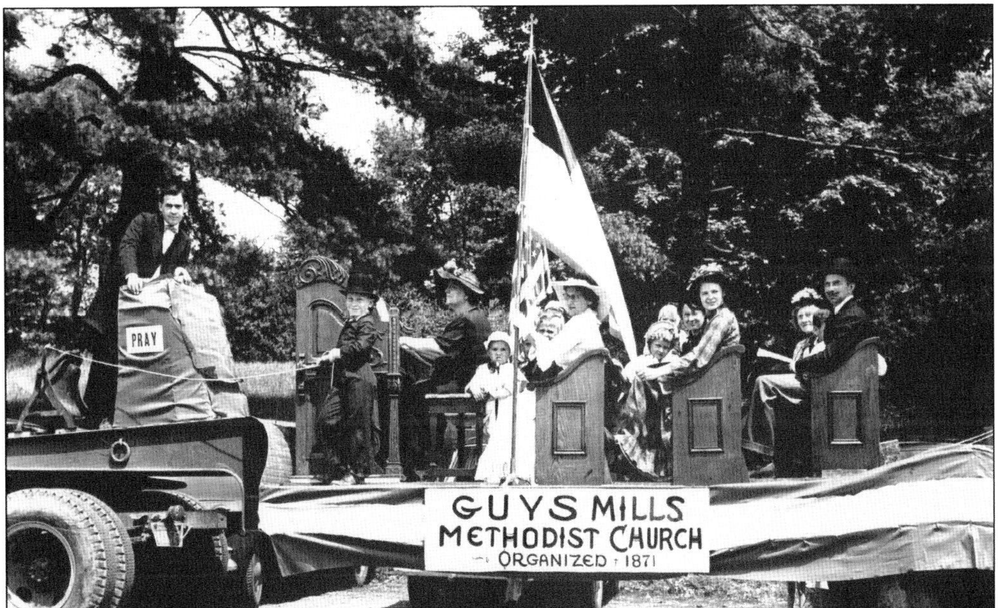

This elaborate Methodist church float about 1952 was constructed on Childs' lowboy. Rev. Gilbert Hoffman stands behind the pulpit while his son Gil Hoffman rings the church bell. Ancinohie Corey plays the organ. Worshippers are identified as (first pew) Doug, Dick and Virginia Gilbert, and Marilyn Childs; (second pew) Lucile Stallard, Henrietta Hoffman, and daughter Barbara Hoffman; (third pew) Karl and Doug Gilbert and Mary Childs. (Author's collection.)

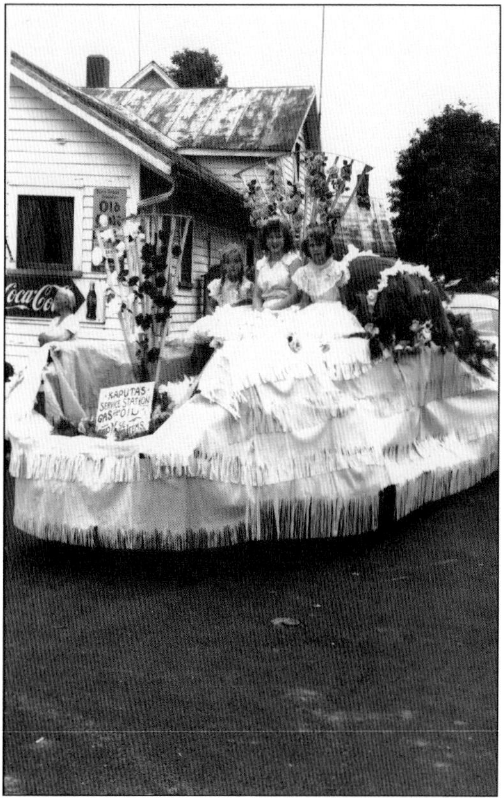

Elaborate Independence Day floats are a long-standing tradition in Guys Mills. This crepe paper confection was sponsored by Kaputa's Service Station and was judged "Best in Parade" in 1957. The princesses are, from left to right, Darlene Kaputa, Sally Kaputa, and Virginia Kaputa. Three thousand spectators watched the parade that year. (Courtesy of Darlene Jablon.)

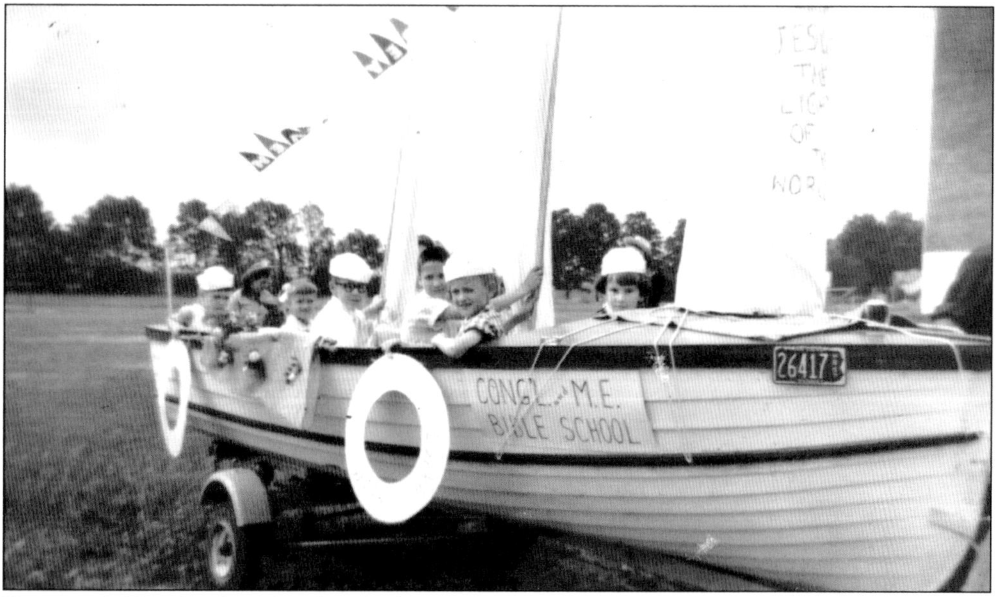

Vacation bible school "sailors," with their "Captain," Virginia Gilbert, are temporarily docked at the school waiting their turn to take sail down Main Street on July 4, 1958. Although the Methodist and Congregational churches did not merge until 1965 to form the United Church of Guys Mills, United Church of Christ, they held joint vacation bible school and cooperated in many other outreaches prior to the merger. (Courtesy of Leatha Humes.)

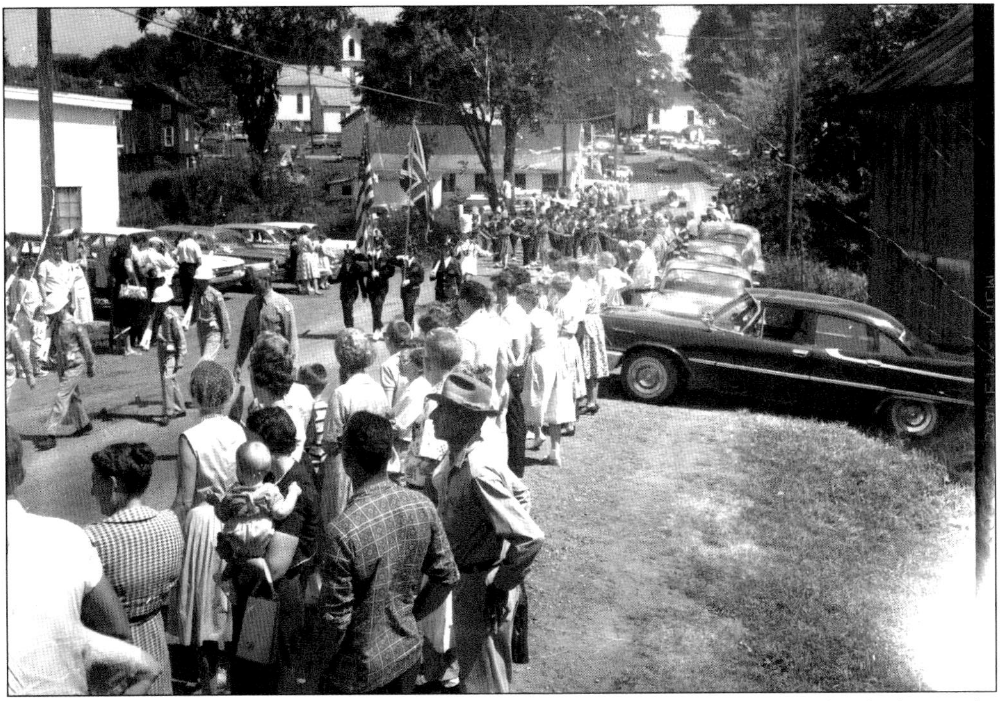

In 1962, the Randolph East Mead Missilemen Marching Band leads the Fourth of July parade. The parades were sponsored by the Randolph Volunteer Fire Department and culminated with fireworks and concessions at the township building. (Courtesy of the Meadville Tribune and author's collection.)

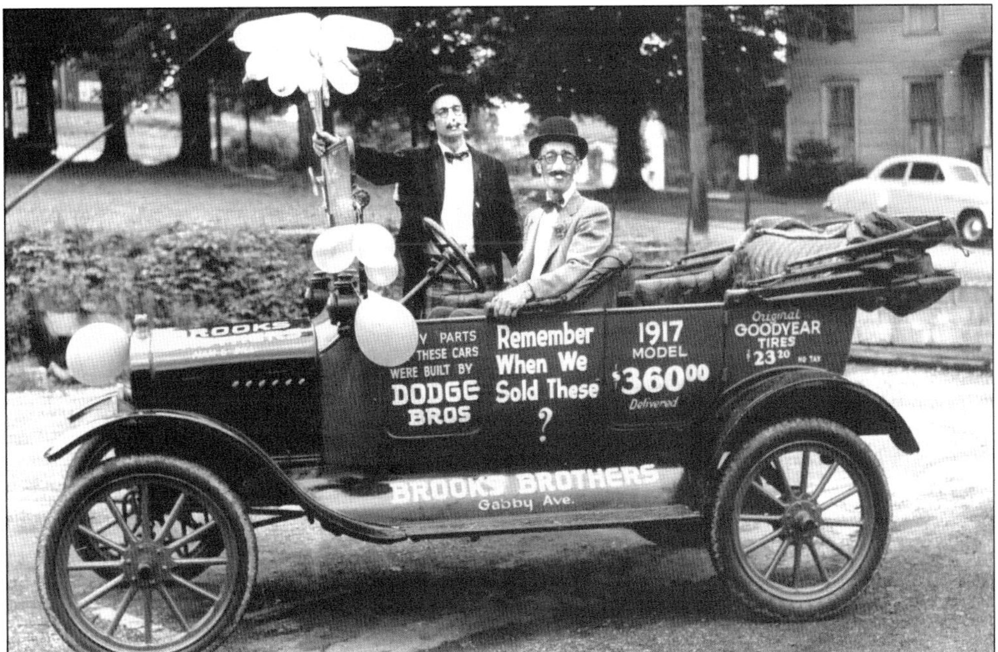

The Guys Mills parades hosted many units from neighboring communities. Brooks Brothers car dealership from Meadville added this entry to the parade. (Courtesy of Brian and Judy Kirberger.)

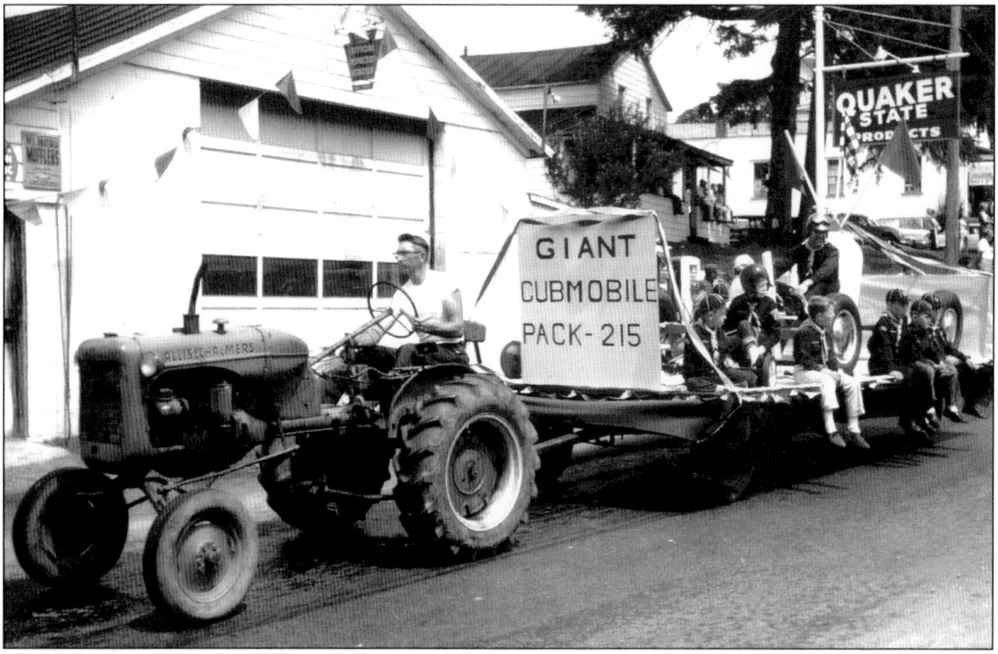

Girl Scouts and Boy Scouts were active in the area for many years. In 1964, Ed Mangus Sr. pulls local Cub Scout pack No. 215 in the parade. Dorcy Bowersox is sitting on the go-cart on the float. Terrill's Garage is in the background, formerly Clate Wygant's Blacksmith Shop then Paul Corey's Service Station. (Author's collection.)

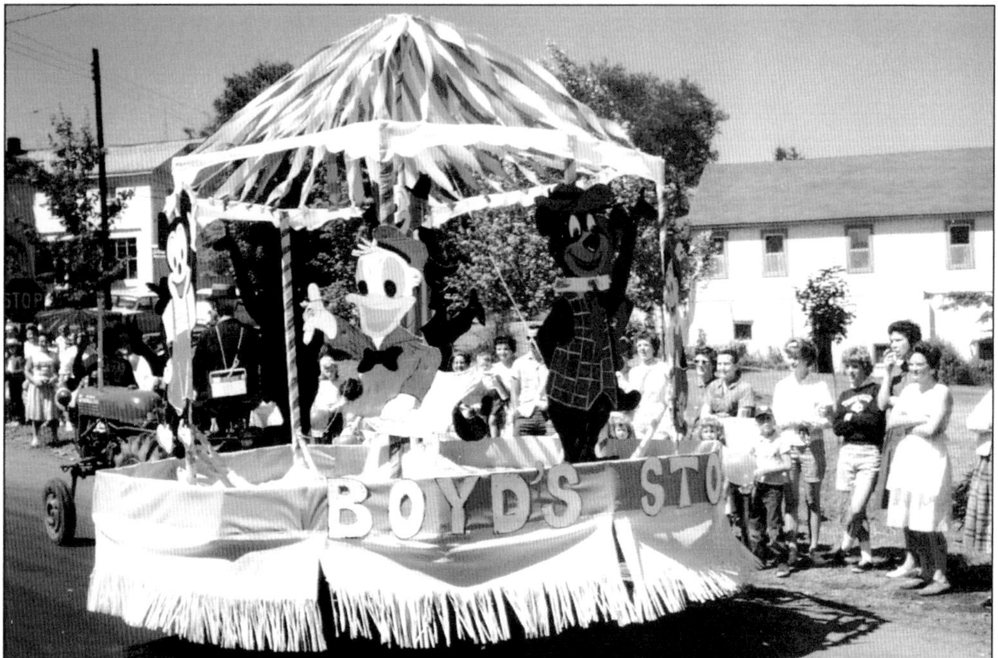

Mickey Mouse, Donald Duck, Yogi Bear, and friends were sponsored by Boyd's Store about 1963. Gene Rumsey designed elaborate floats for Boyd's Store every summer. Otto Graham is driving. (Author's collection.)

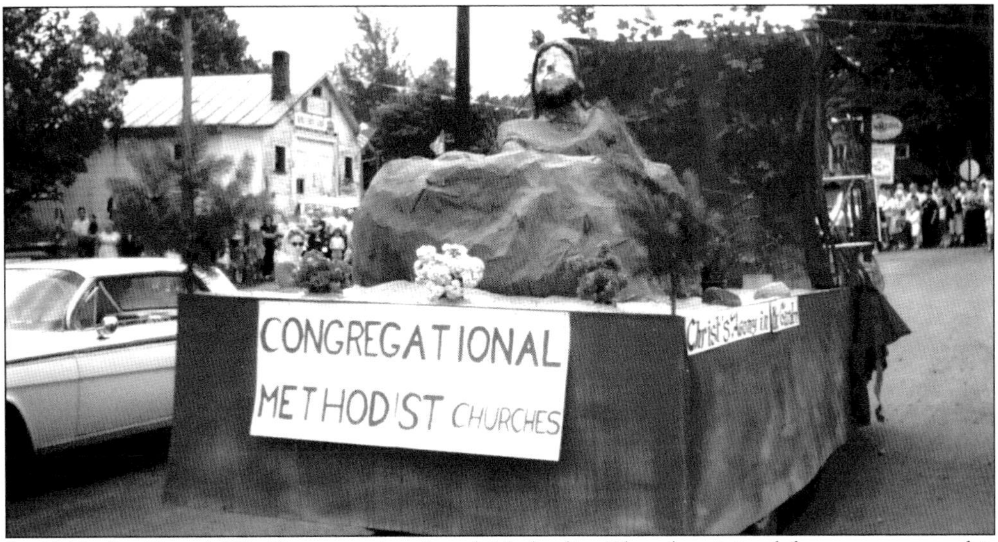

In 1964, the Guys Mills Congregational and Methodist Churches joined forces to create this float of "Christ in the Garden of Gethsemane." The following year they would join forces in a merger to create the United Church of Guys Mills, United Church of Christ. This float won first place in the religious category. Kaputa's Garage is in the background. (Author's collection.)

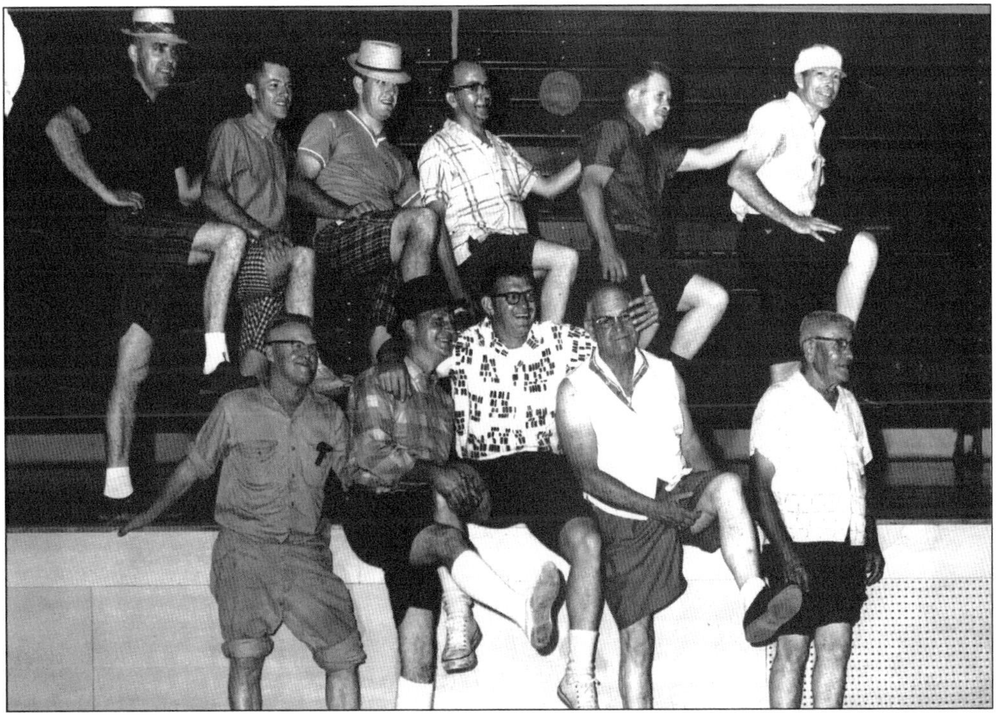

The highlight of the Fourth of July celebration in 1964 was the Men's Beauty Contest to crown the new Mr. Guys Mills. These fun-loving contestants of all ages are making a pathetic attempt at a kick line. Pictured are, from left to right, (first row) Ivan Wright, Victor Armstrong, Gene Rumsey, Harry Burchard, and Joe Fantacci; (second row) Russell Boyd, Ed Moses, David Boyd, Howard Gordon, David Marvin, and Howard Byham. (Courtesy of the Meadville Tribune, Russell and Virginia Boyd, and Brian and Judy Kirberger.)

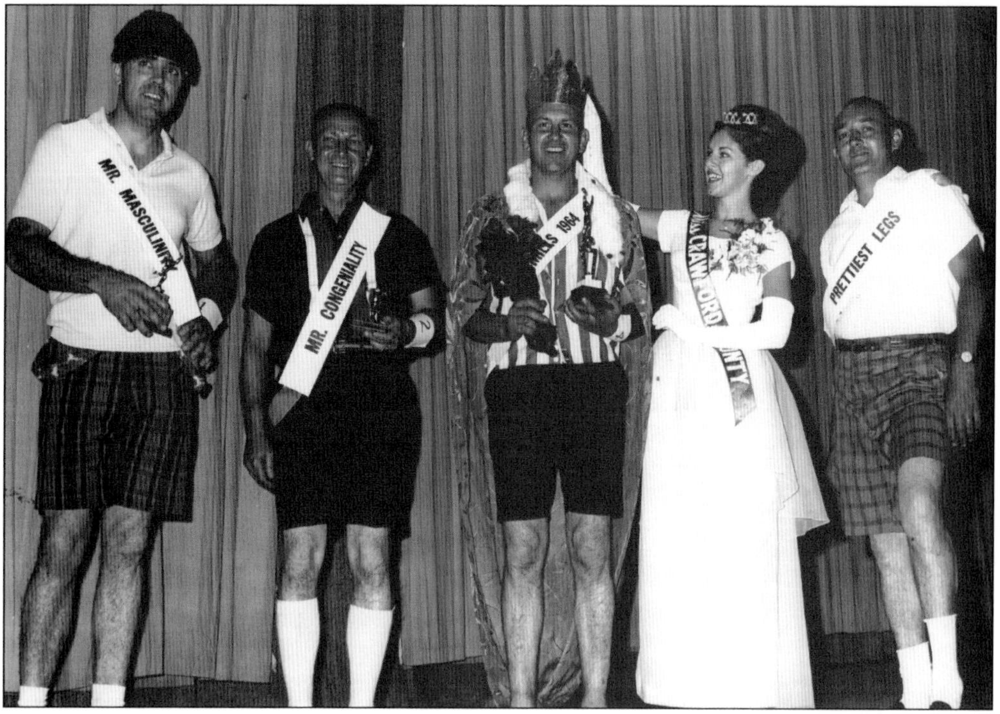

Amid gales of laughter from a sell-out crowd, the judges awarded the 1964 Mr. Guys Mills banner to the lovely Merle Burchard. He was crowned by Miss Crawford County Joyce Curran and was joined on the high school stage by his court: "Mr. Masculinity," Russell Boyd; "Mr. Congeniality," Victor Armstrong; and "Prettiest Legs," Wayne Hollabaugh. (Courtesy of Brian and Judy Kirberger, photograph by Photographic Arts for the Meadville Tribune.)

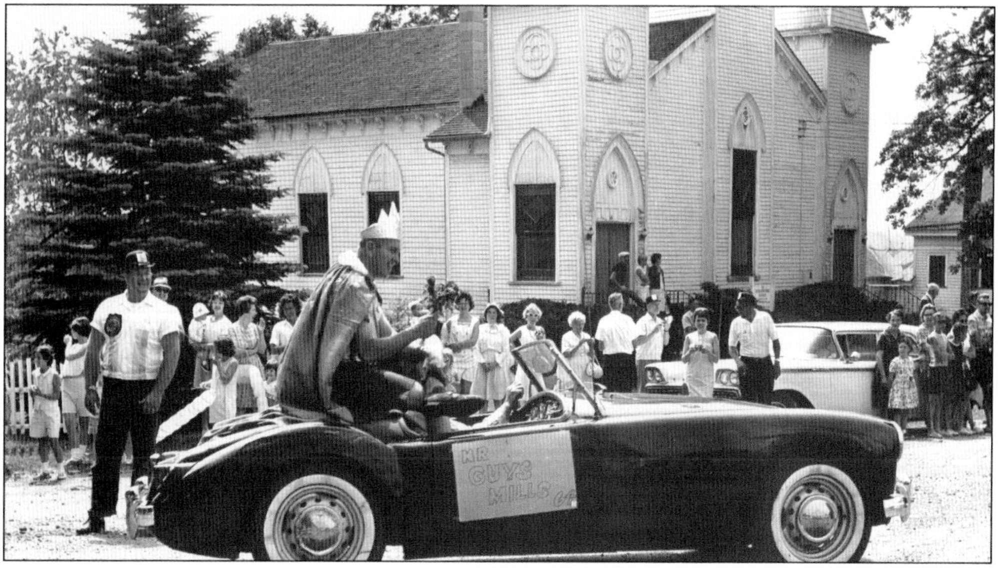

Merle Burchard, Mr. Guys Mills 1964, waves to his loyal subjects below from atop his royal carriage driven by Ford Bailey. Bermuda shorts, the official tinfoil crown, and a plastic flower bouquet complete his regal attire. (Courtesy of Brian and Judy Kirberger, photograph by Photographic Arts for the Meadville Tribune.)

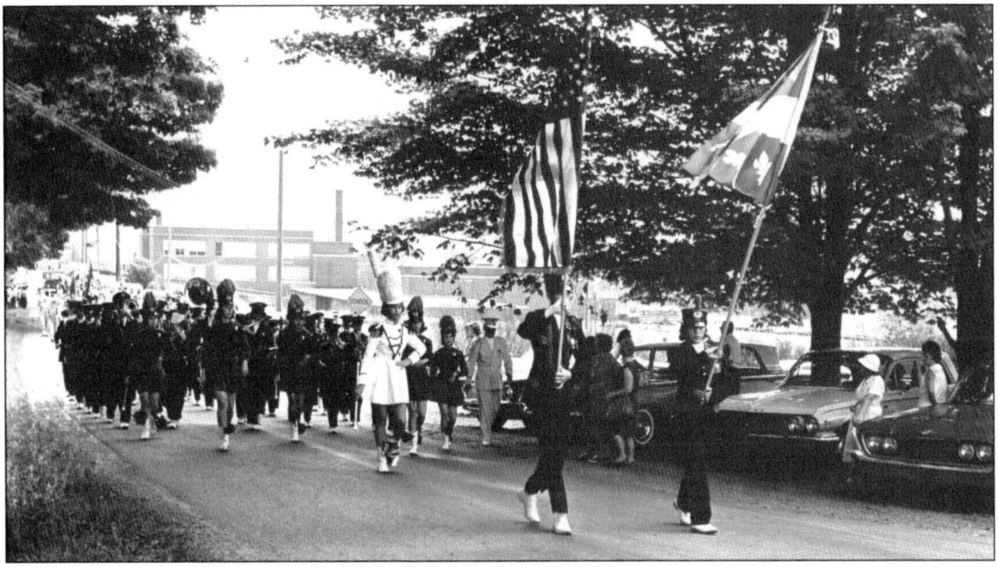

The 1965 Fourth of July parade was perhaps the largest in Guys Mills history with about 80 units. The Randolph Volunteer Fire Department hosted a four-day celebration to honor the village's sesquicentennial. The Randolph East Mead Missilemen Marching Band led the parade under the direction of George Menser. (Courtesy of Brian and Judy Kirberger, photograph by Photographic Arts for the Meadville Tribune.)

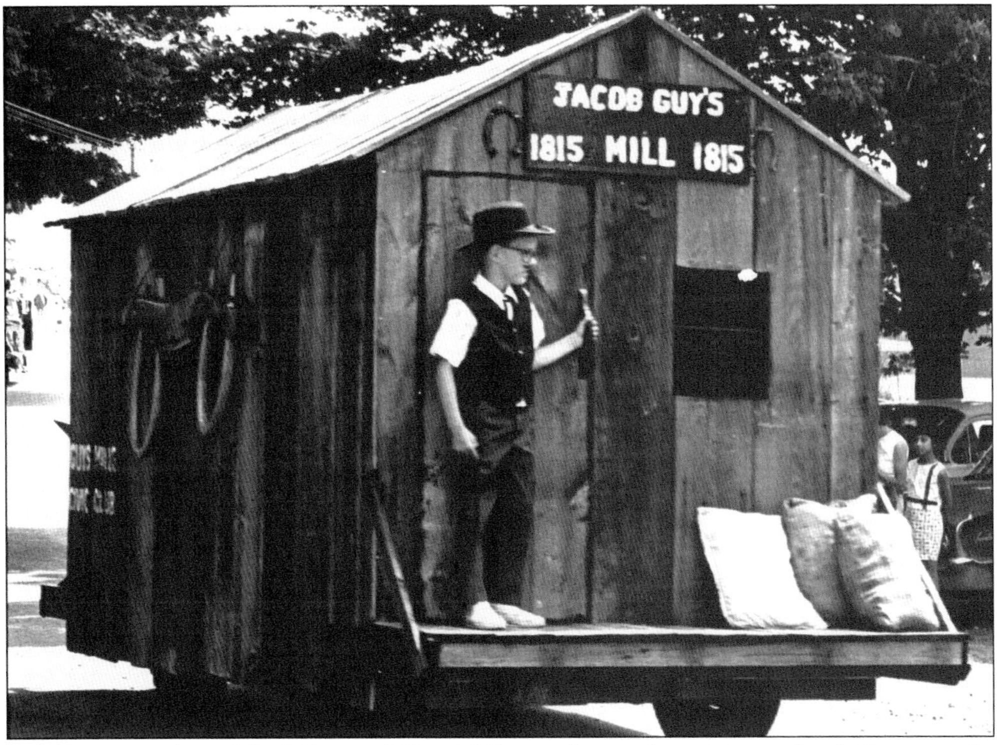

A miniature replica of Guy's Saw and Grist Mill, complete with a miniature Jacob Guy, won the 1965 "Most Original Float" title for its creators, the Guys Mills Women's Civic Club. (Courtesy of Brian and Judy Kirberger, photograph by Photographic Arts for the Meadville Tribune.)

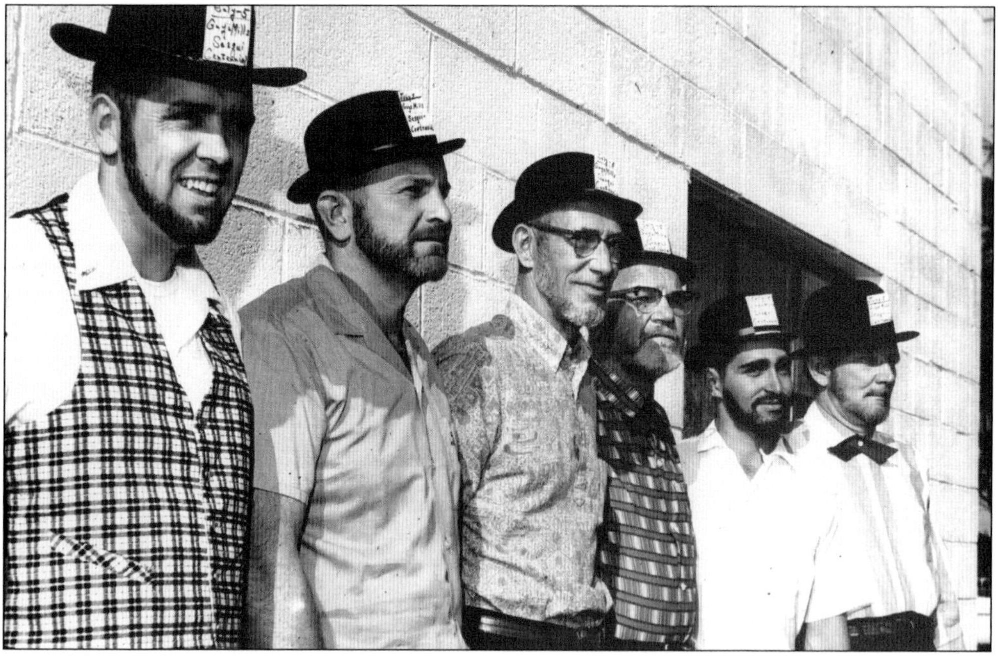

To celebrate the 1965 sesquicentennial, women wore long skirts and sunbonnets, and a beard-growing contest was declared for the men. The beard contestants are, from left to right, Russell Boyd, Clair Burchard, Arthur Smith, Harry Burchard, Brian Kirberger, and Ford Bailey. Clair won the contest, despite cruel rumors that he had his naturally grey beard dyed the night before the judging. (Courtesy of Brian and Judy Kirberger, photograph by Photographic Arts for the Meadville Tribune.)

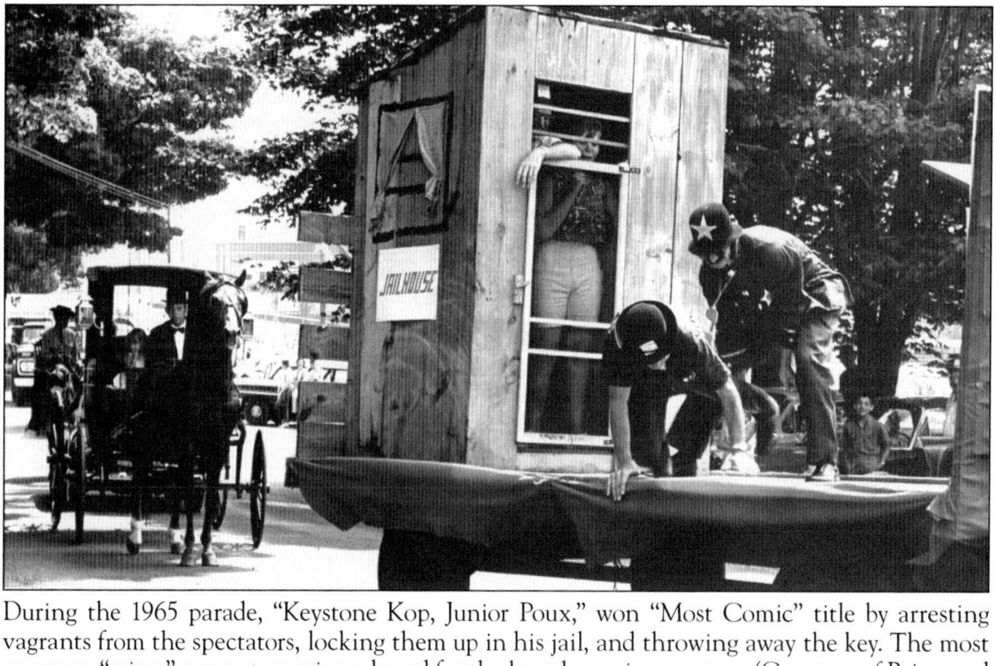

During the 1965 parade, "Keystone Kop, Junior Poux," won "Most Comic" title by arresting vagrants from the spectators, locking them up in his jail, and throwing away the key. The most common "crime" was not growing a beard for the beard-growing contest. (Courtesy of Brian and Judy Kirberger, photograph by Photographic Arts for the Meadville Tribune.)

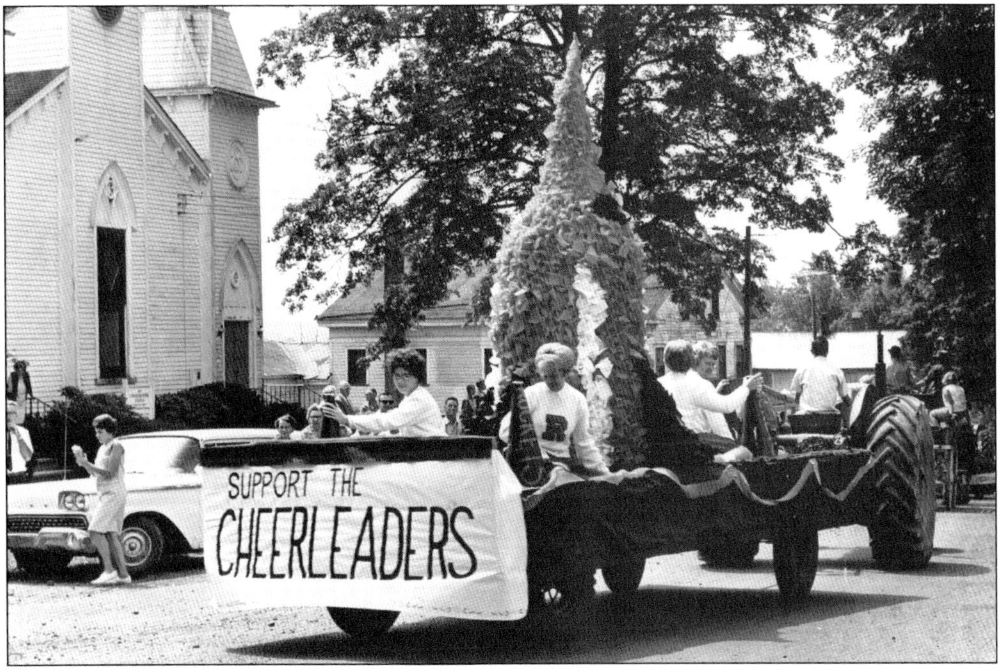

The blazing orange rocket dominated the Randolph Rocket Cheerleaders float and earned them the title of "Best Float" in 1965. (Courtesy of Brian and Judy Kirberger, photograph by Photographic Arts for the Meadville Tribune.)

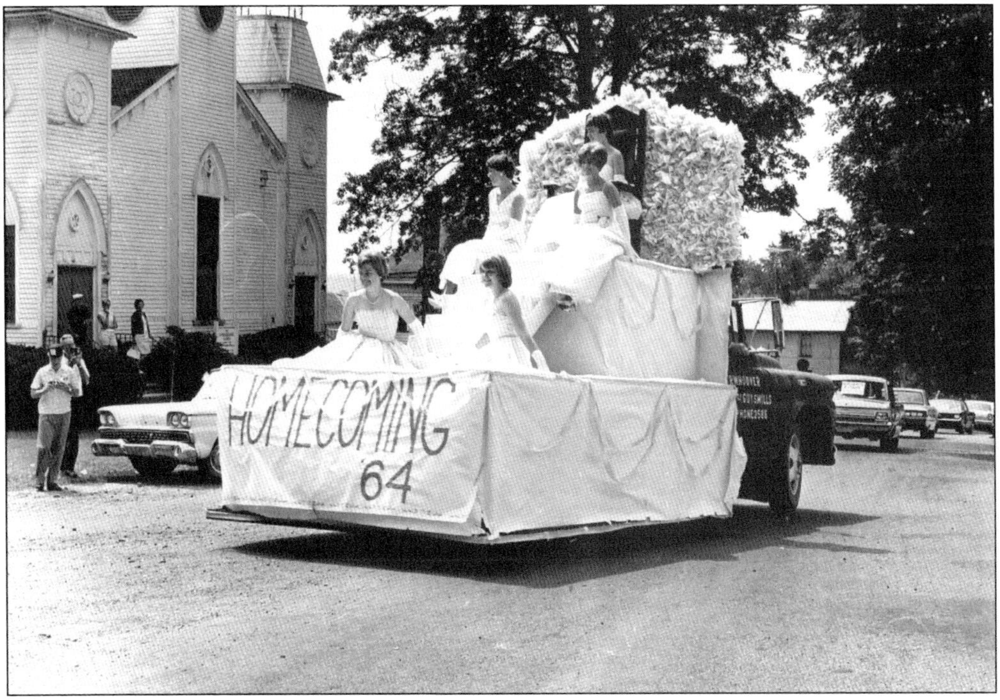

The Randolph East Mead 1964 homecoming queen and her court ride amid a bounty of crepe paper. (Courtesy of Brian and Judy Kirberger, photograph by Photographic Arts for the Meadville Tribune.)

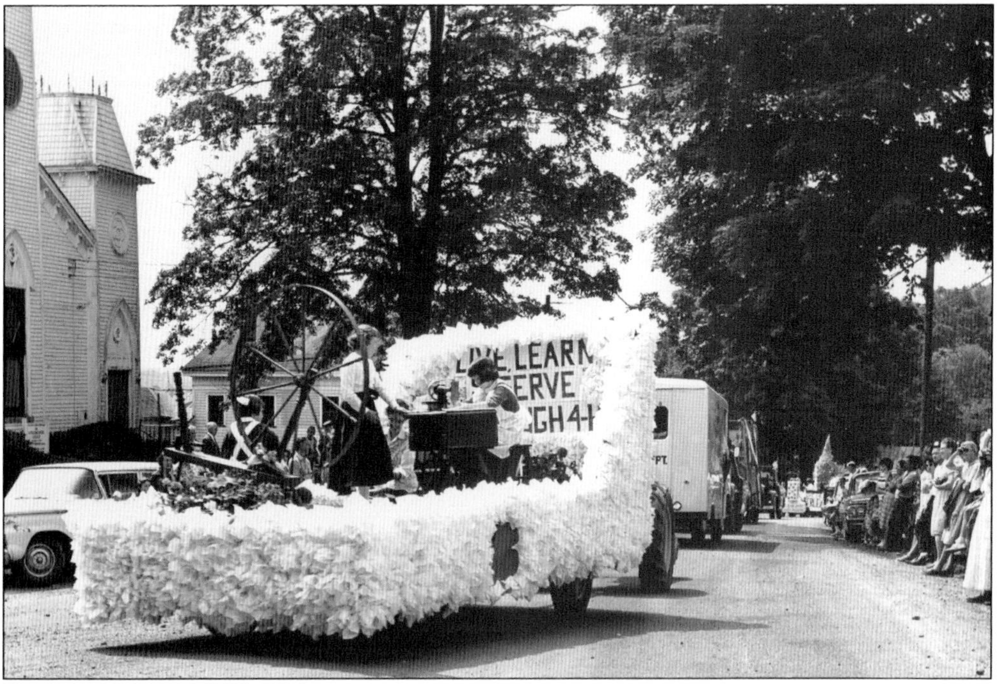

Two 1965 floats commemorated the ways of yesteryear. In the image above, the Sunbeam Sisters 4-H Club won "Best Costumed Float" for their depiction of the history of sewing with a spinning wheel and treadle sewing machine. Seen below is an invitation to "Relive the 1800's," including blacksmithing, butter churning, spinning, and other daily chores of yesteryear. (Courtesy of Brian and Judy Kirberger, photographs by Photographic Arts for the Meadville Tribune.)

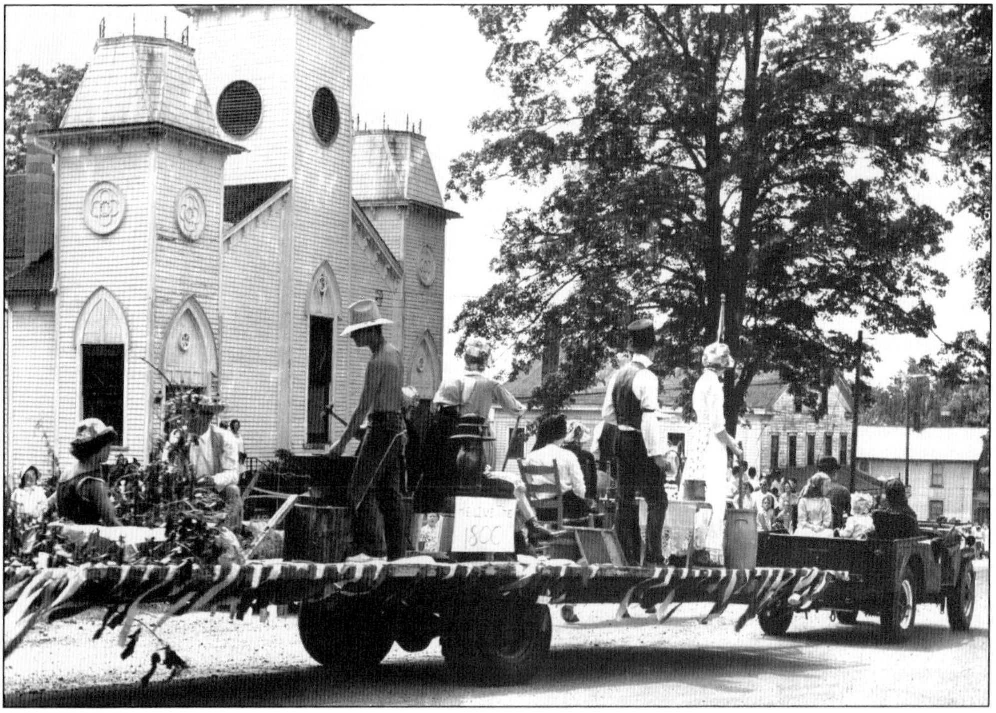

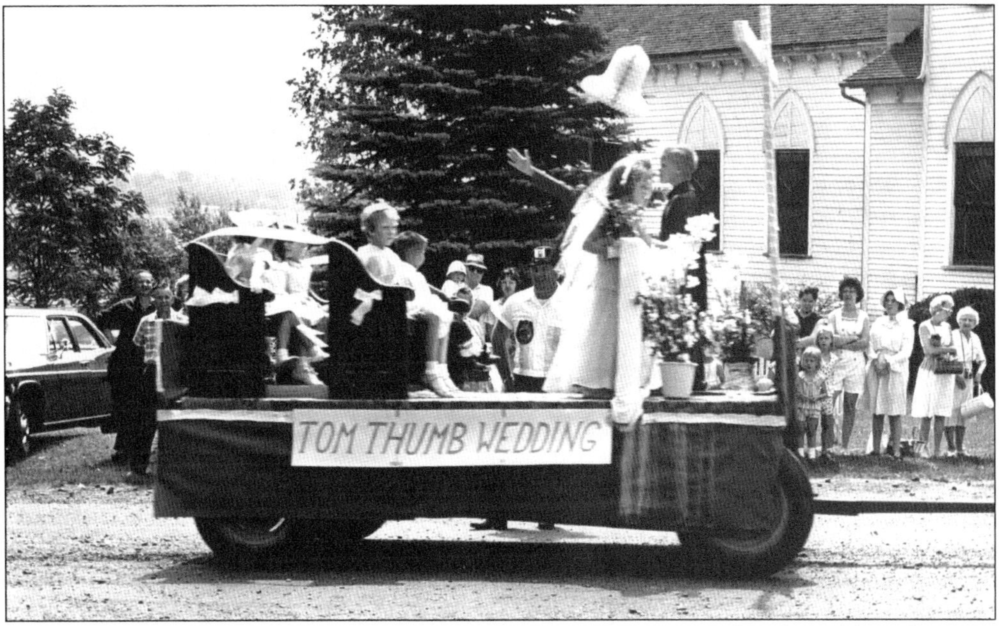

The 1965 "Best Float by a Commercial Establishment" was the "Tom Thumb Wedding" by Peggy Heme's Beauty Shop. The scene is complete with pint-sized minister, bride and groom, guests in small pews, and a tiny wedding bell high above it all. (Courtesy of Brian and Judy Kirberger, photograph by Photographic Arts for the Meadville Tribune.)

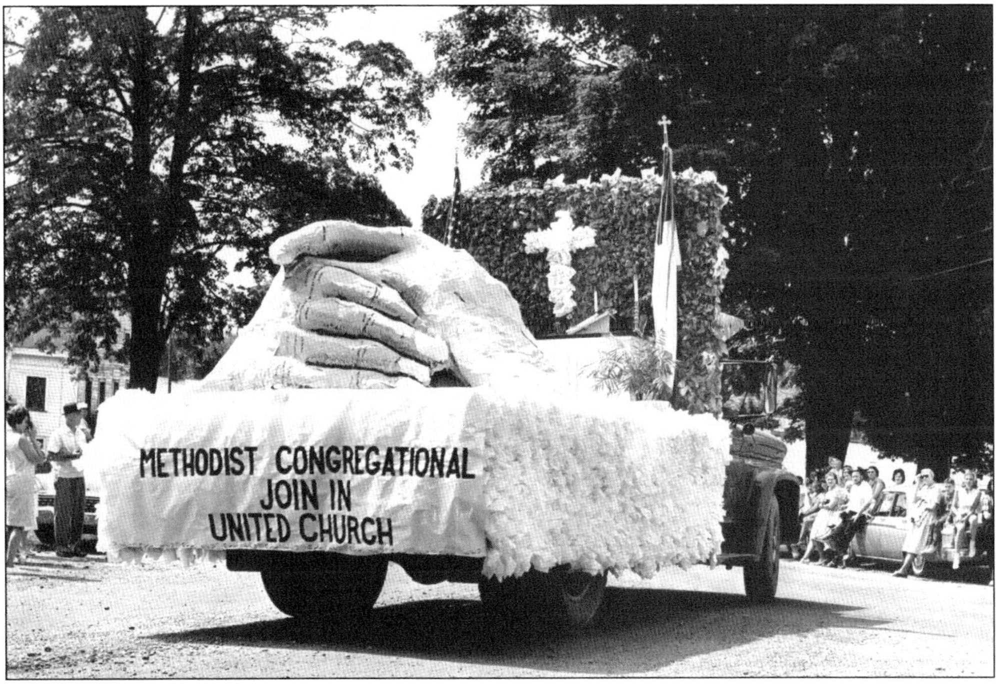

The new United Church of Guys Mills won "Best Religious Float." Signifying Christian unity in "joining hands," the float symbolized the Congregational and Methodist church merger earlier that year. (Courtesy of Brian and Judy Kirberger, photograph by Photographic Arts for the Meadville Tribune.)

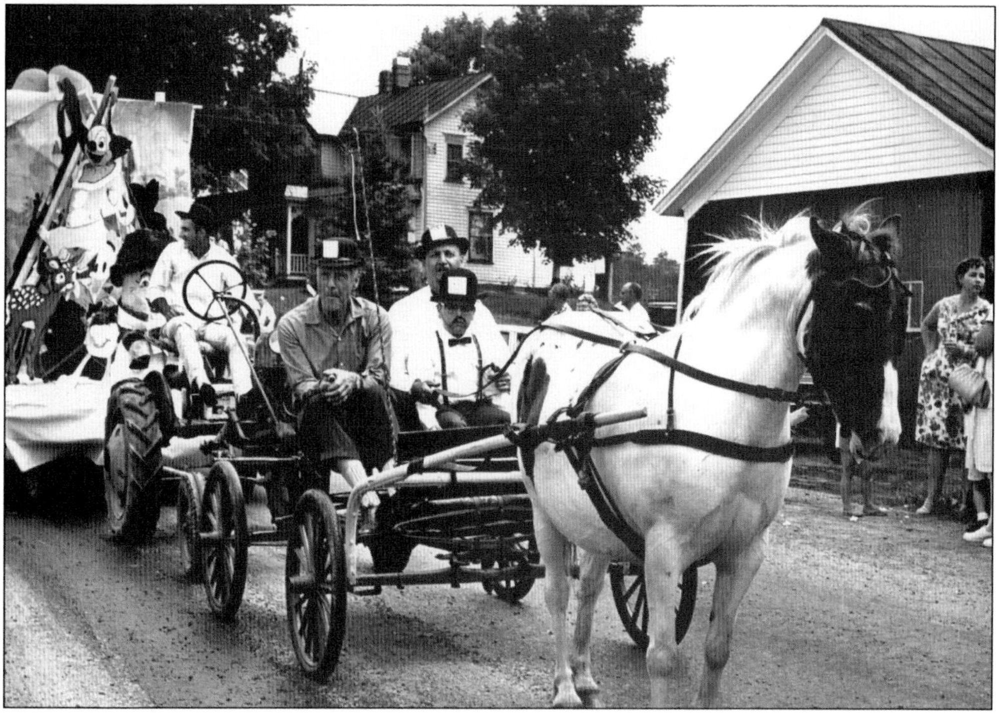

Horsepower was a way of life for Black Ash blacksmith Charlie Armstrong (right), so he must have felt right at home with Victor Armstrong driving with Denny Taylor on his lap in the 1965 parade. (Courtesy of Brian and Judy Kirberger, photograph by Photographic Arts for the Meadville Tribune.)

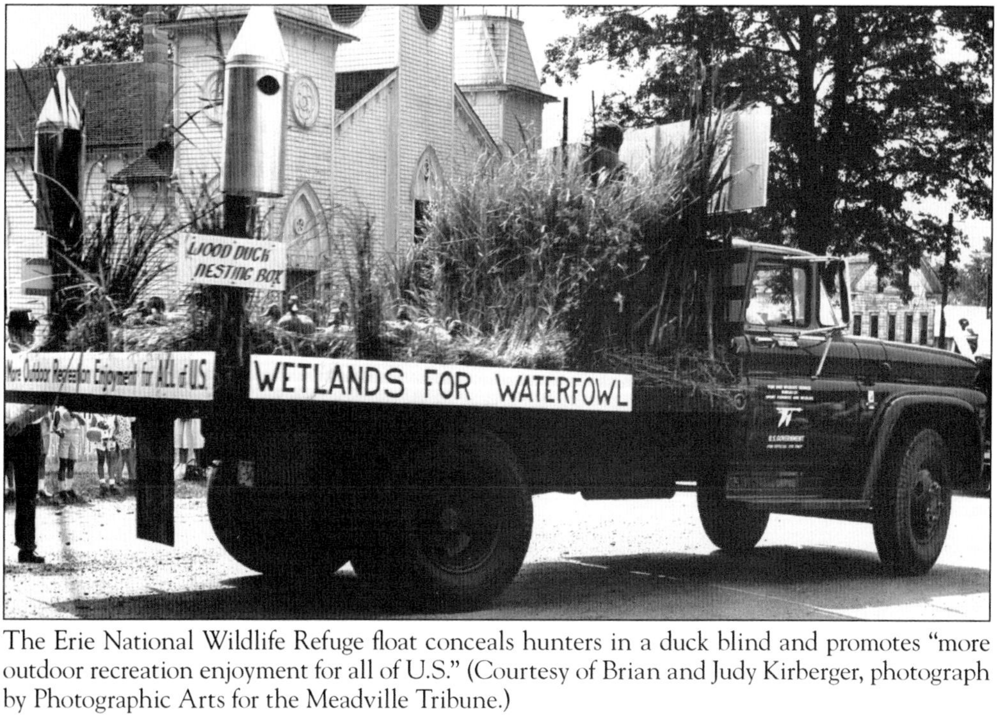

The Erie National Wildlife Refuge float conceals hunters in a duck blind and promotes "more outdoor recreation enjoyment for all of U.S." (Courtesy of Brian and Judy Kirberger, photograph by Photographic Arts for the Meadville Tribune.)

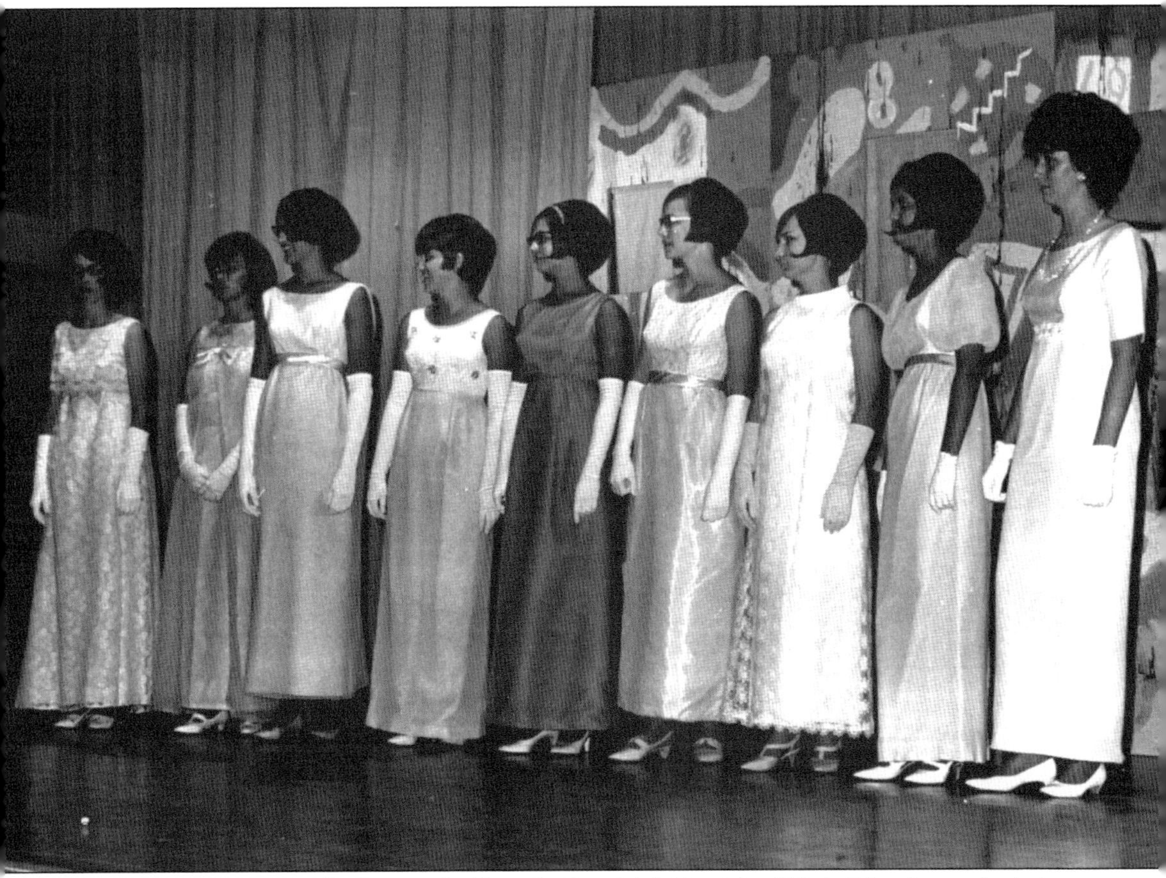

The 1968 Miss Guys Mills Pageant, held on the Randolph East Mead High School stage, had nine contestants. They are, from left to right, Lois Granda, daughter of Robert and Marilyn Granda; Karen Tyler, daughter of Junie and Bertha Tyler; Linda Hollabaugh, daughter of Wayne and Doris Hollabaugh; Kathy Gross, daughter of Butch and Helen Gross; Susan Pierce, daughter of Norman and Helen Pierce; Barb Burchard and Linda Burchard, daughters of Clair and Marjorie Burchard; Cindy Proper, daughter of Richard and Virginia Proper; and Carol Smith, daughter of Amos and Evelyn Smith. Linda Hollabaugh was crowned Miss Guys Mills. (Courtesy of the Meadville Tribune and the author.)